Advances in Intelligent Systems and Computing

Volume 652

Series editor

Janusz Kacprzyk, Polish Academy of Sciences, Warsaw, Poland
e-mail: kacprzyk@ibspan.waw.pl

About this Series

The series "Advances in Intelligent Systems and Computing" contains publications on theory, applications, and design methods of Intelligent Systems and Intelligent Computing. Virtually all disciplines such as engineering, natural sciences, computer and information science, ICT, economics, business, e-commerce, environment, healthcare, life science are covered. The list of topics spans all the areas of modern intelligent systems and computing.

The publications within "Advances in Intelligent Systems and Computing" are primarily textbooks and proceedings of important conferences, symposia and congresses. They cover significant recent developments in the field, both of a foundational and applicable character. An important characteristic feature of the series is the short publication time and world-wide distribution. This permits a rapid and broad dissemination of research results.

More information about this series at http://www.springer.com/series/11156

Bijaya Ketan Panigrahi · M.N. Hoda
Vinod Sharma · Shivendra Goel
Editors

Nature Inspired Computing

Proceedings of CSI 2015

Springer

Editors
Bijaya Ketan Panigrahi
Department of Electrical Engineering
Indian Institute of Technology
New Delhi, Delhi
India

Vinod Sharma
Department of Computer Science and IT
University of Jammu
Jammu, Jammu and Kashmir
India

M.N. Hoda
Bharati Vidyapeeth's Institute of Computer Applications and Management
New Delhi, Delhi
India

Shivendra Goel
Bharati Vidyapeeth's Institute of Computer Applications and Management
New Delhi, Delhi
India

ISSN 2194-5357 ISSN 2194-5365 (electronic)
Advances in Intelligent Systems and Computing
ISBN 978-981-10-6746-4 ISBN 978-981-10-6747-1 (eBook)
https://doi.org/10.1007/978-981-10-6747-1

Library of Congress Control Number: 2017953824

Printed on acid-free paper

This Springer imprint is published by Springer Nature
The registered company is Springer Nature Singapore Pte Ltd.
The registered company address is: 152 Beach Road, #21-01/04 Gateway East, Singapore 189721, Singapore

Preface

The last decade has witnessed remarkable changes in IT industry, virtually in all domains. The 50th Annual Convention, CSI-2015, on the theme "Digital Life" was organized as a part of CSI-2015, by CSI at Delhi, the national capital of the country, during December 02–05, 2015. Its concept was formed with an objective to keep ICT community abreast of emerging paradigms in the areas of computing technologies and more importantly looking at its impact on the society.

Information and Communication Technology (ICT) comprises of three main components: infrastructure, services, and product. These components include the Internet, infrastructure-based/infrastructure-less wireless networks, mobile terminals, and other communication mediums. ICT is gaining popularity due to rapid growth in communication capabilities for real-time-based applications. "Nature Inspired Computing" is aimed at highlighting practical aspects of computational intelligence including robotics support for artificial immune systems. CSI-2015 attracted over 1500 papers from researchers and practitioners from academia, industry, and government agencies, from all over the world, thereby making the job of the Programme Committee extremely difficult. After a series of tough review exercises by a team of over 700 experts, 565 papers were accepted for presentation in CSI-2015 during the 3 days of the convention under ten parallel tracks. The Programme Committee, in consultation with Springer, the world's largest publisher of scientific documents, decided to publish the proceedings of the presented papers, after the convention, in ten topical volumes, under ASIC series of the Springer, as detailed hereunder:

1. Volume # 1: ICT Based Innovations
2. Volume # 2: Next Generation Networks
3. Volume # 3: Nature Inspired Computing
4. Volume # 4: Speech and Language Processing for Human-Machine Communications
5. Volume # 5: Sensors and Image Processing
6. Volume # 6: Big Data Analytics

7. Volume # 7: Systems and Architecture
8. Volume # 8: Cyber Security
9. Volume # 9: Software Engineering
10. Volume # 10: Silicon Photonics and High Performance Computing

We are pleased to present before you the proceedings of Volume # 3 on "Nature Inspired Computing." Presently, the data is growing exponentially. Nature-inspired computing is a major subset of natural computation. It consists of the direct or indirect use of methods inspired by nature to solve problems using a computer. Nature inspired computing is a terminology introduced to encompass three classes of methods: (a) those that take inspiration from nature for the development of novel problem-solving techniques; (b) those that are based on the use of computers to synthesize natural phenomena; and (c) those that employ natural materials to compute. The title covers the main fields of research that compose these three branches, i.e., artificial neural networks, evolutionary algorithms, swarm intelligence, artificial immune systems, fractal geometry, artificial life, DNA computing, and quantum computing. The title also discusses natural computation systems and nature inspired optimization algorithms that are being applied in various domains of human endeavour.

This volume is unique in its coverage. It has received papers from all research domains. The articles submitted and published in this volume are of sufficient scientific interest and help to advance the fundamental understanding of ongoing research, applied or theoretical, for a general computer science audience. The treatment of each topic is in-depth, the emphasis is on clarity and originality of presentation, and each paper is adding insight into the topic under consideration. We are hopeful that this book will be an indispensable help to a broad array of readers ranging from researchers to developers and will also give a significant contribution toward professionals, teachers, and students.

A great deal of effort has been made to realize this book. We are very thankful to the team of Springer who have constantly engaged us and others in this process and have made the publication of this book a success. We are sure this engagement shall continue in future as well and both Computer Society of India and Springer will choose to collaborate academically for the betterment of the society at large. Under the CSI-2015 umbrella, we received over 100 papers for this volume, out of which 25 papers are being published, after rigorous review processes, carried out in multiple cycles.

On behalf of organizing team, it is a matter of great pleasure that CSI-2015 has received an overwhelming response from various professionals from across the country. The organizers of CSI-2015 are thankful to the members of *Advisory Committee, Programme Committee, and Organizing Committee* for their all-round guidance, encouragement, and continuous support. We express our sincere gratitude to the learned *Keynote Speakers* for support and help extended to make this event a grand success. Our sincere thanks are also due to our *Review Committee Members* and the *Editorial Board* for their untiring efforts in reviewing the manuscripts, giving suggestions and valuable inputs for shaping this volume.

We hope that all the participants/delegates will be benefitted academically and wish them all the best for their future endeavours.

We also take the opportunity to thank the entire team of Springer, who have worked tirelessly and made the publication of the volume a reality. Last but not least, we thank the team of Bharati Vidyapeeth's Institute of Computer Applications and Management (BVICAM), New Delhi, for their untiring support, without which the compilation of this huge volume would not have been possible.

New Delhi, India — Bijaya Ketan Panigrahi
New Delhi, India — M.N. Hoda
Jammu, India — Vinod Sharma
New Delhi, India — Shivendra Goel
March 2017

The Organization of CSI-2015

Chief Patron

Padmashree Dr. R. Chidambaram, *Principal Scientific Advisor, Government of India*

Patrons

Prof. S.V. Raghavan, Department of Computer Science, IIT Madras, Chennai
Prof. Ashutosh Sharma, Secretary, Department of Science and Technology, Ministry of Science and Technology, Government of India

Chair, Programme Committee
Prof. K.K. Aggarwal, Founder Vice Chancellor, GGSIP University, New Delhi

Secretary, Programme Committee
Prof. M.N. Hoda, Director, Bharati Vidyapeeth's Institute of Computer Applications and Management (BVICAM), New Delhi

Advisory Committee

- Padma Bhushan Dr. F.C. Kohli, Co-Founder, TCS
- Mr. Ravindra Nath, CMD, National Small Industries Corporation, New Delhi
- Dr. Omkar Rai, Director General, Software Technological Parks of India (STPI), New Delhi
- Adv. Pavan Duggal, Noted Cyber Law Advocate, Supreme Courts of India
- Prof. Bipin Mehta, President, CSI
- Prof. Anirban Basu, Vice President—cum- President Elect, CSI
- Shri Sanjay Mohapatra, Secretary, CSI
- Prof. Yogesh Singh, Vice Chancellor, Delhi Technological University, Delhi
- Prof. S.K. Gupta, Department of Computer Science and Engineering, IIT, Delhi

- Prof. P.B. Sharma, Founder Vice Chancellor, Delhi Technological University, Delhi
- Mr. Prakash Kumar, IAS, Chief Executive Officer, Goods and Services Tax Network (GSTN)
- Mr. R.S. Mani, Group Head, National Knowledge Networks (NKN), NIC, Government of India, New Delhi

Editorial Board

Contents

About the Editors

Dr. Bijaya Ketan Panigrahi is currently an Associate Professor at the Department of Electrical Engineering, Indian Institute of Technology Delhi (IIT Delhi), Delhi, India. His major research areas include power quality, flexible alternating current transmission system (FACTS) devices, power system protection, artificial intelligence (AI) applications to power systems, and nature inspired computing. He is actively working on numerous projects for industry and government. As a member of various professional societies including IEEE (USA), he is also associated with many international journals of repute, in different capacities.

M.N. Hoda is currently a Professor at the Department of Computer Science and the Director of Bharati Vidyapeeth's Institute of Computer Applications and Management (BVICAM), New Delhi. He has over 22 years of academic experience in different capacities. Prior to joining the academic world, he initially worked in the corporate sector as a Software Engineer. He is an expert member of many board-level committees of the Department of Science & Technology (DST), Council of Scientific & Industrial Research (CSIR), and Ministry of Human Resource Development (MHRD). His current areas of research include information system audits, software engineering, computer networks, artificial intelligence (AI), information and communications technology (ICT), and Innovative Pedagogies for 21st Century Teaching Learning Systems. He is a Senior Member of IEEE, CSI, IE (I), ISTE, ISCA, ACM and a fellow of IETE.

Dr. Vinod Sharma is currently a Professor at the Department of Computer Science and IT, University of Jammu, India. He has been the Head of the Department since April 2015. As a member of the Computer Society of India (CSI), he obtained his MCA from the Veermata Jijabai Technological Institute (VJTI), Mumbai, in 1991 and his Ph.D. (Computer Science) from the University of Jammu in 2009.

Dr. Shivendra Goel holds a Ph.D. in Computer Engineering. He completed his MCA (Honours) at Dr. A.P.J. Abdul Kalam Technical University, Lucknow, and his M.Phil. (Computer Science) at Chaudhary (Ch.) Devi Lal University. He is currently an Associate Professor at Bharati Vidyapeeth's Institute of Computer Applications and Management (BVICAM), New Delhi. He worked with Northern India Engineering College (NIEC), New Delhi, and as a Software Engineer at Eagle Information Systems, Noida. Dr. Goel is a Microsoft Faculty Fellow (MFF) and a member of LMCSI and LMISTE.

EasyOnto: A Collaborative Semiformal Ontology Development Platform

Usha Yadav, B.K. Murthy, Gagandeep Singh Narula, Neelam Duhan and Vishal Jain

Abstract With an incessant development of the information technology, ontology has been widely applied to various fields for knowledge representation. Therefore, ontology construction and ontology extension has become a great area of research. Creating ontology should not be confined to the thinking process of few ontology engineers. To develop common ontologies for information sharing, they should satisfy the requirements of different people for a particular domain. Also, ontology engineering should be a collaborative process for faster development. As Social Web is growing, its simplicity proves to be successful in attracting mass participation. This paper aims in developing a platform "EasyOnto" which provide simple and easy graphical user interface for users to collaboratively contribute in developing semiformal ontology.

Keywords Ontology development · Social Web · Semantic web

U. Yadav (✉) · B.K. Murthy · G.S. Narula
CDAC, Noida, India
e-mail: usha.yadav.912@gmail.com

B.K. Murthy
e-mail: bkm@cdac.in

G.S. Narula
e-mail: gagan.narula87@gmail.com

N. Duhan
Department of Computer Engineering, YMCA University of Science and Technology, Faridabad, India
e-mail: neelam_duhan@rediffmail.com

V. Jain
Bharati Vidyapeeth's Institute of Computer Applications (BVICAM), New Delhi, India
e-mail: vishaljain83@ymail.com

B.K. Panigrahi et al. (eds.), *Nature Inspired Computing*, Advances in Intelligent Systems and Computing 652, https://doi.org/10.1007/978-981-10-6747-1_1

1 Introduction

Ontology represents information specific to a particular domain. Ontologies comprise of logical theories that encode knowledge about a particular domain in a declarative way [1, 2]. Terms representing specific domain and the relations between those terms are well described in ontologies. Ontology has become an advanced technology in artificial intelligence and knowledge engineering, playing an increasingly important role in knowledge representation, knowledge acquisition and ontology application. However, ontology creation is known to be a very time-consuming and difficult process. To have common ontologies for information sharing, they should satisfy the requirements of different people. To ensure this, ontology engineering should be a highly collaborative process. Also it is difficult for domain experts to spend much time in developing ontology.

Social Web applications are easy to understand and use for ordinary people. Social Web applications, like wikis and online communities, enable collaboration among people. Collaboration can help in establishing consensus or common understanding required for meaningful information sharing. People can socialize and enjoy on the Social Web. Therefore, the Social Web has proven to be very successful in drawing mass participation, and it is exploding with user-generated contents.

Therefore, this papers to create a platform, named "**EasyOnto**" which aims to be as easy and as simple as possible to enable large number of users who might not have any technical knowledge about ontology can also contribute in creating concepts freely. Section 2 shows related works in developing ontology collaboratively. Section 3 describes problem identification. Section 4 describes detailed explanation of the system is given. Section 5 presented semiformal ontology model.

2 Related Works

Depending upon the different set of requirement, various approaches and methodologies are proposed and implemented.

The myOntology project [3] also uses wikis for community-driven horizontal lightweight ontology building by enabling general users to contribute. The myOntology project proposes to use the infrastructure and culture of wikis to enable collaborative and community-driven ontology building. It intends to enable general users with little expertise in ontology engineering to contribute. It is mainly targeted at building horizontal lightweight ontologies by tapping the wisdom of the community.

Semantic wikis [4] assist in collaborative creation of resources by defining properties as wiki links with well-defined semantics. Collaborative knowledge contributed by various users is presented in more explicit and formal manner, thus enhancing the capabilities of wikis. Using simple syntax, semantically annotating navigational links are encoded between resource pages which show the relations between them. Irrespective of degree of formalization and semantic capabilities, semantic wikis have few common features such as links annotation, context-aware presentation, improved navigation, semantic search and reasoning support.

Dall'Agnol et al. [5] presented a methodology which requires three modules to be done for the ontology creation procedure. These are knowledge gathering, modelling of concepts and ontology evaluation. Web 2.0 allows social tagging process, and Social Web data are annotated and categorized by associating it with tags thus developing folksonomy. Creating and managing these tags collaboratively results in knowledge acquisition. After this phase, folksonomy tags are then converted into ontology elements by the ontology engineers, and then in further ontology evaluation procedure, it is validated.

Buffa et al. [6] had expressed his views on recent research development in semantic wikis. "The use of wikis for ontologies" and "The use of ontologies for wikis" are the most used approach for semantic wikis. Many of the researches done over semantic wikis used the first approach in which the wiki acts as the front end of the collaborative ontology maintenance system. Semantic Media Wiki [7] is an extension to Media Wiki, which permits semantic data to be encoded within wiki pages. Extended wiki syntax helps in encoding the semantic into wiki text. Every article corresponds to exactly one ontological element (class or property). Every annotation in the article makes statements about this element.

The links between the semantic wiki pages are referred to as "Relations". All of this is converted into formal ontology. In paper [8], researchers developed a system to support primary work of ontology development between ontology developers collaboratively, without the need for domain expert to be present.

Folksonimized ontology (FO) is proposed by Wang et al. [9], uses three 3E steps technique, namely extraction, enrichment and evolution. A new blended approach is presented which allows semantic capability of folksonomies is used by ontologies and vice versa. Visual review and visual enhancement tool help in implementing and testing the completed system.

3 Problem Identification

There are number of issues while creating collaborative ontologies. Some of the issues are presented below:

- Common ontology for information sharing should satisfy the requirement of different people. It is challenging to keep the ontology development process easy and simple so as to gain mass participation.
- As each ontology engineer is provided by his own workspace to develop ontology in collaboration, handling concurrency issues among various participants is difficult.

- Creating ontology is very tedious and time-consuming job, so involving domain expert for longer time during the development is not feasible.

Keeping in mind these issues, our objective is to develop very simple and easily understandable system which allows mass users to contribute fully in knowledge acquisition phase. Due to large participation, there will be faster development of knowledge acquisition phase, and it will also not involve the presence of domain expert. Thus, it proves to be very time-efficient methodology for ontology development. Once semiformal ontology belonging to any domain is formed, then domain expert can validate and refine the system.

4 Collaborative Semiformal Ontology Construction System

"EasyOnto" is Social Web application system which allows any interested user to contribute in construction of ontology of any domain of his own choice. Now following stepwise easy and simple procedure, user will contribute in ontology acquisition as shown in Fig. 1. User can follow the sequence or hop to any of the steps presented. As multiple users are performing on the system, similar domains, instance, concepts, semantic annotations will be automatically merged. To show the complete working of the system, knowledge of a particular domain is chosen. Ontology development of "Vehicle" domain is shown. Instances, categories and relation specifying vehicle domain are chosen. At last the conceptual model developed by following the procedure can be used as a knowledge base for any application related to that domain.

Step 1: Choose domain/add new domain

On the main page, user will be shown many domains to choose from to develop ontology for that domain. User can select any domain of his own interest or add new domain. User can add new domain in the textbox provided and click on submit.

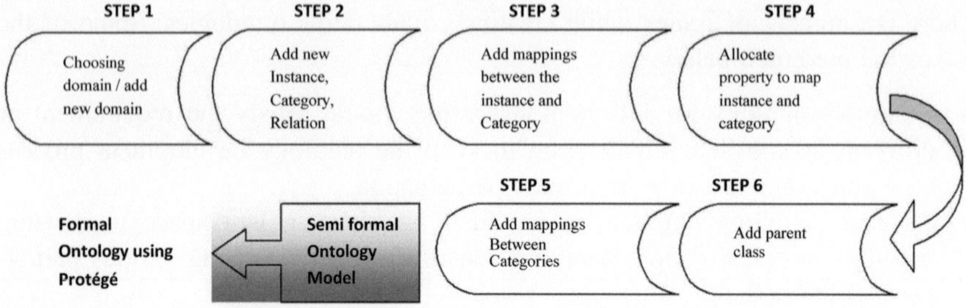

Fig. 1 Collaborative semiformal ontology construction system

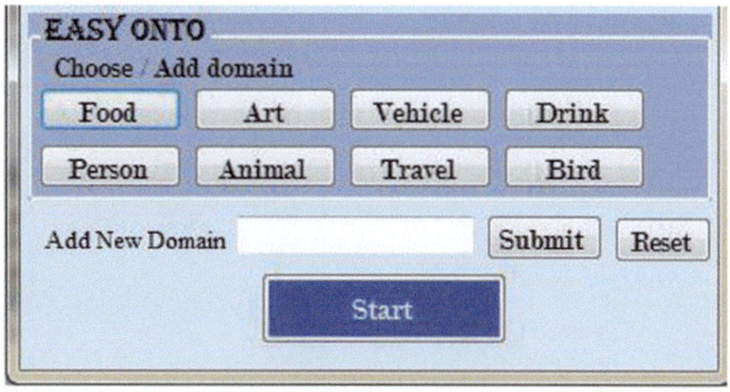

Fig. 2 Choose domain/add new domain

Figure 2 shows various domains to choose from, and "vehicle" domain is chosen by user. Now user needs to click start.

Step 2: Add new instance, category and relation

In this step, user can add instance, category or relations. User need to choose instance, category or relationship by drop-down menu and enter text in textbox provided and click on submit button. Once user chooses any drop-down option, corpus related to that option which is created by other users will be shown to the user. The terms being added will be displayed immediately in corpus. If user does not want to add, he can proceed further by clicking on "Continue" button.

(i) Instance is any term or keyword which belongs to the domain and which can be classified under any category. Figure 3 shows that user selected to add new instances related to vehicle domain like swift desire, pulsar, i20.

(ii) Category is any term which can classify any instances under them. Figure 4 shows that user entered two category "car" and "bike" which is shown in category corpus and click continue.

(iii) Relation refers to the relationship which exists between terms and can be defined. Based on the domain, user can add any relation to relate instance and category. For example

Fig. 3 Add new instance

Fig. 4 Add new category

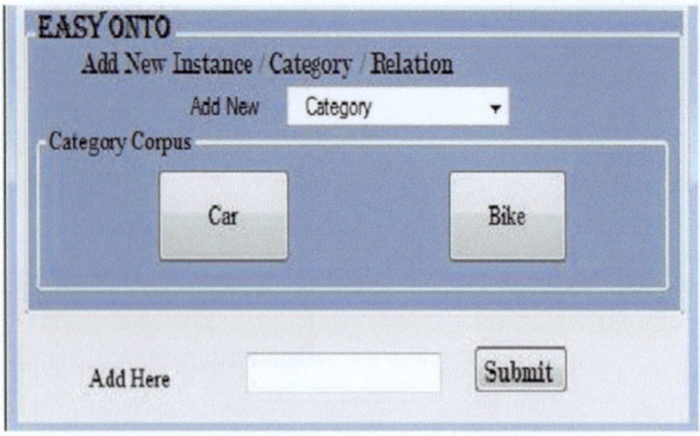

Fig. 5 Add new relation

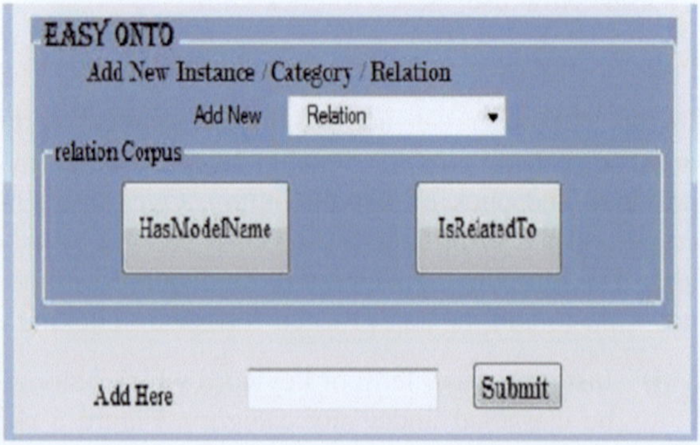

"HasModelName" relation that can be added which is used to relate "Eon" instance and "Car" category as "Car *HasModelName* Eon". This is shown in Fig. 5.

Step 3: **Enrich with semantic annotation**

Semantic annotation refers to any meaning which user wants to associate with the term selected. User need to choose instance or category from their corpus. Once it is chosen, it can be semantically annotated by entering meaningful information about them. Figure 6 shows that with category related to vehicle_model, its meaning "model of a vehicle" is added as a semantic annotation.

User can also choose any relation and provide range of its subject object. Figure 7 shows "HasModelName" relations enriched with "Vehicle_Model" as subject range and "vehicle_type" as object range.

Step 4: **Add relevant mappings between the instance and category**

Instance and categories can also be mapped easily. In this step, instance from instance corpus can be mapped to any category defined in category corpus. For an example, instance such as Eon, i20 can be mapped to "Car" category and pulsar, royal Enfield can be mapped to "Bike" category. User needs to select instance and

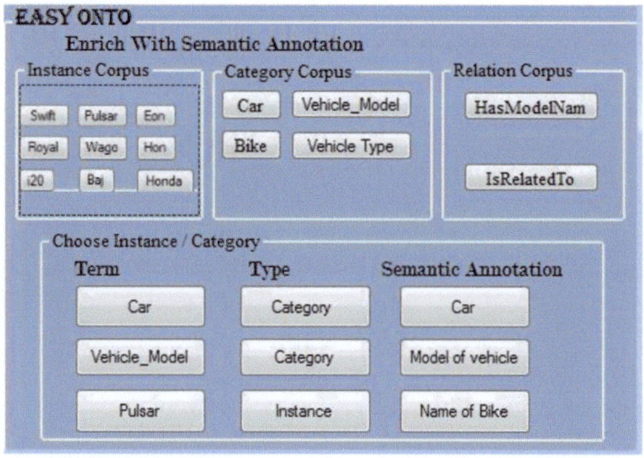

Fig. 6 Enrich term with semantic annotation

Fig. 7 Enrich relation with semantic annotation

category from corpus, and it will be shown in the space provided below the corpuses.

One instance can be mapped to number of categories. For this, user can add as many categories for a specific instance by click on “Add more” button as shown in Fig. 8.

Step 5: Allocate relation to map instance and category

In this step, user can choose relation from relation corpus to appropriately map instance and category. User can pick instance, category and relation and drop them in the space provided. As shown in Fig. 9, various mappings are done.

Step 6: Add parent class

Depending upon the semantic annotation added in step 3, system can automatically assign parent class to some of the instance and category. It depends on the subject and object range added in respect with each relation.

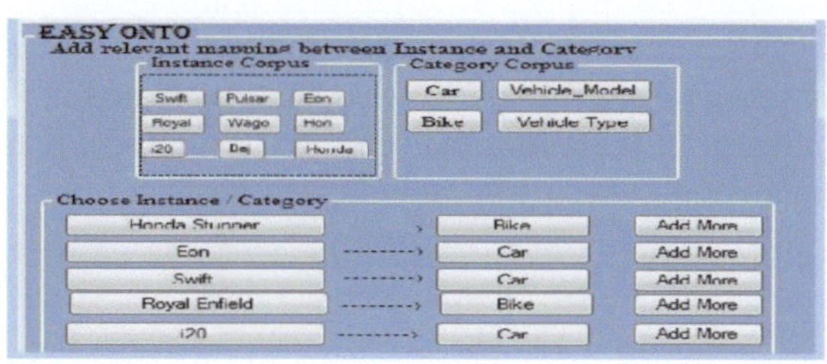

Fig. 8 Add relevant mappings between the instance and category

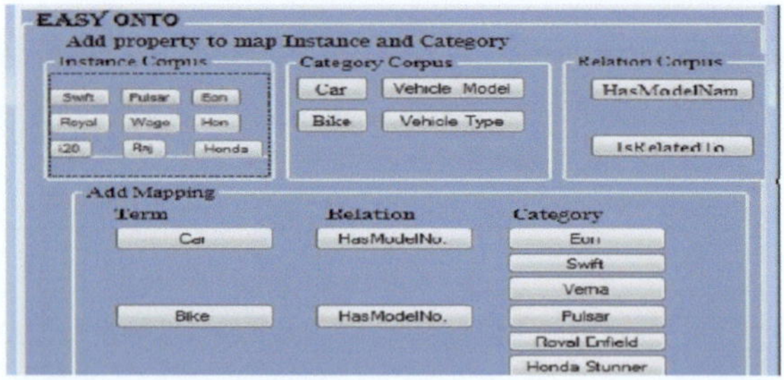

Fig. 9 Allocate relation to map instance and category

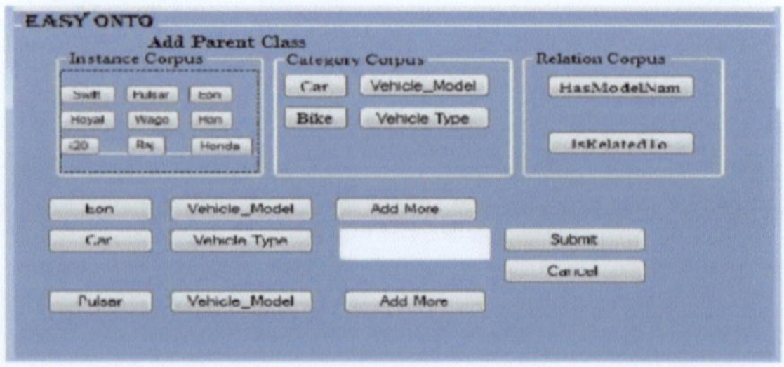

Fig. 10 Add parent class

Suppose the example "Car has modelName Eon". Now the subject range for relation "HasModelName" is vehicle_type and object range is "vehicle_model". So system will autogenerate that "Car" will have vehicle_type as its parent concept and similarly "Eon" will have vehicle_model as its parent class as shown in Fig. 10. Now, if the user wants to add more parent class, he can add by choosing "Add more" button.

Step 7: **Add mappings between categories**

Relations between the categories can also be defined and hence mapping between them can easily be done using relation corpus. The user can pick any category to map other category depending upon some relation and drop down in the space provided. Suppose user adds a new relation in step 1 as "isRelatedTo". In correspond to this relation, user can add mapping between categories.

Figure 11 shows how mapping between categories is done, in which "Car" category is mapped to "Bike" category with the use of "RelatedTo" property. All the data generated till this step are stored in an organized manner in database which can easily be mapped to any formal ontology development tool.

This platform is ready to be validated and refined by the domain experts online by going through the same web pages presented in this section. Once the model is validated, it is ready to be converted into a new ontology using an ontology generation tool, which will be presented next.

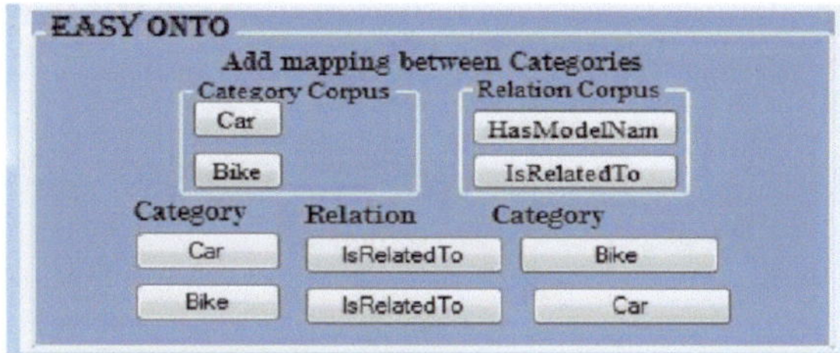

Fig. 11 Add mappings between categories

5 Semiformal Ontology Construction Model

Following the above-explained procedure, system will able to produce semiformal ontology model which can then be validated and refined by refined by domain experts. Once it is validated, formal ontology can be generated either in RDF/OWL format. All the data entered by the user in a system are stored in database in a structured manner which can be easily mapped to ontology elements such as ontology classes, instances and properties. For generating formal ontology, java-based ontology development tool "Protégé" can be used.

Various plug-ins are provided by Protégé to map database values to ontology elements. Converting semiformal ontology to formal ontology is beyond the scope of this paper. Figures 12 and 13 show the layout of formal ontology in Protégé editor.

Representation of generated ontology can be written in OWL or RDF as follows:

<rdf: RDF
Xmlns: rdf ="http://www.w3.org/1999/02/22-rdf#" Xmlns:
rdfs="http://www.w3.org/2000/01/rdf-schmea#"
Xmlns:xsd="http://www.w3.org/2000/10/xmlschema#"><o
wl: ontology rdf: about=" ">
<owl: imports rdf: resource='http://www.owl.org/2001/03/owl#'/>
<owl: label>vehicle</owl:
label></owl: ontology>

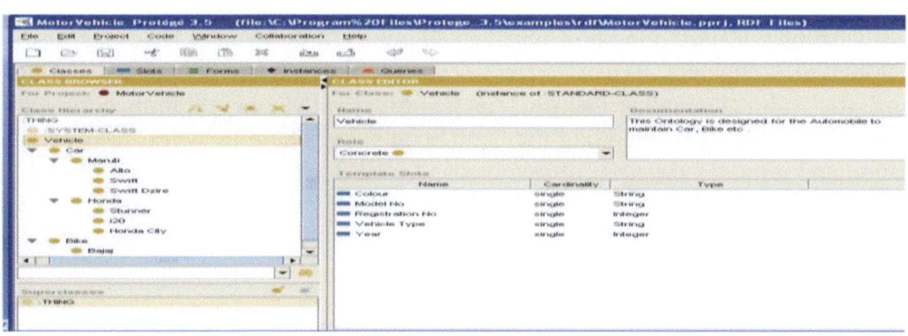

Fig. 12 Ontology design on domain "Motor Vehicle"

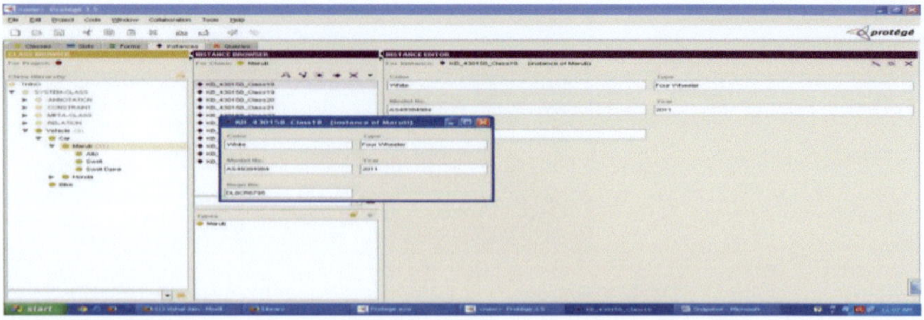

Fig. 13 Defining instances of Maruti

```
<owl: class rdf:ID ="Vehicle">
<owl: subclass of rdf:
resource="#Car"/><owl: subclass of rdf:
resource="#Bike"/>
</owl: class>
<owl: class rdf:ID ="Vehicle">
rdfs:subclass of>
<owl: on property rdf:
resource="#Car"/><owl : on property rdf:
resource="#Bike"/><owl : Datatype Property
rdf: ID="Swift"/><owl : Datatype Property
rdf: ID="Verna"/><owl : Datatype Property
rdf: ID="Pulsar"/>
<owl : Datatype Property rdf: ID="Royal Enfield"/>
</owl:Datatype Property></rdf>
```

6 Conclusion and Future Scope

A Social Web application, named “EasyOnto”, was presented which allows mass participation who does not know much about ontology or does not have expertise of ontology development, to easily create semiformal ontology. This informal ontology, after validation and refinement, can be further converted into formal ontology. This system allows accelerating ontology acquisition phase involves mass participation and removes the need of involvement of domain expert in initial phases of ontology development. Future work involves reusing existing ontology, giving out credit to user who contributes in developing ontology, so as to increase more participation and to improve scalability of the system.

References

1. Cimiano, P.: Ontology Learning and Population from Text: Algorithms, Evaluation and Applications. Springer, New York (2006)
2. Hitzler, P., Krötzsch, M., Rudolph, S.: Foundations of Semantic Web Technologies. Chapman & Hall/CRC (2009)
3. Siorpaes, K., Hepp, M.: myOntology: the marriage of ontology engineering and collective intelligence. In: Bridging the Gap Between Semantic Web and Web 2.0 (SemNet 2007), pp. 127–138 (2007)
4. Schaffert, S.: Semantic social software: semantically enabled social software or socially enabled semantic web? In: Proceedings of the SEMANTICS 2006 Conference, pp. 99–112, OCG, Vienna, Austria (2006)
5. Dall'Agnol, J.M.H., Tacla, C.A., Freddo, A.R., Molinari, A.H., Paraiso, E.C.: The use of well-founded argumentation on the conceptual modeling of collaborative ontology development. In: CSCWD, pp. 200–207 (2011)
6. Buffa, M., Gandon, F., Ereteo, G., Sander, P., Faron, C.: SweetWiki: a semantic wiki. J. WebSemant. **6**(1), 84–97 (2008)
7. Krötzsch, M., Vrandečić, D., Völkel, M.: Semantic MediaWiki. In: Proceedings of the 5th International Semantic Web Conference (ISWC06), pp. 935–942, Springer, Berlin (2006)
8. Zaini, N., Omar, H.: An online system to support collaborative knowledge acquisition for ontology development. In: International Conference on Computer Applications and Industrial Electronics (ICCAIE 2011) 978-1-4577-2059-8/11. IEEE (2011)
9. Wang, S., Zhuang, Y., Hu; Z., Fei, X.: An ontology evolution method based on Folksonomy. In: 2014 International Symposium on Computer, Consumer and Control (IS3C), pp. 336, 339, 10–12 June 2014

Biometric Inspired Homomorphic Encryption Algorithm for Secured Cloud Computing

Yogesh Bala and Amita Malik

Abstract Cloud computing widely uses resource sharing and computing framework over the Internet. Data security is the key objective while sharing data over untrusted environment. This paper presents a novel biometric inspired homomorphic encryption algorithm (BIHEA) for secured data/files transmission over hybrid cloud environment. The proposed algorithm encrypts the user data at run-time by providing the authorized user biometric-feature-based one time password. Every time a user is authenticated by a totally different one time password. The BIHEA provides a good solution to commonly identified theft seen in cloud environment like phishing, shoulder surfing.

Keywords One time password · Homomorphic encryption · Biometric · Cloud computing

1 Introduction

Cloud computing has recently drawn extensive attention to the organization and business community. Cloud computing provides the platform over which the sharing of resources over the Internet can be done efficiently [1]. There are various cloud models that have been developed, and we can describe these models in terms of 'Z as Utility' where Z may represent as hardware infrastructure, application software or storage infrastructure etc. Amazon Microsoft Azure and Salesforce.com are the successfully implemented cloud computing platforms over which the available resources are shared ubiquitously at low costs. Cloud computing implementation in

Y. Bala (✉) · A. Malik
Deenbandhu Chhotu Ram University of Science and Technology,
Murthal, Sonepat, Haryana, India
e-mail: joinyogeshbala@gmail.com

A. Malik
e-mail: amitamalik.cse@dcrustm.org

B.K. Panigrahi et al. (eds.), *Nature Inspired Computing*, Advances in Intelligent Systems and Computing 652, https://doi.org/10.1007/978-981-10-6747-1_2

real time has many challenges. As we know that the major concern of any business organization is the security and confidentially of its information and data.

In the growing era of cloud computing, organizations are placing their data on the cloud to achieve the benefits provided by the cloud such as service flexibility, multitenancy and configurable computing resources which help them to expand their business with minimum effort, time and cost. But the privacy and data security still remains the key concern for the organizations in adoption of clouds. As the data is in the hand of third party, many encryption algorithms have been proposed by researchers to provide the security to stored data. Uma Somani et al. [1] have implemented the concept of RSA encryption along with the digital signature that results in enhancing the data security of cloud in cloud computing. Yu et al. [2] have described a cryptographic method that improves the security and confidentiality of prioritized information on cloud server. Tirthani and Ganesan [3] have presented Diffie-Hellman Key Exchange algorithm using elliptic curve cryptography for efficient transfer of encrypted data. In this paper, authors have used a traditional one-tier authentication which is vulnerable to security attacks. Arasu et al. [4] have proposed the method that concatenates message, hash function and key which helps in ensuring the authenticate message delivery. The method implements a single-tier authentication and hence not a suitably strong for cloud environment. Rivest et al. [5] introduced the concept of homomorphic encryption which enables the computation of encrypted data without using the secret key. Thus, it facilitates to perform operations on the encrypted data without decrypting it. Before the introduction of homomorphic encryption, it was not possible to perform operation on encrypted data, so we have to decrypt the data on the cloud server before performing any calculation on the data. So, the homomorphic encryption allows the cloud provider to perform the operations on encrypted data without decrypting it.

In this paper, we address this open issue and propose a two-tier bio-inspired homomorphic encryption algorithm that provides a secured data access scheme at two layers over unreliable cloud computing media. Our proposed system is based on the knowledge that in real-time scenarios, all the information/message can be encrypted by defining a key component. The same secret keys are shared among users which allow a user to decrypt the encrypted data, only if the key matches with the generated key. Key is generated using the biometric-feature-based algorithm in which multiple keys are created that are dependent on the biometric feature of user in real-time scenario. At a time, one key is passed to the other user as one time password for authentication and to decrypt the stored data at cloud servers [6–10]. Such a design also brings about confidentiality, security and authorization of data access on cloud. Only the data owner can grant the permission to access the data, without any such permission the user will not be able to access the data.

The rest of the paper is organized as follows. Section 2 discusses the homomorphic encryption algorithm. Section 3 presents the proposed BIHE algorithm. In Sect. 4, we analyse our proposed system in terms of its security features and time complexity. We conclude this paper in Sect. 5.

2 Homomorphic Encryption Algorithm

Homomorphic encryption is the cryptography technique that enables to communicate multiple number of parties in cooperation to generate the ciphertext without the knowledge of plain text. Thus, homomorphic encryption applies the algebraic operations on the ciphertext, without deciphering it to plain text. The homomorphic encryption technique can be expressed as follows.

Consider $E(x)$ be the function defined for performing encryption and m_1 and m_2 be two plain texts. C_1 and C_2 are the ciphertexts given as in Eqs. 1 and 2.

$$c = E(m)_{11} \tag{1}$$

$$c = E(m)_{22} \tag{2}$$

$$c \times c = E(m + m)_{1212} \tag{3}$$

Equation 3 performs the algebraic operations x on C_1 and C_2 as shown in Eq. 3. Here + is also the mathematical operation applied over messages. In this paper, homomorphic encryption is chosen as an encryption method to encrypt the user data over cloud.

3 Biometric Inspired Homomorphic Encryption Algorithm

This section presents a BIHEA. The BIHEA allows the data to be encrypted using key generated as one time password (OTP) from iris of the registered user over the cloud, which is used as a key to decrypt ciphertext only in one time process.

Figure 1 describes the system architecture of BIHEA algorithm. In the first step, the scanned retinal image of cloud user is taken as an input to BIHEA. The reason for choosing the iris in proposed algorithm is that retinal vessels of a specific cloud user have unique feature which have the least chance of matching with other.

Thereafter, the input image is resized into 505 × 598 to make the choice of the data pool get powerful enough that it can generate highly random data. We can either use RGB or greyscale image. RGB image is used in this work. The input RGB image is converted into greyscale image. Grey images are used to extract the edges (retinal vessels) of a retinal image. Retinal vessels are often used for authentication purpose. Fovea is fixed in retinal image, but optical disc can move. All the blood vessels are connected to the optical disc. Feature points are collected from the edge extraction process of a retinal image. So, extracted feature points from retinal image can be different for a same person. These different feature points are useful to create OTPs. In this proposed approach, random numbers of variable length are generated using the retinal feature points.

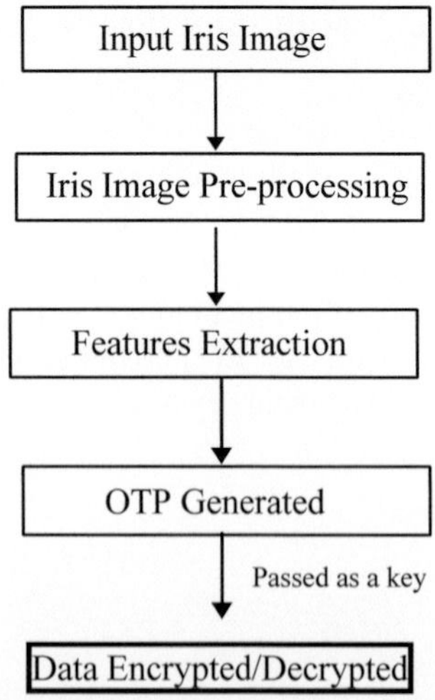

Fig. 1 System architecture of BIHEA encryption and decryption

This random number of variable length is used as OTP. OTP is valid only for a single session. Every time a user wants to enter the system, a new OTP is generated.

Both encryption of data and decryption of data are based on homomorphic encryption method. The BIHEA algorithm is described as follows:

Step-1: *Generation of OTP*

In this, we take the first component which is the scanned image of the registered user as input. Retina is a powerful biometric factor to generate the OTP. After that we resize the image according to the requirement. In our work, we have resized the image to 505×598. Now as we have taken the RGB image, we convert the image into greyscale. The reason for converting into greyscale image is that RGB image has three channels whereas greyscale image has only one channel, thus it eases in the computation of Euclidean distance. Next step is to extract the edges of greyscale retinal image. Now, the intensity value of a point in the image is either 0 or 1. Edges (blood vessels) gone through the points have intensity value 1, and rest of the image points have intensity value 0. The points (x, y) which have intensity (I) value 1 are taken for further use. Now, distance is calculated from (0, 0) to each point. We have used 'Sobel' method to extract the edges of a retinal image. We store those distance value in the matrix that are multiple of 7, i.e. $D\%7 == 0$. This calculation is done to confuse the hacker. They do not know which numbers are used in the system to generate the OTP. There may be possibility of duplicity in the matrix. Thus, duplicate number checking process is used to filter the duplicate number from D matrix, and it is stored in final matrix, M. A random number (N) is selected from the range $4 \leq N \leq 7$. Now, N numbers are selected randomly from the final matrix M. N is taken randomly to create variable length number. Finally, permutation of N numbers is done to generate the variable length random number called OTP.

Step-2: *BIHEA Encryption Technique Using OTP as a Key*

Input the data of cloud users and converts the data into its respective ASCII value. After the conversion into ASCII, we have to make equal length data of both users as we have to perform the mathematical operation on it. If the length is not same, then firstly we select the data whose length is small and append it with white space. Thereafter, data of both cloud users is converted into 16-bit binary data format. Now in order to perform the operation of encryption, we firstly randomly generate a number between 1 and 100 and then add integer obtained by multiplying the OTP generated in previous step with 19, in each bit of ASCII data. The arithmetic + operation is performed over resulted data of cloud users and stored on the cloud server.

Step-3: *BIHEA Decryption Technique Using OTP as a Key*

In cloud when any registered user needs the data of other registered cloud user, the request is sent by the user to the cloud server to retrieve the data. Thereafter, request is accepted by cloud server, and it delivers the stored data to the requisitioned. After receiving the data from the cloud, it will decrypt the received data using the same biometric inspired OTP key. User converts both data, i.e. its own data and decrypted data, into 16-bit binary format. They perform the exclusive OR operation on these two 16-bit binary data, and the result obtained is converted into the decimal value. Finally, we convert decimal value, i.e. respective ASCII value, into the corresponding ASCII characters. Hence, we get the data of the other registered cloud user.

4 Results and Discussion

The proposed BIHEA scheme tries to mitigate the security attacks such as unauthorized access of data, information disclosure during sharing, accessing and sharing the data of one user with other users without the permission and acknowledgement of data owner.

A. *Breach of Data Access*

The proposed BIHEA system explained in Sect. 3 which give permission to the user having an OTP is authorized to access the data. Only the data owner is authorized to issuing of OTP scan. The data cannot be accessed either by the Cloud Storage Provider or by the users, if they do not have the OTP. The imposition of the access control policy is guaranteed even if the Cloud Storage Server is not within the reach of the data owner or if it is malicious and untrusted as the access to the data or information depends on the OTP generated by the data owner. Breach of data access can happen in two possible situations.

(1) The OTP with which the data can be decrypted is acquired by the unauthorized user or attacker, without the any knowledge or help by the Cloud Storage Provider. To access such an OTP, the attacker will have to know (a) iris of the

registered user, (b) random number generated, and (c) randomly chosen integer, e.g. '19', which is multiplied with the OTP used as a key. The knowledge of these three secrets is impossible. So, it is hardly possible for an attacker to access such an OTP without any help from the Cloud Storage Provider.

(2) The other possible situation is that the OTP with which the data can be decrypted is acquired by the unauthorized user or attacker, with the knowledge or help by the Cloud Storage Provider. To access such an OTP, the iris of the registered user or the knowledge of randomly chosen value for the OTP must be known to the attacker. As OTP is delivered to user in the form of short message service (SMS), it is not possible for the attacker to calculate OTP from SMS. The SMS message is kept in secret and private by the user, so the attacker could not access the key. In brief, it is impossible for the attacker to access the key even with if Cloud Storage Provider helps the attacker.

B. *Data Disclosure during Sharing*

The data in the cloud environment is always in its encrypted form whether it is shared or any computation is done on the data; however, it may be encrypted with different keys, at different stages. Thus, the data is not decrypted at any point of instant before delivering the computational results to the requested user, who is authorized to access the data. Hence, it guarantees that the entire process of sharing does not allow leaking of any part of the information to unauthorized user.

To access the decrypted information during the sharing process, an unauthorized user must have the key or knowledge of iris pattern of registered user and method of generation of OTP using that pattern with the random generated numbers. From the above analysis, it is determined that the data cannot be decrypted by the unauthorized user. To decrypt message, the attacker needs the key used.

C. *Time Complexity*

Finally, the time complexity of BIHEA with the existing RSA, DES and AES encryption is done. It is clearly evident from the bar graphs shown in Figs. 2, 3, 4 and 5

Fig. 2 Computation time comparison of DES, AES, RSA and BIHEA

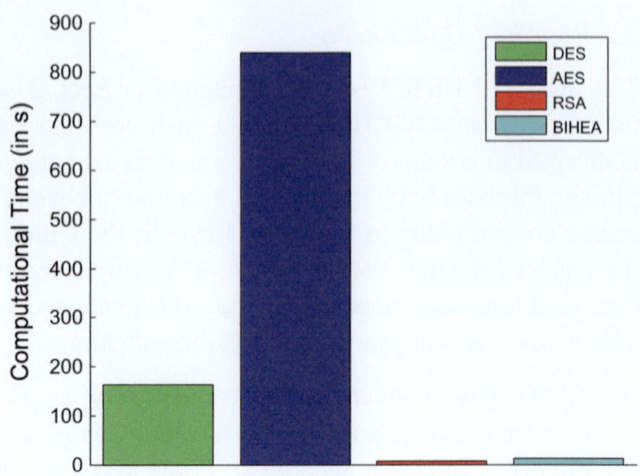

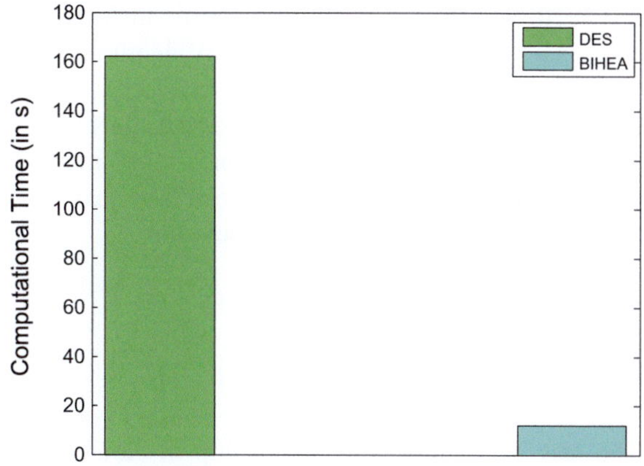

Fig. 3 Bar chart of DES algorithm in comparison to BIHEA

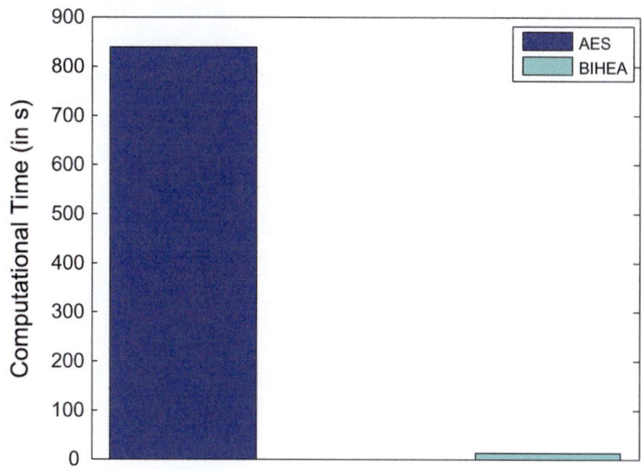

Fig. 4 Bar chart of AES algorithm in comparison to BIHEA

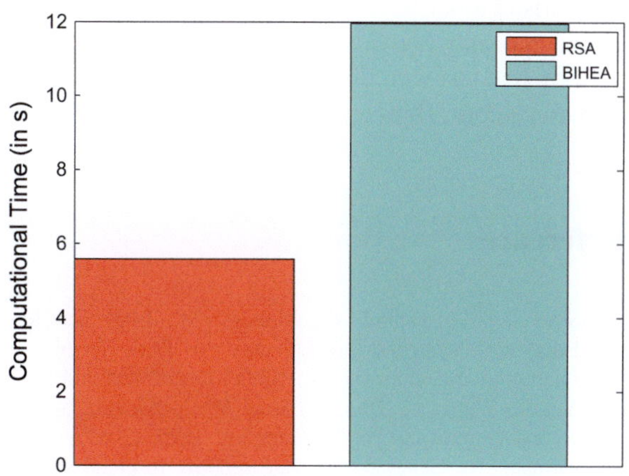

Fig. 5 Bar chart of RSA algorithms in comparison to BIHEA

that BIHEA takes less time in comparison to AES and DES encryption algorithm, but takes more time in comparison to RSA algorithm. RSA algorithm takes least time for execution, but it is more vulnerable to attacks. Thus, researchers proposed AES and DES encryption algorithms that reduce the effects of attacks, but on the other hand, the algorithm complexity increases, hence takes more time to execute. The proposed BIHEA offers both the advantages, i.e. it takes less time to execute and is more resistant to the attacks due to its two-tier architecture.

5 Conclusion

The lack of infrastructure ownership in cloud computing results in lack of user interest for storing its valuable data over the cloud. Thus, it becomes essential to develop the user's trust in cloud for sharing its data over the cloud environment. In this paper, we have proposed a biometric inspired homomorphic encryption algorithm (BIHEA) which is successfully implemented. The proposed encryption system has two-tier mechanism that means user data is encrypted using a secret key that is generated using iris of the user and generates the ciphertext which can be decrypted with a singular decryption key obtained as OTP from the registered user. This system allows the re-encryption of the user data, by altering the encryption key without decrypting the data. Thus, BIHEA provides a good system for sharing the user data on the cloud securely. The proposed system protects user data from unauthorized access and allowing enforcing the sharing policies as stated by the data owner.

We have performed thorough study and analysis of various security schemes before finalizing the proposed system and proof that the system allows user to securely share the data over untrusted cloud servers. The security analysis of the proposed BIHEA system infers that it can prevent number of security attacks and provide strong trusted environment for sharing the user data over untrusted cloud in comparison to DES, AES and RSA schemes. In the future, replay attack can also be considered and prevented using Time Stamp in BIHEA. It is also foreseen to perform real test with distributed computing on existing cloud servers like Amazon, Salesforce.com, Hadoop along with MATLAB tool.

References

1. Somani, U., Lakhani, K., Mundra, M.: Implementing the Digital Signature with RSA Encryption algorithm to Enhance the Data Security of cloud in cloud computing 1st International Conference on Parallel Distributed and Grid Computing. IEEE (2010)
2. Yu, S., Wang, C., Ren, K., Lou, W.: Achieving Secure, Scalable, and Fine-grained Data Access Control in Cloud Computing. IEEE (2010)
3. Tirthani, N., Ganesan, R.: Data security in cloud architecture based on diffie hellman and elliptical curve cryptography IACR Cryptology, ePrint Archive 49 (2014)

4. Arasu, S.E., Gowri, B., Ananthi, S.: Privacy-preserving public auditing in cloud using HMAC algorithm," International Journal of Recent Technology and Engineering, IJRTE **2**(1) (2013)
5. Ronald L. Rivest, Leonard Adleman, and Michael L. Dertouzos.: On Data Banks and Privacy Homomorphisms, chapter On Data Banks and Privacy Homomorphisms Academic Press. pp. 169–180 (1978)
6. Jansen W.A.: Cloud Hooks: Security and Privacy Issues in Cloud Computing 44th Hawaii International Conference on System Sciences (2011)
7. Miranda, M., Pearson, S.: A Client-Based Privacy Manager for Cloud Computing COMSWARE'09. Dublin, Ireland (2009)
8. Wang, J., Mu, S.: Security issues and countermeasures in cloud computing in 2011 IEEE International Conference on Grey Systems and Intelligent Services, pp. 843–846 (2011)
9. A. Tripathi and A. Mishra (2011) Cloud computing security considerations in 2011 IEEE International Conference on Signal Processing, Communications and Computing (ICSPCC), pp. 1–5
10. Mathisen E.: Security challenges and solutions in cloud computing in 2011 Proceedings of the 5th IEEE International Conference on Digital Ecosystems and Technologies Conference (DEST), pp. 208–212 (2011)

Relevance Feedback Base User Convenient Semantic Query Processing Using Neural Network

P. Mohan Kumar and B. Balamurugan

Abstract In today's world, people prefer Internet applications for fulfilling their needs. One cannot give guarantee for all applications get completed and all completed are not to the level of user satisfactory. Most of the solutions exist only for major cases such as optimal response, nearby output, similar answer, failure, fraudulences. Some may be discarded by the user itself, but all applications cannot be left as that, few holds significance. At the outset, we strive to provide solutions for such significant applications to the level of user satisfactory. In this paper, a way is analysed to reprocess such applications by taking the relevance feedback based on their input and obtained output and reaches their convenience using semantic intelligence and neural networks.

Keywords Feedback · Intelligence · Semantic cache · Neural network

1 Introduction

The growth rate of Internet users for various applications increases day to day due to the busy scenarios of life schedule. Any user whenever he/she tend to access the Internet for relevant information retrieval, they fed a word, sentence, or an URI/URL, a query and event base click, irrespective of precise imprecise input how far the obtained data is correct. Various researches have been made and proved with respect to the criteria as query form, response time, semantic and syntactic base, data conversion mode, intelligence inference base, knowledge acquisition, query expansion and dynamic adaptation during run-time, etc. But the main issue is how far the obtained output is exact based on the input given and are they satisfied with that result. In this paper in order to answer this question, we provide road map as first we give definition for satisfaction and dissatisfaction, general aspects why this arise, existing techniques proved by researchers based on type of data, system

P. Mohan Kumar (✉) · B. Balamurugan
VIT University, Vellore, Tamil Nadu, India
e-mail: pmohankumar@vit.ac.in

B.K. Panigrahi et al. (eds.), *Nature Inspired Computing*, Advances in Intelligent Systems and Computing 652, https://doi.org/10.1007/978-981-10-6747-1_3

architecture for proposed approach, work principle, sample data set with neural network approach as how this data can be trained and tuned to map the relevance and conclude with mapping the converged output to the user convenience by semantic intelligence agent, which follows the discussing with pros and cons of the designed algorithm.

2 Related Work

Query processing is the core activity of the database system irrespective components used. Though the work is, at the outset considered it is mandatory to see the problem of query folding activity [1], i.e. determining if and how a query can be answered from the given set of resources such as previous cached results, materialized views, metadata, ontologies, as shown in [2] are not much concentrated. We emphasize intelligence from the user feedback. We extract only the representation of satisfiability, equivalence and implication relational aspects to compare with derived set of relations. Anyhow, we took the unsatisfied result only and strive for satisfiability towards intelligence. As a preliminary notion, we need to follow some rules which are represented in below table and detailed description followed for processing as specified in Dunham. The notion of "similar" in the mind of the user may fluctuate depending on the query, the history of retrievals observed and the user. If there is a significant discrepancy between the similarity as calculated by the system and the notion of similarity in the user's mind, the results are destined to be unsatisfactory. This problem has served as the impetus for what is known as "Relevance Feedback" (RF). Relevance feedback retrieval systems prompt the user for feedback on retrieval results and then use this feedback on subsequent retrievals with the goal of increasing retrieval performance.

3 System Work Flow

The proposed work flow is explained in the generalized system architecture. It has the following components GUI where the user can interface in order to give input, view resultant as well as post the feedback if the obtained output is not satisfactory. Semantic intelligence agent plays a vital role for the system in overall for server as well as client services. It holds major four components; one resultant cache which stores all the processed output, which is for future use. Then the feedback cache to store the user feedback information for the unsatisfactory output. Neural network layer for tuning the incoming user information and mapping relevant to the processor to execute with respect to the system semantics prior stored and vice versa. Query log which contains all the query details used for reprocessing. SQL server is the actual query processor, which retrieves the required information for user query. Data log holds the information about data storage in database. Whenever user gives

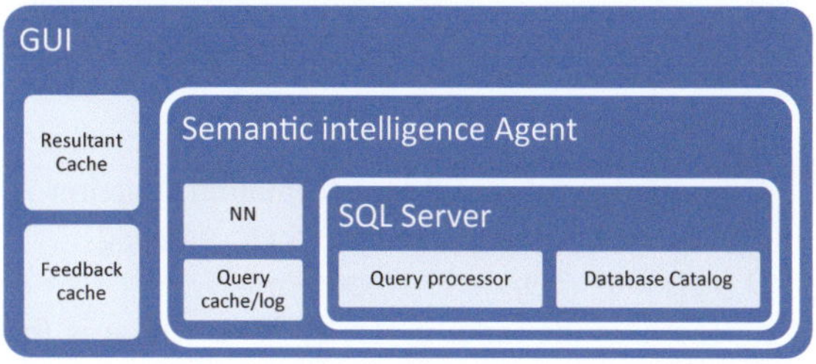

Fig. 1 Generalized system architecture

the input, the system checks for its validity; if it is OK, then it checks prior processed log; if so, then the relevance existence is checked in resultant cache and displayed else if it is newer, it will be allowed for processor and executed. The output displayed to the user after logging the necessary details in query log. During the first time, the proxy (intelligence agent) acts as validator and the NN acts as input layer to the query processor. Since we concentrate on relevance feedback based on user satisfactory identification, we see from unsatisfactory query results alone (Fig. 1).

The network model stores the relevance given by the semantic intelligence agent and output from the processor and finds the exactness. The NN training is detailed in the above session.

4 Proposed Algorithm

4.1.2 Query processor (query_id, attribute, relation, tuple value, operation).

{//information given by semantic intelligence inference engine relation, operator, attributes value, output of NN layer;
If (query== exact)
Fetch the relevance result from query cache and submit to event mapping agent ().
Else If (query ==partial)
Process as probe and remainder query execute perform dynamic mapping and submit to event mapping agent. Else
If (query ==mismatch) Display the invalid. Exit.}

4.1.3 User feedback processing in interactive mode

4.1.3.a User online(feedback)//learning mode

Input: user feedback.//initial weights of the neuron in the layer are initially “0”;

The first set of output obtained from query processor is stored as weights in all the neurons. Let its weight be $w_i, S_i(0) = w_i \quad 0 \leq i \leq n-1$

$S_i(0)$ output of node i at time t and w_i is the initial value between 0 and 1.

The activation and weight computation during iteration is calculated as

$$S_i(x+1) = fs\sum_{i=0}^{n=1} \text{witi}(0), \quad 0 \leq j \leq n-1$$

F_s continuous sigmoid transformation function

F_s(net$j$) = 1/1 + exp[−(net$j$ − theta$_{a_j}$)/theta$_{a_0}$]

O_s(net) = Fs(net$j$) + Fs1(net$k$)End.

F_s1(net$k$) is the input given by NN2 which is the output processed by offline.

The above process is repeated output between at least two iteration become more similar, i.e. alike exact.Return;End}

4.1.3.b User feedback processing in offline mode

User offline(feedback)//supervised mode

User given feedback from the SIA is tested with the neurons. The average weight be between [0, 1]. It can be allowed to train as $w_{new} = w_{old} - \alpha\, \partial E/\partial w_{old}$, where α is the learning rate, the error be E = (target − output)^2, and the actual output is measured by the sigmoid, a real function sc: IR ! (0, 1) defined by the expression sc (x) = 1/1 + e − cx. The final output Fs1(net$k$) = f(x)(1 − f(x) end

Based on these function measure, the output is given to the query processor.

5 Experimental Analysis

ATM utilization of a customer and resolving inconveniences via net/mobile-banking interface. We chose user case as a customer utilizing ATM facility on his home branch, i.e. a bank ATM where customer having account, customer utilizing authorized other related bank ATM's, customers viewing or posting their status towards net-banking, mobile-banking or personal approaches. User invokes bank application towards mobile-banking and gets activated based on the id and password validity; the home page is displayed in GUI. He/She can view his prior problem status and invoke new application or continue to the prior application by posting his request as feedback. Further, he/she can continue in an interactive mode or post a feedback and continue later. The SIA analyses the given feedback information and finds the relevance by comparing the semantic contents stored and passed as input to the NN1. In NN1, this input is stored as initial weights with new values and passed to processor. The obtained output will be displayed to the user after storing this information in NN2. If the user is satisfied, he/she can exit else he/she can again post relevance feedback. These inputs are again parsed by the SIA and given to NN1. Here again, the input weight is added to the prior existing weight. From here onwards the NN process starts. NN1 is used to decide the input validation and consistency [3]. NN1 acts as a learning mode, where the weights are adjusted by itself based on the incoming feedback input as well as prior stored value. Further in order to find the exactness, it will take the output obtained from the NN2 which is a supervised mode processor; it will be used during the offline. It will be detailed in offline mode. This process will be repeated until the system converges or the user satisfies [4, 5]. The parsed data is passed as and input to the NN2 which is supervised layer. It makes use of the SIA to load its initial weight which is the target weight. The incoming input will be trained by the NN2 iteratively by the assistance of the relevance given by the SIA [6] related to the problem and displayed to the user as output. Here, the exactness with any variance will be displayed. User can view his output and he/she may repeat based on his convenience [7]. We tested few samples and we find the significance of our proposed approach.

5.1 Research Results

In this section, we show how the samples were acquired, display the success rate of this system and examine the cause of failure of some sample.

5.1.1 Samples Tested. Day-Wise Report

See Tables 1, 2 and 3.

Table 1 Problem samples

Day 1	Problem type	Validity	Fault type	Status	Mode
User A	DD	Valid	System	Resolved	Offline
User B	ATM	Invalid	User card	Unresolved	Online
User D	RTGS	Valid	System	Resolved	Online
User E	Loan account	Valid	System	Resolved	Offline

Table 2 Proposed system performance significance

S. No.	Day	No. of users	Problem type	Mode of request	Rate of success	Rate of failure	Rate of success	Rate of failure
					Existing system	Existing system	Proposed system	Proposed system
1	01	50	DD	Offline	40(90%)	10(10%)	48(98%)	2(2%)
2	02	100	ATM	Online	97(97%)	3(3%)	100(100%)	0(0%)
3	03	70	NEFT	Online	60(93%)	10(17%)	65(95%)	5(5%)

Table 3 Failure causes and reasons

S. No.	Problem type	Mode	Status	Reason
1	ATM	Online	Failure	Timed out, money not available, txn overlapping (rare)
2	DD	Offline	Failure	Account No. wrong entry, signature invalid amount insufficient

5.1.2 Graphical Representation for the System Output

The system output status is plotted as graph with various modes, initially, the output related to problems posted in offline mode as shown in Fig. 2 and in similar online mode in Fig. 3. Here, we took the sample problems such as ATM, DD and NEFT [7–10] transactions for group of customers of particular bank with collective branches in particular town (Figs. 4 and 5).

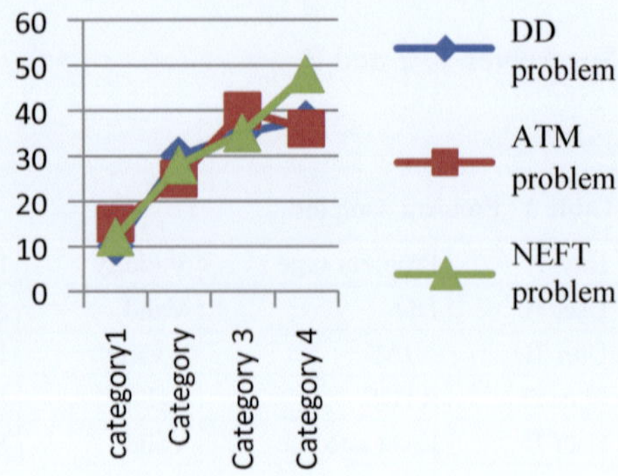

Fig. 2 User problems with offline

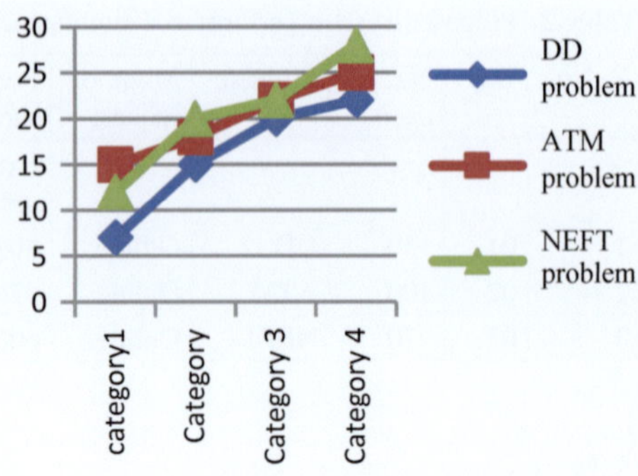

Fig. 3 User problem with online

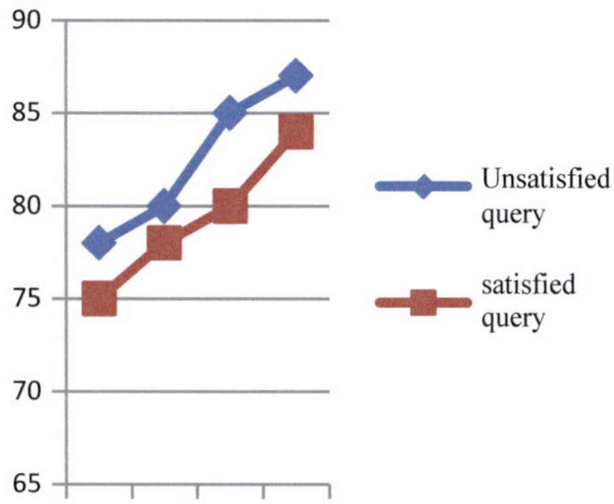

Fig. 4 Proposed system response time

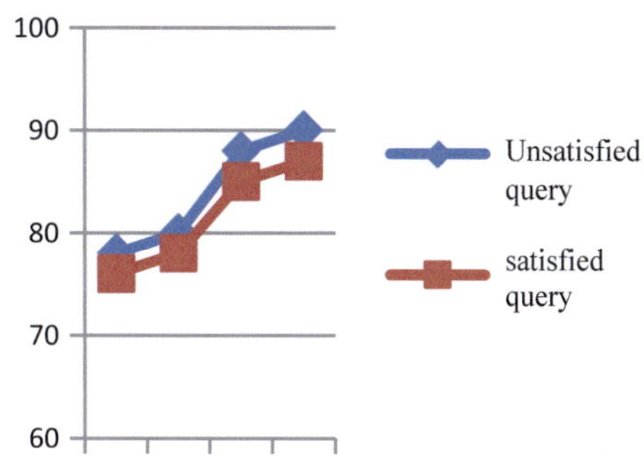

Fig. 5 Existing system time response

6 Conclusion

This paper discusses the issues about the processed query user inconvenience. It analyses and provides all the relevant cause to the level of user judgment. The sample is tested with the real-time application scenario with respect to online as well as offline mode. The designed model along with query processor and the semantic intelligence agent collectively strive to bring the satisfactory output relevant to the user prior posted input query, corresponding to the feedback posted based on processed output by processing iteratively. This can be enhanced to large set with image-based applications in future.

References

1. Ren, Q., Dhunam, H.: Semantic caching and query processing Technical report (1998)
2. Sheshasaayee, A., Jasmine, C.: Relevance feedback techniques Implemented in CBIR: current trends and issues. Int. J. of Eng. Trends Technol. (IJETT) **10**(4), 166–175 (2004) (ISSN: 2231-5381)

3. A Briefing Given to the SC 2003 Education Program on Knowledge Discovery in Databases, Nov 16 2003. NCSA (2003)
4. Veera Jyothi, B., Shanker, U., Neural network approach for image retrieval based on preference elicitation. Int. J. Comput. Sci. Eng., **02**(04), 934–941 (2010)
5. Mistry, D.: Survey of relevance feedback methods in content-based image retrieval. Int. J. Comput. Sci. Eng. Technol. (IJCSET) (ISSN: 2229-3345)
6. Durai, CRB.: Improved content based image retrieval using neural network optimization with genetic algorithm. Int. J. Emerg. Technol. Adv. Eng. **2**(7) (2012)
7. Modaghegh, H., Javidi, M., Sadoghi Yazdi, H., Pourreza, H.R.: Learning of relevance feedback using a novel kernel based neural network. Aust. J. Basic Appl. Sci. **4**(2), 171–186 (2010)
8. Wasilewska, A., Neural networks Tutorial. State University of New York
9. Chu, K.K., Chang, M., Hsia, YT.: A Hybrid Training Mechanism for Applying Neural Networks to Web-based Applications. In: IEEE International Conference on Systems, Man and Cybernetics. (2004)
10. Zhang, Z., Chung-E Data Mining Approach for Network Intrusion Detection. Department of Computer Science. California State University (2002)

Comparative Analysis of Decision Tree Algorithms

Mridula Batra and Rashmi Agrawal

Abstract Decision trees are outstanding tools to help anyone to select the best course of action. They generate a highly valuable arrangement in which one can place options and study possible outcomes of those options. They also facilitate users to make a fair idea of the pros and cons related to each possible action. A decision tree is used to represent graphically the decisions, the events, and the outcomes related to decisions and events. Events are probabilistic and determined for each outcome. The aim of this paper is to do detailed analysis of decision tree and its variants for determining the best appropriate decision. For this, we will analyze and compare various decision tree algorithms such as ID3, C4.5, CART, and CHAID.

Keywords Ensemble · ID3 · C4.5 · CART · CHAID

1 Preface

A decision tree is a grid or tool that is used to support decisions which include various alternatives, including event outcomes, cost of resources used, and its usage [1]. It is one way to exhibit an algorithm. Applications of decision trees are typically used in research and analysis of decision.

There are three types of nodes in decision tree:

1. Decision nodes are symbolized by squares.
2. Chance nodes are denoted by circles.
3. End nodes are signified by triangles.

M. Batra (✉) · R. Agrawal
Manav Rachna International University, Faridabad, India
e-mail: rashmi.sandeep.goel@gmail.com

B.K. Panigrahi et al. (eds.), *Nature Inspired Computing*, Advances in Intelligent Systems and Computing 652, https://doi.org/10.1007/978-981-10-6747-1_4

There are two types of decision trees:

- *Classification tree*: This tree is used to predict label of the class to which the data belongs.
- *Regression tree*: These are generally used where the class label is a real number.

2 Techniques of Decision Tree

Here are some techniques, often called *ensemble* methods, which are used to build more than one decision tree [2–4]:

- *Bagging*: Bagging is used to build many decision trees by continually resampling guided facts with alternate, which determines the tree for a consent calculation.
- *Random forest*: This type of classifier selects a numerals of decision trees randomly to enhance classification rate.
- *Boosted trees*: Boosted trees represent classification and regression problems.
- *Rotation forest*: In this ensemble method, principal component analysis (PCA) is applied initially on every decision tree.

3 Decision Tree Classification

This is referred as one of the most accepted methods for knowledge discovery. It methodically examines the information contained huge facts to reveal valuable rules and relationships, and generally, it is used for the purpose of prediction. If we compare with other data mining methodologies, this is extensively applicable in various areas [2–8].

4 Algorithms

4.1 ID3
4.2 C4.5 (enhancement of ID3)
4.3 CART
4.4 CHAID

4.1 ID3 (Iterative Dichotomizer 3) Algorithm

ID3 stands for Iterative Dichotomizer 3. This algorithm produces a decision tree from given dataset. This algorithm is mainly used for natural processing and machine learning domain.

The algorithm starts with the actual set '**S**' as the first node. After every iteration, it iterates through every unused attribute of the set '**S**' and calculates the entropy.

4.1.1 Properties

ID3 does not assure an optimal solution. It is based on choosing the most appropriate attribute to split the dataset on every iteration. In this algorithm, backtracking is used to improve the search in order to find the best decision tree.

ID3 can over fit to the guided facts, to avoid over fitting, we should make use of smaller trees instead of using larger ones. This algorithm results in miniature trees and does not provide the optimal least feasible tree solutions.

4.1.2 Data Description

The test facts which occur in ID3 have some prerequisites:

- Attribute-value description—The similar fields should express every illustration, having predetermined amount of assessments.
- Predefined classes—In this algorithm, predefined fields are used.
- Discrete classes—The output classes of the dataset must be discrete. Constant groups are split into indistinct classes.
- Attribute Selection

In ID3, information gain calculates which attribute is the most appropriate. Information gain is a method used to measure the suitability of attributes to the target class. The attribute which is having the highest information gain is considered the most valuable attribute for classification. To define gain, we first need to have an idea from information theory called entropy. Entropy measures the amount of information in an attribute.

4.1.3 Information Gain

Information gain IG(A) is the compute of the difference in entropy from start to end the set S is split on an attribute A.

$$\mathrm{IG}(A, S) = H(S) - \sum_{t \in T} p(t) H(t)$$

where

- $H(S)$ the entropy of set S
- T the subsets created from splitting set S by attribute A such that $S = \bigcup_{t \in T} t$
- $p(t)$ the proportion of the number of elements in t to the number of elements in set S
- $H(t)$ the entropy of subset t.

$H(S)$ (or information gain IG(A)) measure the field with smallest entropy. The algorithm persists on every division and considers only those fields which have never measure earlier.

Recursion on a subset can bring a halt in any of the following cases:

- Each component in the subset belongs to the parent class, and the current node becomes the end node.
- If more attributes cannot be selected, then the end node is labeled with the general class of the subset.
- An end node is created and labeled with the general class when no attribute is matched with the parent set.

In this algorithm, every non-terminal node represents the chosen field on which data was divided, and terminal node represents the group tag of concluding detachment of the division.

4.2 C4.5 Algorithm

C4.5 is an addition of ID3 algorithm. C4.5 algorithm is also known as statistical classifier. This algorithm also uses the concept of information entropy like ID3. C4.5 algorithm splits the attributes into subsets of one class or other. The field having the maximum information gain finds the results.

It has some foundation cases.

- If the samples fit in the similar groups, it creates an end node for the chosen group.
- If a previously unseen class is found, then this algorithm creates a higher decision node with the expected value.

Expansion of ID3 algorithm

- Handling both continuous and discrete attributes—For holding the constant fields, the algorithm splits the list into smaller lists with attributes having values above threshold and having values equal to or less than the threshold values.
- Handling training data with missing attribute values—In this algorithm whose attribute values are not known are not used in information gain.

4.3 CART Algorithm

CART stands for classification and regression tree. It is the decisive classification tree algorithm. CART is nowadays used as a tool data mining. Other algorithms have tried to match the accuracy of CART algorithm but are unable to do so. CART algorithm is an effective tool to disclose the data relationships which remain hidden using other data analytical tools. This algorithm is widely acceptable tool for predictive modeling.

4.4 Introduction to CHAID

CHAID stands for *chi*-squared Automatic Interaction Detector [9]. This algorithm effectively gives up multi-way frequency tables and is used for marketing research.

Both CHAID and CART algorithms build trees, and every non-terminal node defines a split condition to provide the best possible prediction or classification.

Following are the steps for algorithm:

- The algorithm prepares categorical predictors by approximating equal number of observations.
- In this step, the algorithm merges the categories which are less significant and have a different dependent variable.
- In this step, the algorithm splits the variable having smallest value.

5 Conclusion

Predictive accuracy is an active area of research, and giving general recommendation on this topic is difficult. In this paper, we have studied in detail different decision tree algorithms.

References

1. Demsar, J.: Statistical comparisons of classifiers over multiple data sets. J. Mach. Learn. Res. **7**, 1–30 (2006)
2. Cormode, G., Muthukrishnan, S.: An improved data stream summary: the count-min sketch and its applications. J. Algorithms **55**(1), 58–75 (2005)
3. Yadav, S.K., Bharadwaj, B., Pal, S.: A data mining application: a comparative study for predicting student's performance. Int. J. Innovat. Tech. Creat. Eng. **1**(12), 13–19 (2011)
4. Aher, S.B., Lobo, L.M.R.J.: A comparative study of classification algorithms. Int. J. Inf. Tech. Knowl. Manag. **5**(2), 239–243 (2012)

5. Singhal, S., Jena, M.: A study on WEKA tool for data preprocessing, classif ication and clustering. Int. J. Innov. Technol. Explor. Eng. (IJITEE) **2**(6), (2013). ISSN: 2278–3075
6. Breiman, L., Friedman, J.H., Olshen, R.A., Stone, C.J.: Classification and regression trees. Chapman & Hall/CRC, New York (1984)
7. Belsley, D.A., Kuh, E., Welsch, R.E.: Regression diagnostics: identifying influential data and sources of collinearity. New York (1980)
8. Breiman, L., Friedman, J.H., Olshen, R.A., Stone, C.I.: Classification and regression Trees. Wadsworth, Belmont, CA (1984)
9. Xu, M., Wang, J., Chen, T.: Improved decision tree algorithm: ID3+. Intell. Comput. Signal Process. Pattern Recogn. **345**, 141–149 (2006)

Analysing the Genetic Diversity of Commonly Occurring Diseases

Shamita Malik, Sunil Kumar Khatri and Dolly Sharma

Abstract It is generally believed that the existence of all organisms present on this earth has their point of convergence in a common gene pool. The current species passed through an evolutionary process which is still underway. The theoretical assumptions relating to the common descent of all organisms are based on four simple facts: first, they had wide geographical dispersal; second, the different life forms were not remarkably unique and did not possess mutually exclusive characteristics; third, some of their attributes which apparently served no purpose had an uncanny similarity with some of their lost functional traits; and last, based on their common attributes these organisms can be put together into a well-defined, hierarchical and coherent group, like a family tree. Phylogenetic networks are the main tools that can be used to represent biological relationship between different species. Biologists, mathematicians, statisticians, computer scientists and others have designed various models for the reconstruction of evolutionary networks and developed numerous algorithms for efficient predictions and analysis. Even though these problems have been studied for a very long time, but the computational model built to solve the biological problems fail to give accurate results while working on real biological data, which could be due to the premises on which the model is based. The objective of this paper is to test and analyse the transmission of commonly occurring diseases to fit into more realistic models. The problems are not only important because we need to know how they came into existence and how they migrated, but also helpful for the treatment of such diseases and drug discovery.

S. Malik (✉)
Amity School of Engineering and Technology, Noida, Uttar Pradesh, India
e-mail: smalik@amity.edu

S.K. Khatri
Amity Institute of Information Technology Noida, Noida, Uttar Pradesh, India
e-mail: skkhatri@amity.edu

D. Sharma
Computer Science and Engineering, Shiv Nadar University, Greater Noida, India
e-mail: dolly.sharma@snu.edu.in

B.K. Panigrahi et al. (eds.), *Nature Inspired Computing*, Advances in Intelligent Systems and Computing 652, https://doi.org/10.1007/978-981-10-6747-1_5

Keywords Phylogenetic reconstruction · Algorithms · Genetic diversity · Substitution model · Biological relationships

1 Introduction

Phylogeny is the evolutionary history of a genetically related species or a group of life forms. In excellent contingency, this may really be distinguished, and the most significant point of biological process reconstruction is to explain biological relationships that species or group descend from common ancestry. Thus, we can easily say that phylogenetic analysis plays a significant role in modern biological applications. These applications are ancestral sequence reconstruction, multiple sequence alignment, recombination and hybridisation [1, 2]. In phylogenetics, relationships are represented as a branching diagram known as tree. These branches are known for lineage distance which may split into independent branches or hybridise or sometimes may even become extinct. There are three divisions of relationship: monophyly, paraphyly and polyphyly [3]. Monophyly and paraphyly groups have a single ancestral origin. Monophyletic groups always have all the descendants from the same origin. On the other hand, if one lineage emerging from a monophyletic group is removed, then the group is named as para-phyletic. In polyphyletic groups, characters absent from the most recent ancestor lead to the formation of this group type [4]. Each homologous sequence could be treated as a single character trait. This single character trait is responsible for the phylogenetic reconstruction. Change of these character traits is also helpful in phylogenetic inference. For this to work, one needs to arrange DNA sequences. This process is called sequence alignment. So, it is believed that phylogenetic reconstruction among data set materials may be a useful aid in the understanding of the existence of a disease, disease migration pattern, treatment of such diseases and drug discovery. An assortment of distinctive methodologies is currently available for investigation of genetic diversity. These methods depend on performance data, pedigree data, agronomic data, biochemical data, morphological data and DNA-based data.

In this study to get the moderately correct and unbiased estimates of phylogeny, we intend to focus on the following:

(i) Sampling strategies of the data sets
(ii) Genetic distance
(iii) Genetic relationships
(iv) Reconstruction of phylogeny and
(v) Bootstrapping

2 Methods

The use of statistical tools and techniques, such as computing the selection of substitution model, computing mean diversity within the subpopulation as well within entire population, is an important requirement, followed by reconstruction of phylogenetic network using any efficient algorithm such as ReTF [5]. After reconstruction process, bootstrapping is performed to understand the results derived from different types of datasets. It focuses on statistical analysis techniques with the already defined algorithm. It is more helpful with both features in analysis of genetic diversity at the intraspecific level in disease finding.

In this study, commonly occurring virus data sets from National Centre for Biotechnology Information have been used to perform the analysis. Many viruses that were earlier present in only a few parts of the world are now spreading throughout the world; these include HIV1, Ross River virus, H1N1, Rift Valley Fever virus, Ebola, Zika virus, Japanese encephalitis virus, louping ill virus, chikungunya virus and West Nile virus. The spread of these viruses is related to climate change and other environmental factors. In this study, our emphasis will be on HIV1, H1N1 and Ebola viruses. Viruses are considered to be polyphyletic; it means that can they have many evolutionary origins. Keeping this in mind, different strands of data sets are taken for analysis. Once a data set is ready, we run multiple sequence alignments. There are widely available software which are used for alignments, e.g. ABA, ClustalW, DNA Alignment, MUSCLE, Phylo, T-Coffee. In this study, we have used ClustalW to arrange the sequences. Multiple sequence alignments (MSA) are used to arrange three or more biological sequences. Initially, when we get the data, each strand is of a different length; at the same time, some gaps are present. Aligning such sequences is a tedious process; therefore, computational algorithms are used to align such sequences. Once alignment is done, we will be using ReCons algorithm [5] to find the list of most conserved motifs. These conserved motifs depend on p-value calculations after using PMS5 [6]. The list of motifs with predefined threshold value is used to find the best substitution model. This substitution model describes the process from which a sequence of characters is recast into another set of traits. Substitution model is used for various aims. Primarily, it is used to construct the evolutionary trees. Sometimes it is used to simulate sequences to test newly designed algorithms. Many different substitution models are used, but the very old and renowned model general time reversible (GTR) is widely accepted. This model was created by Simon Tavare in 1986. It is the most general, independent, finite-sites, time-reversible model. With the help of motif lists that were the output of ReCons [7] algorithm and on the basis of statistical analysis of substitution model, phylogenetic network is reconstructed. Bootstrapping is the process of evaluating the relative strength of the newly constructed phylogenetic network to the original tree. In this, each interior branch of tree is compared. This resampling process is repeated several hundred times, and each interior branch is assigned a bootstrap value (Fig. 1)..

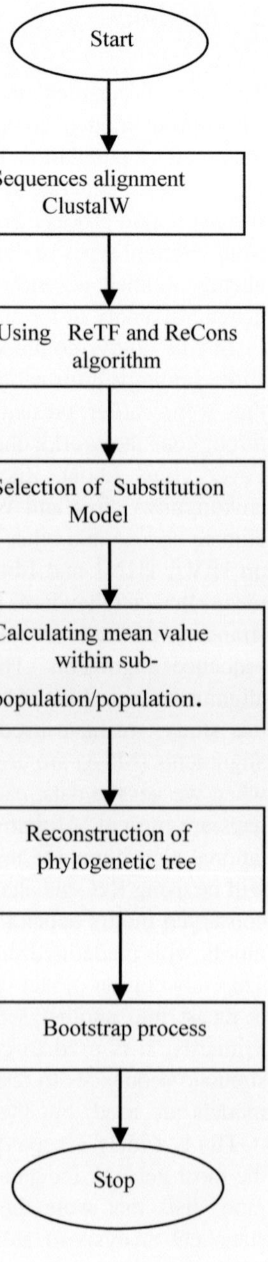

Fig. 1 Steps in analysis of viruses data sets

3 Results

To get correct phylogeny, we consider the following parameters.

Step 1 *Analysing the data samples on the basis of motif using (ReCons) algorithm with* statistical *analysis*

DNA sequences are taken from National Centre for Biotechnology Information. Sequences are arranged using ClustalW algorithm. Once sequences are arranged, PMS5 is used to find the motifs with constrains *(l, d)* where *l* is the length of motif and *d* is the allowed number of mutation. We get hundreds to thousands of motifs. Here ReCons algorithm [5] is used to find the list of most conserved motifs. Predefined threshold is taken into account when looking for the conserved motifs (Table 1).

Step 2 *Selection of substitution model*

Selection of best substitution depends on maximum likelihood fits of 24 different nucleotide substitution models. Models with the most reduced Bayesian information criterion (BIC) are acknowledged for representing the best substitution pattern. For every substitution model, maximum likelihood value (lnL), Akaike AICc value, information criterion and the parameters are presented in the tables below [8]. Discrete Gamma distribution (+G) having five rate division with consideration that a chunk of sites are evolutionary invariable (+I) can be used to present the non-consistency in the evolutionary rates. Gamma shape parameter and invariant sites are depicted at relevant points. There were a total of 1137 positions in HIV, 2300 in H1N1, 4322 in Ebola. These evolutionary analyses were conducted in MEGA6 [9]. An inherent obstacle in evolutionary analysis is the choice of appropriate selection of the best substitution model. AICc [10] or BIC [11] mostly use theoretical metrics. A researcher usually estimates up to three parameters to describe the substitution model. The most important factor that should be considered is the rate multiplier which is responsible for the overall substitution model. Secondly, one or more parameters are used to describe the relative rates at which nucleotides replace each other. This is called general time reversible (Tables 2, 3, 4).

Step 3 *Analysing the data samples on the basis of gene diversity within the subpopulation and within the entire population*

Genetic diversity is a necessary feature of all living organisms. It provides the resource for the progressive adaption of the population to ever-changing setting. It describes naturally genetic difference among individuals of the same species. This

Table 1 Threshold table for data sets

Threshold	Data sets of viruses		
	HIV1 motifs count	H1N1 motifs count	Ebola motifs count
0.993–0.999	11	8	12
0.899–0.992	32	28	26

Table 2 Substitution model analysis for HIV1 virus

Model	Parameters	BIC	AICc
HKY+G	32	11752.89	11505.2
TN93+G	33	11762.41	11506.98
HKY+G+I	33	11762.64	11507.21
GTR+G	36	11769.78	11491.15
TN93+G+I	34	11772.15	11508.99
GTR+G+I	37	11779.53	11493.16
HKY+I	32	11792.57	11544.88
TN93+I	33	11802.31	11546.88
GTR+I	36	11808.68	11530.05
HKY	31	11814.78	11574.82
TN93	32	11824.32	11576.63
GTR	35	11832.74	11561.84
T92+G	30	11842.88	11610.66
T92+G+I	31	11852.62	11612.67
T92+I	30	11880.42	11648.2
T92	29	11899.82	11675.34
K2+G	29	11958.68	11734.2
K2+G+I	30	11968.42	11736.2
K2+I	29	11996.94	11772.46
K2	28	12026.42	11809.68
JC+G	28	12272.59	12055.85
JC+G+I	29	12282.33	12057.85
JC+I	28	12305.65	12088.91
JC	27	12314.24	12105.24

is also called quasi-species. These variations help in the survival of genes even after climatic changes. Also, there is genetic drift which can be described as increase or decrease of population by chance over a period of time. Genetic drift is common issue after population bottleneck. Initially while analysing the genetic diversity, sequencing of DNA clones is obtained from multiple plaques. These plaques were descending from plaque-purified genomes. This approach is further used to calculate mutation rate used for genetic diversity (Table 5).

Genetic diversity is important for two reasons. If the population of an organism contains a large gene pool, then we can easily analyse its chances of surviving and flourishing. A small gene pool has limited genetic variability. Some people could have acquired characteristics making them, especially resistant to diseases. Sometimes there is likelihood that they may have different attributes that increase their chances for survival. In nature, the “fittest” people survive and go ahead to reproduce—Darwin termed this procedure “natural selection”. Secondly, genetic diversity also reduces the incidence of unfavourable inherited traits. When the group is small, the chances to breed within the group increase manifold. This helps to maintain the genetic make-up of the individual.

Table 3 Substitution model analysis for H1N1 virus

Model	Parameters	BIC	AICc
T92	29	4267.496	4036.756
HKY	31	4271.173	4024.526
T92+I	30	4277.456	4038.762
T92+G	30	4277.456	4038.762
TN93	32	4280.265	4025.665
HKY+G	32	4281.133	4026.532
HKY+I	32	4281.133	4026.532
T92+G+I	31	4287.415	4040.768
TN93+I	33	4290.225	4027.671
TN93+G	33	4290.225	4027.671
JC	27	4290.449	4075.617
HKY+G+I	33	4291.092	4028.538
K2	28	4294.018	4071.232
TN93+G+I	34	4300.184	4029.677
JC+I	28	4300.408	4077.622
JC+G	28	4300.409	4077.623
K2+I	29	4303.977	4073.237
K2+G	29	4303.978	4073.237
GTR	35	4308.689	4030.229
JC+G+I	29	4310.368	4079.628
K2+G+I	30	4313.937	4075.243
GTR + G	36	4318.631	4032.219
GTR+I	36	4318.648	4032.236
GTR+G+I	37	4328.591	4034.226

Step 4 *Analysing the reconstruction of phylogenetic networks*

There are two commonly used approaches for inferring phylogenies. The first approach is phenetic approach. In this approach, inference is not drawn regarding any historical relationships; only the distance between species is measured. In order to create tree, hierarchal clustering approach is used. Other approach is cladistics, in which all possible paths of evolution are considered. Each node is inferred during the process and choosing an optimal tree according to some model of evolutionary history. In this study, we will be focusing on cladistics approach. The algorithm used to reconstruct the phylogenetic network is maximum likelihood. This method was introduced by Felsenstein [12]. This method does not impose any constraint on the constancy of biological process rate among lineages. It assigns quantitative possibilities to mutational events, instead of simply counting them. This methodology compares doable biological process trees on the premise of their ability to predict the discovered information. The tree having the maximum probability of deriving the detected sequences can be picked. To check the correctness of reconstructed tree, bootstrap process [13] is used. Bootstrap is basically the confidence level of

Table 4 Substitution model analysis for Ebola virus

Model	Parameters	BIC	AICc
TN93+I	33	55541.97	55193.84
HKY	31	55542.28	55215.26
TN93	32	55542.5	55204.92
HKY+G	32	55543.08	55205.5
TN93+G	33	55543.32	55195.19
TN93+G+I	34	55554.14	55195.46
HKY+I	32	55554.7	55217.12
HKY+G+I	33	55555.46	55207.34
GTR	35	55577.19	55207.97
GTR+G	36	55578.18	55198.41
GTR+I	36	55585.04	55205.26
GTR+G+I	37	55590.71	55200.39
T92	29	55606.82	55300.89
T92+G	30	55607.73	55291.25
T92+I	30	55618.6	55302.12
T92+G+I	31	55620.26	55293.23
K2	28	56192.22	55896.84
K2+G	29	56192.99	55887.06
K2+I	29	56204.75	55898.82
K2+G+I	30	56205.25	55888.77
JC	27	56479.4	56194.57
JC+G	28	56480.78	56185.4
JC+I	28	56491.93	56196.55
JC+G+I	29	56493.32	56187.39

Table 5 Genetic diversity within subpopulation and within entire population

Genetic diversity	Viruses		
	HIV1	H1N1	Ebola
Mean diversity within subpopulation	218.00	117.00	221.00
Mean diversity in entire population	312.00	227.00	309.00

phylogenetic network. In this process, sampling is done for each *n* nucleotides' data set. From each succession data set, n nucleotides are haphazardly picked with replacements, giving rise to *a* row of *b* columns each. From this new matrix, a tree is reproduced. After that, topology of this tree is compared to that of the original tree. Each inside branch is given a score value that represents confidence of reconstruction of phylogeny. If the bootstrap value for a given interior branch is 65% or higher, then the topology at that branch is considered "correct". The following analysis is performed on the HIV1, H1N1 and Ebola data sets (Table 6).

The results of reconstruction of phylogenetic network using ReTF algorithm [5] are shown in Figs. 2, 3 and 4.

Table 6 Stages of analysis during reconstruction of phylogenetic networks

Phylogenetic reconstruction analysis	
Statistical analysis method	Maximum likelihood
Phylogeny test	
Test of phylogeny	Bootstrap phylogeny test
No. of bootstraps	500
Substitution model	
Substitution type	Nucleotide
Model	GTR
Performance	
No. of threads	1

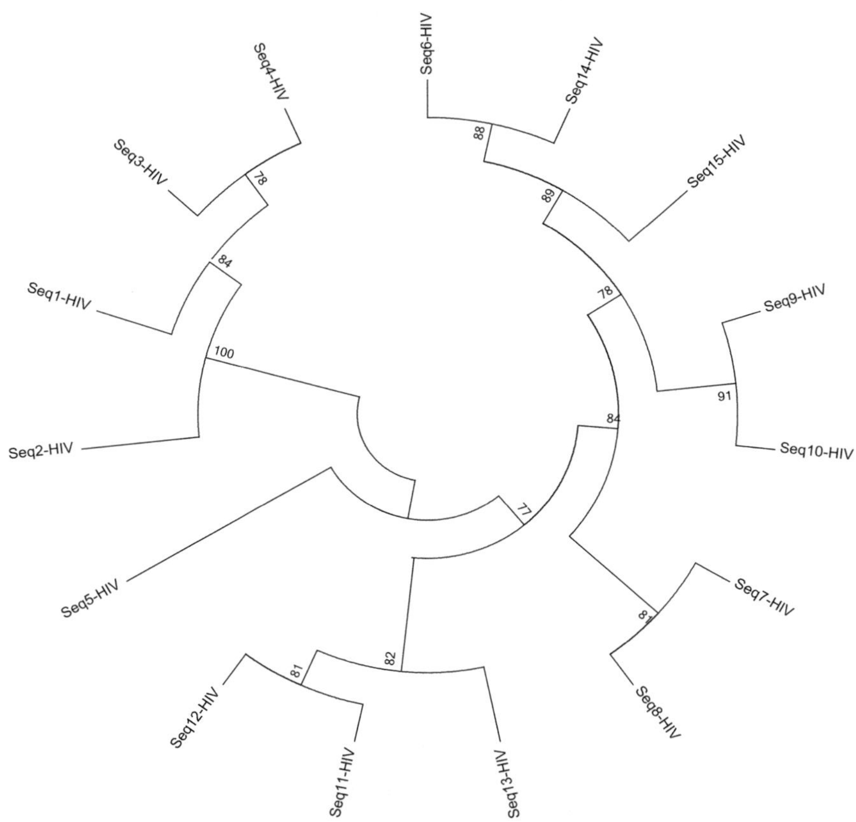

Fig. 2 Bootstrap analysis of HIV1 using ReTF algorithm

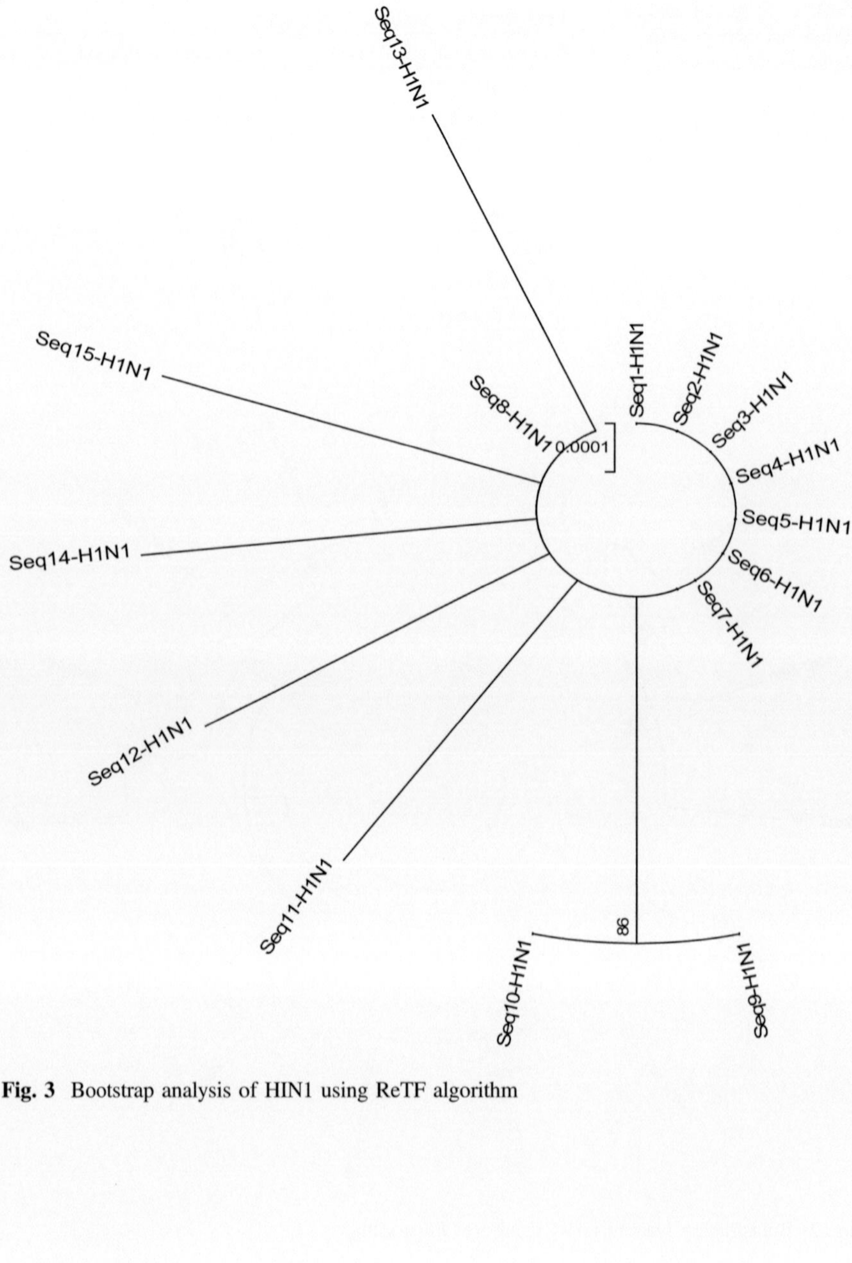

Fig. 3 Bootstrap analysis of HIN1 using ReTF algorithm

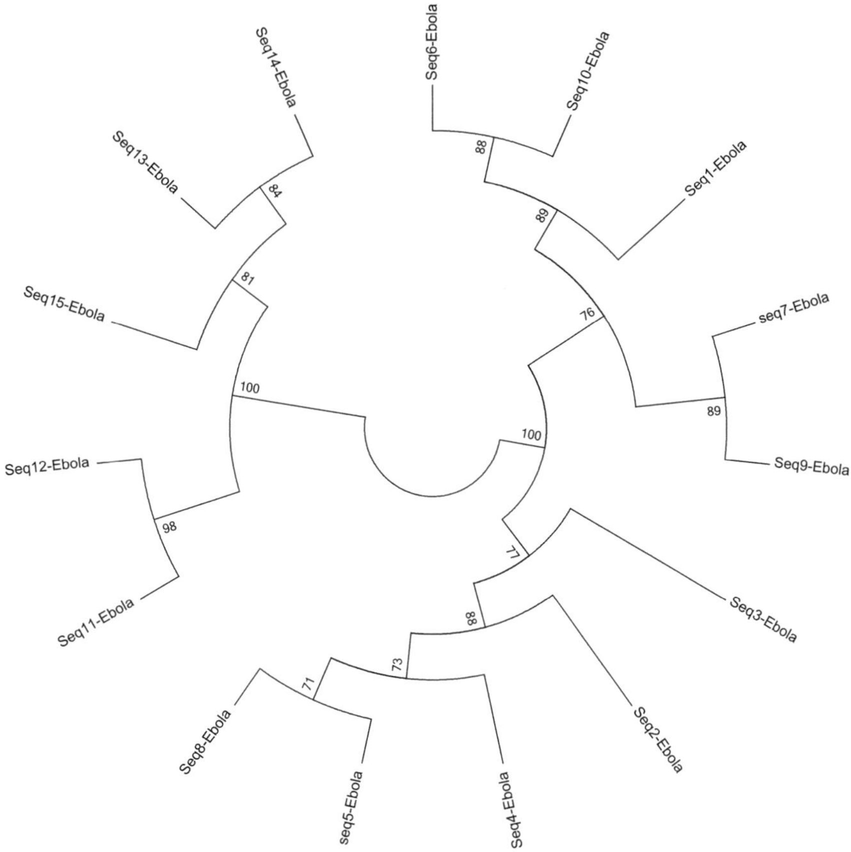

Fig. 4 Bootstrap analysis of Ebola using ReTF algorithm

4 Conclusions

The transmission of infectious diseases is an inherently ecological process. It involves interactions among different species. Although current studies have been able to shed light on the diversity of disease origin, the mechanisms underlying these effects stay unclear in several cases. In this, we conducted examination on a worldwide scale to test whether the diversity of human diseases, some of them in charge of high rates of morbidity and mortality. In this study, we also guaranteed to get the list of highly conserved motifs. The program is sure to report all sets of motifs with lowest parsimony scores. These are calculated with regard to the phylogenetic tree relating the different input species. Further, the computation of genetic diversity within the subpopulation and entire population easily shows the presence of disease and its variances. At last, reconstruction of phylogenetic network helps in tracing phylogeny of the diseases. Subsequent to controlling for direct puzzling impacts applied by distinctive strands of information taken, our discoveries demonstrate that human disease increments occur with the assorted diversity and structure of disease types.

Acknowledgements The authors thank Dr. Ashok K. Chauhan, Founder President, Amity University, for his encouragement, guidance and providing the necessary infrastructure for research.

References

1. Magner, L.N.: A history of the life sciences, revised and expanded. CRC Press (2002)
2. Jain, R., Rivera, M.C., Lake, J.A.: Horizontal gene transfer among genomes: the complexity hypothesis. Proc. Natl. Acad. Sci. **96**(7) (1999)
3. Nelson, G.: Historical biogeography: an alternative formalization. Syst. Zool. **23**(4) (1974)
4. Kitching, I.J.: Cladistics: The Theory and Practice of Parsimony Analysis, No. 11. Oxford University Press (1998)
5. Malik, S., Sharma, D.: Reconstructing phylogenetic network with ReTF algorithm (rearranging transcriptional factor). In: 2013 IEEE 13th International Conference on Bioinformatics and Bioengineering (BIBE), IEEE (2013)
6. Dinh, H., Rajasekaran, S., Kundeti, V.K.: PMS5: an efficient exact algorithm for the (ℓ, d)-motif finding problem. BMC Bioinform. (2011)
7. Malik, S., Sharma, D.: Detecting history of species using mining of motifs in Phylogenetic Networks. In: Proceedings of the 2014 International Conference on Information and Communication Technology for Competitive Strategies. ACM (2014)
8. Nei, M., Kumar, S.: Molecular Evolution and Phylogenetics. Oxford University Press, New York (2000)
9. Tamura, K., Stecher, G., Peterson, D., Filipski, A., Kumar, S.: MEGA6: molecular evolutionary genetics analysis version 6.0. Mol. Biol. Evol. (2013)
10. Hurvich, C.M, Tsai, C.L.: Regression and time series model selection in small samples. Biometrika (1989)
11. Schwarz, G.: Estimating the dimension of a model. Ann. Stat. (1978)
12. Felsenstein, J.: Evolutionary trees from DNA sequences: a maximum likelihood approach. J. Mol. Evol. (1981)
13. Felsenstein J.: Confidence limits on phylogenies: an approach using the bootstrap. Evolution (1985)

Alternate Procedure for the Diagnosis of Malaria via Intuitionistic Fuzzy Sets

Vijay Kumar and Sarika Jain

Abstract Malaria is a disease, which affects many people around the globe. In this study, we propose a fuzzy diagnosis approach for the clinical diagnosis of the type of malaria which affects the patient. By the help of the prescribed method, one can easily diagnose the type of malaria, without conducting any laboratory test. On the basis of relation between symptoms and various types of infection present in patients, we develop hypothetical medical information-based case study of patients with assigned degree of membership, non-membership, and intuitionistic index. By using the procedure, we can easily diagnose the type of malaria; for example, patient p_1 is suffering from *Plasmodium malariae* (*Pm*), p_2 is suffering from *Plasmodium ovale* (*Po*), p_3 is suffering from *Plasmodium falciparum* (*Pf*), and p_4 is suffering from *Plasmodium vivax* (*Pv*) and *P. malariae* (*Pm*). Also, we can develop a computer program for the proposed procedure.

Keywords Intuitionistic fuzzy sets (IFSs) · Medical information · Normalized hamming distance

1 Introduction

Malaria is potentially a disastrous tropical disease caused by an organism known as *Plasmodium*. The organisms are exposed to persons by biting them by infected *Anopheles* mosquitoes, a female mosquito. WHO [1], it is estimated that there were about 216 million cases of malaria with an estimated 655,000 deaths in 2010.

V. Kumar (✉) · S. Jain
Department of Mathematics, Faculty of Engineering, Manav Rachna International University, Faridabad, India
e-mail: drvijaykumarsudan@gmail.com

B.K. Panigrahi et al. (eds.), *Nature Inspired Computing*, Advances in Intelligent Systems and Computing 652, https://doi.org/10.1007/978-981-10-6747-1_6

Around 40% of the world's population is at the risk of malaria. There are four types of malaria to infect a person. They are *Plasmodium vivax* (*Pv*), *Plasmodium ovale* (P*o*), *Plasmodium malariae* (*Pm*), and *Plasmodium falciparum* (*Pf*). Out of these four types, *P. falciparum* is the most lethal parasite that causes most infections and deaths. The general symptoms of malaria include headache, vomiting, high fever, and flu-like symptoms (fever, loss of appetite, rigors, tiredness, nausea, slight jaundice, abdominal pain, diarrhea, enlarged liver, and spleen (sometimes not palpable), etc.). The treatment of malaria is prescribed solely on the basis of symptoms, when a parasitological diagnosis is not possible. WHO [1] recommends that all cases of suspected malaria can be confirmed using parasite-based diagnostic testing (either microscopy or rapid diagnostic test). Microscopy is a routine test, whereas polymerase chain reaction (PCR) and serology technique are more accurate than microscopy, but is expensive and requires a specialized reference laboratory. Thus, it is important to set a correct diagnosis and to identify the type of malaria present in patients. Clinical diagnosis is based on the signs and symptoms present in a patient and physical findings by examination. Adlassnig [2, 3], Ahn [4], Albin [5], Sanchez [6], Yao and Yao [7] described the applications of fuzzy theory to medical diagnosis. Atanassov [8], De and Biswas [9], Kumar [10], Gupta [11], Szmidt [12–14] described the concept of generalized fuzzy theory and using the application of intuitionistic fuzzy sets and proposed medical decision-making methods. Akhtar [15], Tangpukdee [16], and Rosanas et al. [17] elaborated diagnostic methods of malaria. In the proposed work, we will discuss the clinical method of distances for the diagnosis of the type of malaria.

1.1 Intuitionistic Fuzzy Sets (IFSs)

Atanassov [8] proposed intuitionistic fuzzy sets. In this paper, we propose a method of distances between IFSs Q and R. In our consideration, we are using normalized Hamming distance between two intuitionistic fuzzy sets (IFSs) which is defined as:

$$d(s(p_i), d_k) = \frac{1}{2n}\sum_{j=1}^{n} \left[\left|\mu_j(p_i) - \mu_j(d_k)\right| + \left|v_j(p_i) - v_j(d_k)\right| + \left|\pi_j(p_i) - \pi_j(d_k)\right| \right] \tag{1}$$

where $0 \le d(s(p_i), d_k) \le n$.

2 Clinical Diagnosis Approach

Medical diagnosis is a skill to analyze patient's health status from an available set of inputs. It is only possible by the intensive collaboration between physicians and mathematicians. Usually, a diagnosis process starts with the patient complaints about the situation to doctor interactively during an interview, and the doctor analyzes the situation through the set of available symptoms as well as by measuring physical metrics such as blood pressure, body temperature, some related laboratory tests. The diagnosis is then governed by considering the whole available information about the patient, on the basis of that best possible treatment is proposed, and the whole process might be iterated. In each iteration, the diagnosis might be reconfigured, refined, or even rejected. The major task of the process is to get rid of the disease. Intuitionistic fuzzy sets successfully handle the uncertain situations carried by medical diagnosis system. Adlassnig [2, 8], Ahn [4], let $S = \{\text{headache, Vomiting, highfever, flu like synptoms}\}$ be the set of symptoms of malaria, $D = \{Pv, Po, Pm, Pf\}$ be the set of the types of malaria present in a patient, and $P = \{p_1, p_2, p_3, p_4\}$ be the set of suspicion patients of malaria. We can estimate the type of malaria in particular patient using the information given in the tables.

In order to check the applicability of the method, we frame a hypothetical medical information base of symptoms and the type of malaria for each patient as.

Table 1 Symptoms of the corresponding type of malaria

R	*Plasmodium vivax*		*Plasmodium malariae*		*Plasmodium falciparum*		*Plasmodium ovale*	
Symptoms	μ_R	ν_R	μ_R	ν_R	μ_R	ν_R	μ_R	ν_R
Headache	0.4	0.0	0.7	0.0	0.3	0.3	0.1	0.7
Vomiting	0.3	0.5	0.2	0.6	0.6	0.1	0.2	0.4
Highfever	0.1	0.7	0.0	0.9	0.2	0.7	0.8	0.0
Flu like symptoms	0.4	0.3	0.7	0.0	0.2	0.6	0.2	0.7

Table 2 Patients and the available set of symptoms for the types of malaria

Q	Headache		Vomiting		Highfever		Flu like symptoms	
Patients	μ_Q	ν_Q	μ_Q	ν_Q	μ_Q	ν_Q	μ_Q	ν_Q
p_1	0.8	0.1	0.6	0.1	0.2	0.8	0.6	0.1
p_2	0.0	0.8	0.4	0.4	0.6	0.1	0.1	0.7
p_3	0.8	0.1	0.8	0.1	0.0	0.6	0.2	0.7
p_4	0.6	0.1	0.5	0.4	0.3	0.4	0.7	0.2

Table 3 Diagnostic levels of patients and their corresponding type of malaria

	Plasmodium vivax	*Plasmodium malariae*	*Plasmodium falciparum*	*Plasmodium ovale*
p_1	0.325	0.25	0.275	0.65
p_2	0.475	0.625	0.375	0.15
p_3	0.387	0.462	0.275	0.512
p_4	0.275	0.275	0.325	0.437

From Tables 1 and 2, our purpose is to diagnose the type of malaria for each patient associated with the set of available symptoms and characterize for each type of malaria. The lowest distance obtained points out the type of malaria present in a patient. Using (1), the distance measure for each patient from the type of malaria based on symptoms is given in the Table 3.

From Table 3, we conclude that patient p_1 is suffering from *P. malariae*, p_2 is suffering from *P. ovale*, p_3 is suffering from *P. falciparum*, and p_4 is suffering from *P.vivax* and *P. malariae*.

3 Conclusion

In this paper, a generalized fuzzy method is proposed, which is an alternative method for the diagnosis of the type of the malaria from an available set of symptoms present in the patient and its causes for the type of disease. It is possible to classify the type of malaria present in the patients by using the mentioned method. Also, we can develop a computer program of the said algorithmic approach, which may help the doctors in the process of easy diagnosis.

References

1. WHO.: World Malaria Report (2011)
2. Adlassnig, K.P.: CADIAG-2: Computer-Assisted Medical Diagnosis using Fuzzy Subsets, pp. 219–242. Approx. Reasoning in Decision Anal. N.H. Pub. Co., New York (1982)
3. Adlassnig, K.P.: Fuzzy set theory in medical diagnosis. IEEE Trans. Syst., Man, and Cybern. (SMC) 16, 260–265(1986)
4. Ahn, J.Y., Kim, Y.H., Mun, K.S., Oh, S.Y., Han, B.S.: A fuzzy method for diagnosis of headache. IEICE Trans. Inf. Syst. E91-D (4), 1215–1217(2008)
5. Albin, M.A.: Fuzzy Sets and Their Application to Medical Diagnosis. Doctoral Dissertation. University of California, Berkley (1975)
6. Sanchez, E.: Solutions in Composite Fuzzy Relation Equation: An Application to Medical Diagnosis. Fuzzy Automata and Decision Process, Elsevier (1977)
7. Yao, J.F., Yao, J.S.: Fuzzy decision making for medical diagnosis based on fuzzy number and compositional rule of inference. Fuzzy Sets Syst. 120, 351–366 (1981)
8. Atanassov, K.T.: Intuitionistic fuzzy sets. Fuzzy Sets Syst. **20**(1), 87–96 (1986)

9. De, S.K., Biswas, R.: A.R.: An application of intuitionistic fuzzy sets in medical diagnosis. Fuzzy Sets Syst. **117**, 209–213 (2011)
10. Kumar, V., Bharti, I., Sharma, Y.K.: Fuzzy diagnosis procedure of the types of glaucoma. Int. J. Appl. Inform. Syst. **1**(6), 42–45 (2012)
11. Gupta, P., Kumar, V.: Application of intuitionist fuzzy sets (IFS) in medical diagnosis of headache. In: Proceedings of 4th International Conference on Quality, Reliability and Infocom Technology (ICQRIT) (Trends and Future Directions), Narosa, pp. 356–359 (2011)
12. Szmidt, E., Kacprzyk, J.: On measuring distances between intuitionistic fuzzy sets. Notes IFS. **3**(4), 1–13 (1997)
13. Szmidt, E., Kacprzyk, J.: Distances between intuitionistic fuzzy sets. Fuzzy Sets Syst. **114**(3), 505–518 (2000)
14. Szmidt, E., Kacprzyk, J.: Intuitionistic fuzzy sets in some medical applications. In: Proceedings of 7 Fuzzy Days on Computational Intelligence: Theory and Applications. pp. 148–151 (2001)
15. Akhtar, S., Maimoon, S., Wilkinson, A., Gowardhan, V., Mahore, S.: Feasible choices in diagnostic methods of malaria. J. Vector Borne Dis. **47**, 151–154 (2010)
16. Tangpukdee, N., Duangdee, C., Wilairatana, P., Krudsood, S.: Malaria diagnosis: a brief review. Korean J. Parasitol. **47**(2), 93–102 (2009)
17. Rosanas, U., Anna, M.D., Betuela, I., Barnadas, C., Iga, J., Zimmerman, P.A.: Comparison of diagnostic methods for the detection and quantification of the four sympatric *Plasmodium* species in field samples from Papua New Guinea. Malaria J. **9**, 361 (2000)

A Deadline-Aware Modified Genetic Algorithm for Scheduling Jobs with Burst Time and Priorities

Hitendra Pal, Bhanvi Rohilla and Tarinder Singh

Abstract Scheduling plays a vital role in our real life, same as CPU scheduling majorly affects the performance of computer system. For better performance, scheduling depends upon the parameters of jobs (arrival time, burst time, priority, etc.). Different algorithms have been used to find the above factors. Many algorithms such as FCFS, SJF, round-robin, priority are applied, but all these techniques provide a sequence of jobs relevant to their properties. Developing an appropriate sequence using previously known algorithms takes exponential time. This paper proposes an efficient method for process scheduling using a deadline-aware approximation algorithm, where required schedule has a certain weightage of priority and burst time of job. Here, GA and modified GA are compared in terms of number of iterations, number of test cases, requirement percentage and tardiness (fitness value). The results demonstrate that modified GA approach produces solutions very close to the optimal one in comparison with GA.

Keywords CPU scheduling · Optimization · Genetic algorithm · Crossover

H. Pal (✉) · T. Singh
Department of Computer Engineering, Delhi Technological University,
Shahbad Daulatpur, Main Bawana Road, Delhi, India
e-mail: hitendra18pal@gmail.com

T. Singh
e-mail: tarinders23@gmail.com

B. Rohilla
Department of Mechanical and Automation Engineering, IGDTUW,
New Delhi, India
e-mail: rbhanvi@gmail.com

B.K. Panigrahi et al. (eds.), *Nature Inspired Computing*, Advances in Intelligent Systems and Computing 652, https://doi.org/10.1007/978-981-10-6747-1_7

1 Introduction

CPU scheduling is one of the most important functionalities of the operating system, and the scheduling of jobs play a vital role in the performance and efficiency of CPU. The major functionality of this task is to maximize the efficiency and finally enhance the performance. The problem of getting a flexible or robust solution for scheduling problems is of utmost importance for real-life applications. For an optimal solution, it may take exponential time which is not feasible. We have an approximation algorithm to find an optimal or nearby optimal solution in polynomial time. Genetic algorithm is one of the approximation base algorithms inspired by nature and popularized by Holland [1] and De Jong [2].

A basic GA consists of five components, namely random number generator, fitness evaluation unit, the genetic operators, selection (Reproduction), crossover, and mutation operations. The basic algorithm is summarized below:

STEP 1: Initialize population
STEP 2: Repeat
STEP 3: Evaluation
STEP 4: Selection
STEP 5: Crossover
STEP 6: Mutation
STEP 7: Until requirements are met.

1.1 Scheduling Criteria

1.1.1 CPU Utilization

The amount of time CPU is busy in performing useful task divided by the total amount of time. In 99% of jobs, 99% of the execution time is spent on a particular bunch of lines. To increase utilization, the page which consists of those lines must reside in main memory.

1.1.2 Throughput

Throughput is the rate at which a number of processes complete their execution per unit time.

1.1.3 Turnaround Time

It is the total time when a process arrives in the ready state till the process completes its execution and moves to terminate state.

1.1.4 Waiting Time

Waiting time is the total time spent by process in ready queue.

1.1.5 Response Time

Response time is the time between when a process is brought into main memory and the time first spent in ready queue before it starts execution.

1.1.6 Tardiness

Difference between job completion time and its deadline time.

1.1.7 Makespan

When several jobs are competing for execution, makespan is the time from the starting of first job to the end of last job run.

1.2 The Problem Statement

Let there be N pre-emptive processes (jobs) $(j_1, j_2, \ldots, j_n)$ [3] that are waiting to be processed by a single processor system. Each job j_i has its arrival time a_i, burst time b_i and priority p_i, respectively.

The objective is to find the schedule that satisfies the following constraints:

1. CPU should process every job.
2. Processes are independent and complete for resources.
3. We have two schedules of N processes, one ordered by their burst times and the other according to their priorities, and a third schedule needs to be generated whose completion time is nearby and before the deadline time of that schedule (sequence of jobs). The completion time of this schedule is called as optimal solution, and the schedule is called the optimal solution schedule.

2 Related Work

This section presents a comprehensive study of genetic algorithm (GA) with scheduling work in last the 2–3 decades. GA is widely used in many engineering fields, and its effective optimization performance was verified in the literature [4]. GA is based on mechanics of natural selection in the biological system. GAs are implemented in different application areas, specifically in combinational problems, such as scheduling [5, 6]. In general, scheduling problems have been proved to be NP-complete, and so to find an optimal solution, it takes exponential time, which is not feasible in real life. GAs play a vital role in finding nearby optimal solution for optimization and search problems in polynomial time [7]. The guided random search-based algorithms typically generate multiple candidate solutions sampled from a feasible solution space and use a guided search for exploration. A host of evolutionary swarm intelligence techniques such as genetic algorithms [8], particle swarm optimization [9], ant colony optimization [10], simulated annealing [11], and Tabu search [12, 13] have been successfully applied to scheduling. There are a plethora of algorithms for scheduling processes on single processor or multiple processor systems. Some of the most well-known algorithms among them are shortest-job-first (SJF) scheduling, first come, first serve (FCFS) scheduling, priority scheduling and round-robin (RR) scheduling [14].

In Xu et al. [15], authors proposed a multiple priority queueing genetic algorithms which work on parallel heterogeneous computing systems for task scheduling. Here, the role is to minimize the makespan by efficiently assigning subtask to priority depending on resource needed. In Neshat et al. [16], authors present a technique of CPU scheduling using Fonseca and Fleming's genetic algorithm (FFGA) in which author considers three parameter: burst time, priority, and I/O device service time, and these parameters are taken as multiobjective for FFGA. In Patel and Solanki [17], authors present a hybrid scheduling algorithm using genetic approach which involves some software tool which produce a comprehensive simulation of a numbers of CPU scheduling algorithm. In Moin et al. [18], authors present hybrid nature-inspired technique to solve job shop scheduling (JSSP) in which author proposed multiparents crossover and test the performance on various benchmark functions of JSSP test problem. In Umbarkar [19], author presents a dual population generation genetic algorithm which solves the constrain of local optimal which sometime arise during finding of optimize solution of a problem. In genetic algorithm, solution sometimes stuck in local optimal author verified his method against 9 problems in author paper. In Yan-Fang and Yue [20], authors present a genetic algorithm to solve dynamic job shop scheduling approach which is fine for a dynamic, changeable agile manufacturing system. In Butt and Akram [21], authors present a fuzzy decision-making system for CPU scheduling of a multitasking operating system in which author provides intelligence to schedule a jobs with dynamic priority using fuzzy logic. Author found that the results are more improved than previous fuzzy-based CPU scheduling algorithm. In Bhadula et al. [22], authors present a comparison among genetic algorithm, shortest-job-first

(SJF) and priority scheduling for solving CPU scheduling problem. The results demonstrate that author's genetic approach is nearly optimal to SJF and far better than priority scheduling.

3 Proposed Work

We have two schedules, one according to SJF and the other according to priority. We know that considering only SJF and neglecting priorities give us optimal total turnaround time (TAT), which is not possible in real-life applications as the processes come with different priorities and may have a deadline also. Hence, a schedule which has optimal or nearly optimal turnaround time considering the above factor of the jobs is required.

If the priorities of the jobs are neglected and sequences are executed according to their CPU bursts, then we may end up with a sequence where the process with lowest burst time has the highest I/O burst and vice versa executed first; in such cases, SJF schedule may not give optimal TAT. Hence, both the priorities of the jobs in schedule and their burst times are considered in this algorithm.

In the proposed algorithm, we have taken two schedules, one ordered according to SJF and other according to their priorities. Let the weightage of TAT according to priority in the optimal schedule be w_p (requirement percentage); i.e., new required schedule should contain w_p % of priority and $(1 - w_p)$ % of SJF in the solution. The optimal schedule whose completion time is nearby or equal to deadline time is obtained by variation of w_p.

Let required time,

$$\text{RT} = w_p * \text{sch\_priority} + \left(1 - w_p\right) * \text{sch\_sjf} \tag{1}$$

where

sch_priority Total turnaround time (TAT) according to priority scheduling.
sch_sjf Total turnaround time (TAT) according to shortest-job-first (SJF) scheduling.

Require time (RT) is the total turnaround time (TAT) of some schedule whose completion time is nearby or equal to deadline time, and we have to find that schedule or a schedule who's TAT is nearby RT. It may happen that there is no schedule with that RT; therefore, we go for a schedule whose TAT is nearby RT.

3.1 Fitness Function

Find schedule with minimum tardiness.

$$\text{Tardiness} = \text{modulus}\ [\text{completiontime} - \text{required time(RT)}] \quad (2)$$

$$\text{Fitness value} = \text{tardiness value.}$$

Completion time = TAT of schedule (sequence of jobs) which is generated during genetic algorithm or to be taken as part of initial population. Priority scheduling is applied to find this TAT.

Required time (RT) from Eq. (1).

3.2 Genetic Algorithm

STEP 1: Initialize population: The initial population contains 50 chromosomes representing schedule of N jobs. Each chromosome contains priorities of N jobs, and each priority is unique. Priority is assigned randomly to each job using Poisson distribution.
STEP 2: Repeat
STEP 3: Evaluation
STEP 4: Selection
STEP 5: Crossover
STEP 6: Mutation
STEP 7: Until requirements are met.

3.3 Modification in GA (MGA)

STEP 1: Choosing an Encoding scheme.
STEP 2: Initialize population: The initial population contains only two chromosomes representing the schedule of N jobs, one ordered according to their priorities and the other according to the CPU bursts.
STEP 3: Repeat
STEP 4: Evaluation fitness function which is tardiness from Eq. (2).
STEP 5: Selection
STEP 6: Crossover
STEP 7: Mutation
STEP 8: Until requirements are met.

3.3.1 Encoding Scheme

The basis of genetics is a chromosome which consists of genes. To represent a gene, we require some encoding schemes. Various types of encoding schemes are as follows:

1. Binary encoding
2. Permutation encoding
3. Value/real encoding
4. Octal and hexadecimal encoding.

In our algorithm, we have used value encoding scheme.

3.3.2 Crossover Operator Phase

Here, two-point crossovers are used. For crossover operation, two individuals are selected based on minimum fitness value from the current population. Apply two-point crossover operation on parent chromosome to generate new offspring chromosome. A new set of sequence vector is generated for new offspring. Compute the cost for that offspring; compute the fitness of updated individual. Replace the worst parent and associated chromosome with new best offspring and its chromosome, if it is better, update individuals.

3.3.3 Mutation Operator Phase

If mutation criteria are met (it is randomly 3 times out of 100 times), then select two individuals based on minimum fitness value from current population for mutation operation. Apply mutate operation (swap operation) to generate new chromosomes (new offspring). Compute the fitness value for that offspring. Replace the worst parent and associated chromosome with new best offspring and its chromosome if it is better, update individuals.

4 Experiment and Result

For the experiment, we have randomly generated input set using Poisson distribution with some factors which are taken for experiment (shown in Table 1). A number of test cases are 20 with random number of processes. The algorithm is implemented in C; the result from Figs. 1, 2, 3, 4, 5, 6, 7, 8, 9, and 10 is examined

Table 1 Randomly Generated Input Set

	Mean	Variance	Range
Process	50	30	[20–80]
Arrival	5	5	[0–10]
Burst	20	19	[1–39]
Priority	25	24	[1–49]

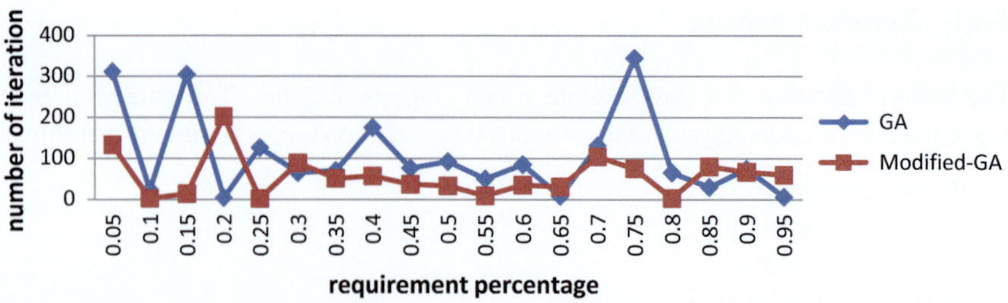

Fig. 1 Test Case (65 processes) for solution Tardiness

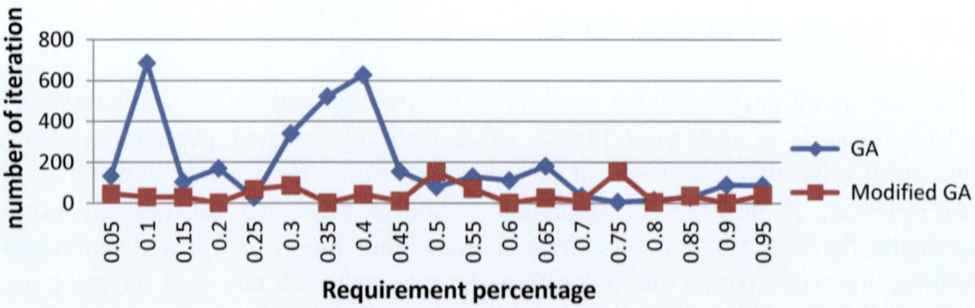

Fig. 2 Test Case (79 processes) for solution Tardiness

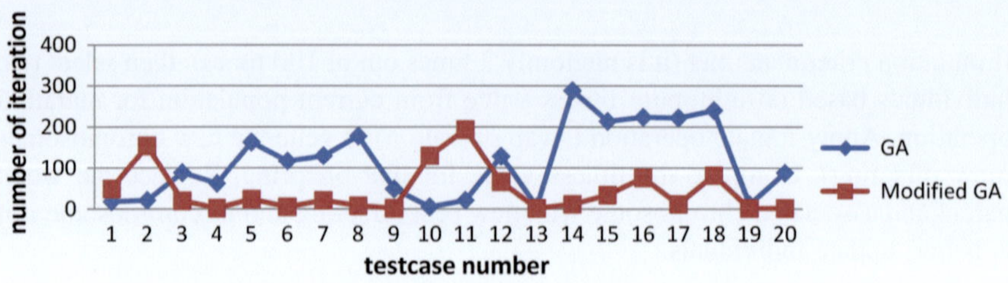

Fig. 3 Requirements Percentage (0.3) for solution Tardiness

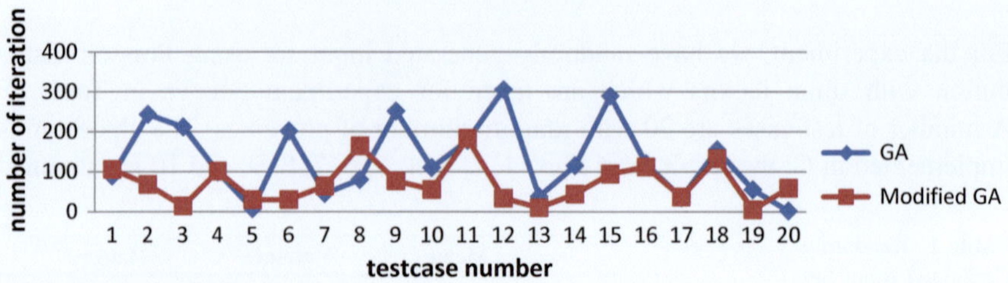

Fig. 4 Requirements Percentage (0.5) for solution Tardiness

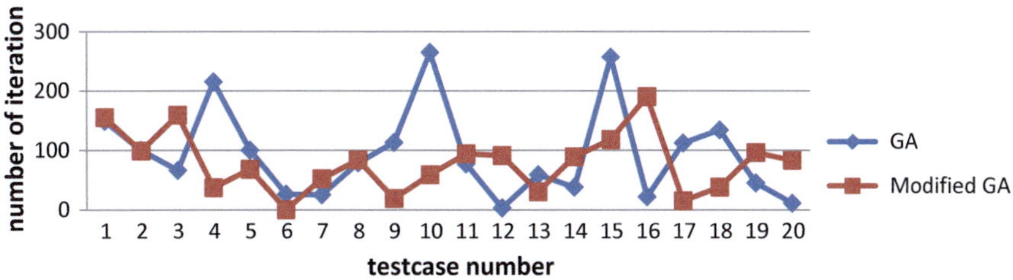

Fig. 5 Requirements Percentage (0.7) for solution Tardiness

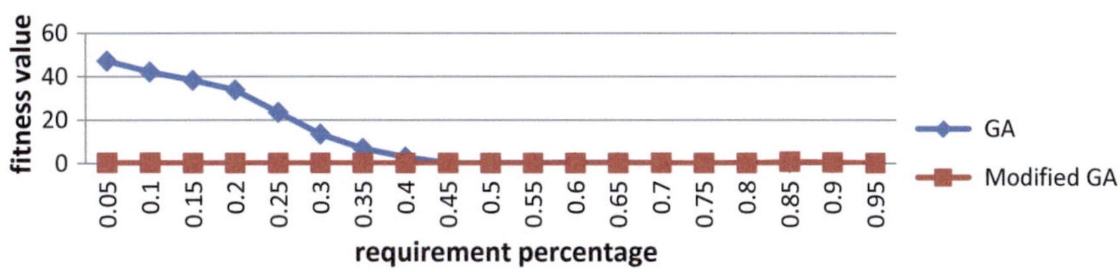

Fig. 6 Test Case (65 processes) for solution Tardiness/Fitness Value

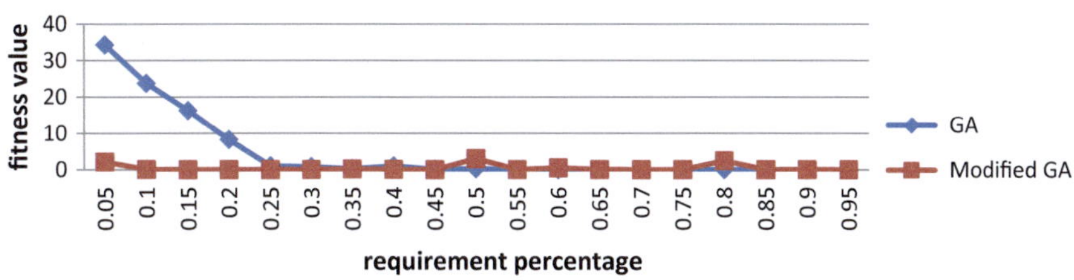

Fig. 7 Test Cases (79 processes) for solution Tardiness/ Fitness Value

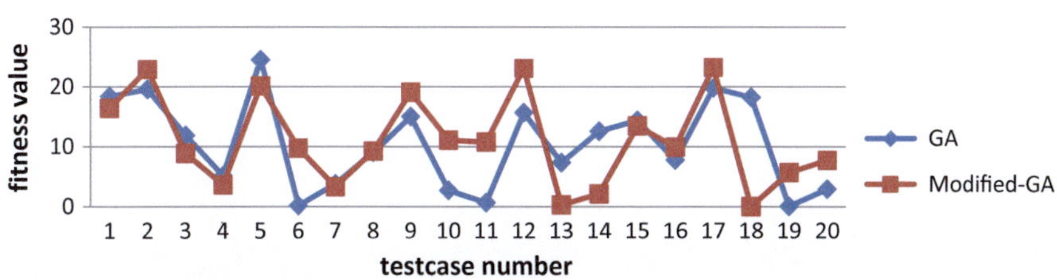

Fig. 8 Requirements Percentage (0.3) for solution Tardiness/Fitness Value

with a system having 4 GB RAM, i5 2.6 GHz processor, run on compiler GCC on Linux operating system, and result from Figs. 11, 12, 13, and 14 is examined with a system having 2 GB RAM, i5 2.5 GHz, run on compiler Microsoft Visual C++ on Window 8.

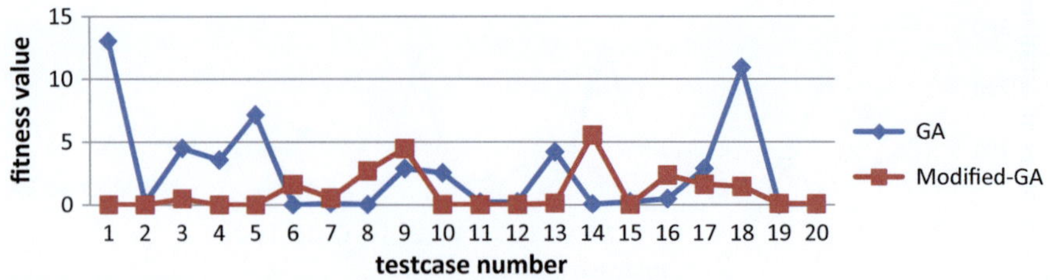

Fig. 9 Requirements Percentage (0.5) for solution Tardiness/Fitness Value

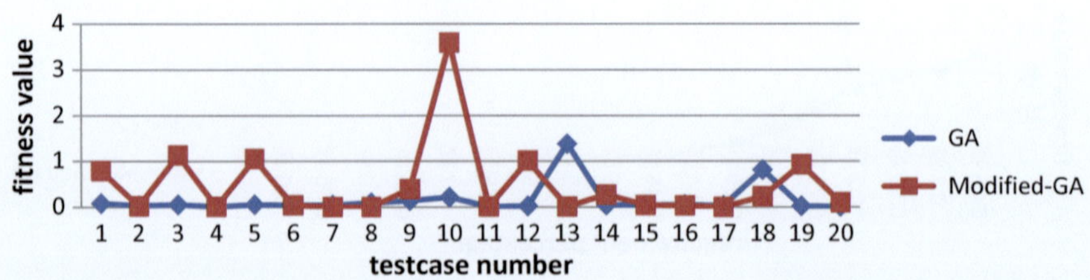

Fig. 10 Requirements Percentage (0.7) for solution Tardiness/Fitness Value

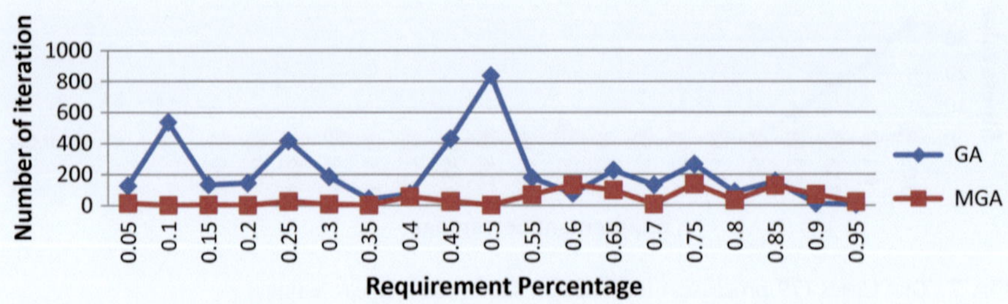

Fig. 11 Test Case (65 processes) for solution Tardiness/Fitness Value

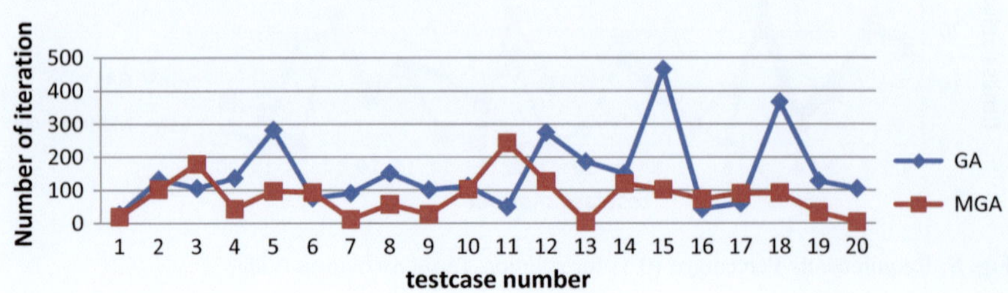

Fig. 12 Requirements Percentage (0.5) for solution Tardiness

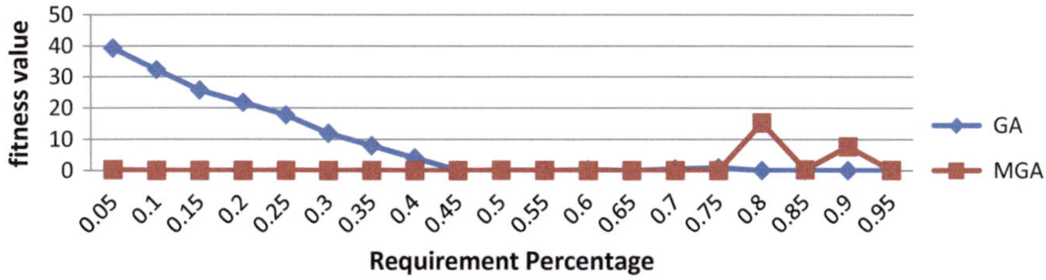

Fig. 13 Test Case (65 processes) for solution Tardiness/Fitness Value

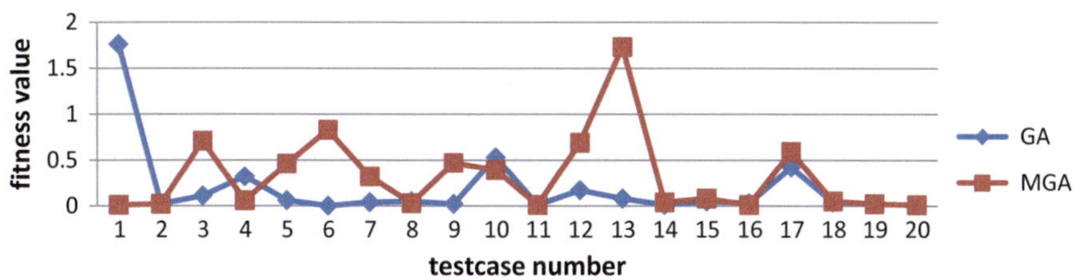

Fig. 14 Requirement percentage (0.5) for solution Tardiness/Fitness Value

In GA, the numbers of chromosomes are 50, and the mutation probability is 0.03.

In (modified GA) MGA, the number of chromosomes is 2, i.e. one according to SJF and other according to priority, and the mutation probability is 0.03.

For all algorithms, maximum number of cycle (MAXCYCLE): 1000.

Number of iterations indicates solutions converge towards deadline after each iteration.

Requirement percentage is weightage of sch_priority (w_p) in the optimal schedule.

In Fig. 1, a test case which has 65 numbers of processes is taken into consideration. The graph represents that the number of iterations in which solution (tardiness) converges with the variation in requirement percentage.

In Fig. 2, a test case which has 79 numbers of processes is taken into consideration. The graph represents the number of iterations in which solution (tardiness) converges with the variation in requirement percentage.

In Fig. 3, requirement percentage is 0.3. The graph represents the number of iterations in which solution (tardiness) converges with different number of test cases.

In Fig. 4, requirement percentage is 0.5. The graph represents the number of iterations in which solution (tardiness) converges with different number of test cases.

In Fig. 5, requirement percentage is 0.7. The graph represents the number of iterations in which solution (tardiness) converges with different number of test cases.

In Fig. 6, a test case which has 65 numbers of processes is taken into consideration. The graph represents the solution (tardiness/fitness value) converges with the variation in requirement percentage.

In Fig. 7, a test case which has 79 numbers of processes is taken into consideration. The graph represents the solution (tardiness/fitness value) converges with the variation in requirement percentage.

In Fig. 8, requirement percentage is 0.3. The graph represents the solution (tardiness/fitness value) converges with the different number of test cases.

In Fig. 9, requirement percentage is 0.5. The graph represents the solution (tardiness/fitness value) converges with the different number of test cases.

In Fig. 10, requirement percentage is 0.7. The graph represents the solution (tardiness/fitness value) converges with the number of test cases.

In Fig. 11, a test case which has 65 numbers of processes is taken into consideration. The graph represents the number of iterations in which solution (tardiness) converges with the variation in requirement percentage.

In Fig. 12, requirement percentage is 0.5. The graph represents the number of iterations in which solution (tardiness) converges with different numbers of test cases.

In Fig. 13, a test case which has 65 numbers of processes is taken into consideration. The graph represents the solution (tardiness/fitness value) converges with the variation in requirement percentage.

In Fig. 14, requirement percentage is 0.5. The graph represents that the solution (tardiness/fitness value) converges with the different number of test cases.

5 Conclusion

Process scheduling problems are a combinatorial problem in which selection and arrangement of jobs are key factors. Different algorithms and techniques are developed to find the above factor. Genetic algorithm is one of the approximation techniques which provide nearby desirable optimal solution. In this paper, a deadline-aware approximation algorithm is applied in which MGA performance is much better than GA in almost all cases. The future work is intended towards an efficient hybrid approximation algorithm that will be treated as decision-making system.

References

1. Holland, J.H.: Adaptation in Natural and Artificial Systems. University of Michigan Press, Ann Arbor (1975)
2. De Jong, K.A.: Adaptive system design: a genetic approach. IEEE Trans. Syst. Man Cybern. **10**, 566–574 (1980)

3. Xhafa, F., Abraham, A.: Computational models and heuristic methods for grid scheduling problems. Future Gener. Comput. Syst. **26**, 608–621 (2010)
4. Goldberg, D.E.: Genetic Algorithms in Search. Optimization and Machine Learning. Addison Wesley, Boston (1989)
5. Yao, W., et al.: Genetic Scheduling on Minimal Processing Elements in the Grid. Springer, Berlin (2002)
6. Fayad, C., Petrovic, S.: A Genetic Algorithm for the Real-World Fuzzy Job Shop Scheduling. Innovations in Applied Artificial Intelligence, pp. 524–533. Springer, Berlin (2005)
7. Biegel, J.E., Davern, J.J.: Genetic algorithms and job-shop scheduling. Comput. Ind. Eng. **19**, 81–91 (1990)
8. Fogel, D.B.: Evolutionary algorithms in theory and practice. Complexity **2**(4), 26–27 (1997)
9. Li, H., Wang, L., Liu, J.: Task scheduling of computational grid based on particle swarm algorithm. In: Third International Joint Conference on Computational Science and Optimization (CSO), vol. 2, pp. 332–336, May 2010
10. Li, K., Xu, G., Zhao, G., Dong, Y., Wang, D.: Cloud task scheduling based on load balancing ant colony optimization. In: Chinagrid Conference (ChinaGrid), 2011 Sixth Annual, pp. 3–9, Aug 2011
11. Houshmand, M., Soleymanpour, E., Salami, H., Amerian, M., Deldari, H.: Efficient scheduling of task graphs to multiprocessors using a combination of modified simulated annealing and list-based scheduling. In: Third International Symposium on Intelligent Information Technology and Security Informatics (IITSI), pp. 350–354, April 2010
12. Shanmugapriya, R., Padmavathi, S., Shalinie, S.: Contention awareness in task scheduling using tabu search. In: IEEE International Advance Computing Conference, IACC 2009, pp. 272–277, March 2009
13. Wong, Y.W., Goh, R., Kuo, S.-H., Low, M.: A tabu search for the heterogeneous dag scheduling problem. In 15th International Conference on Parallel and Distributed Systems (ICPADS), pp. 663–670, Dec 2009
14. Gaba, V., Parashar, A: Comparison of processor scheduling algorithms using genetic approach. Int. J. Adv. Res. Comput. Sci. Softw. Eng. **2**(8), 37–45 (2012)
15. Xu, Y., Li, K., Khac, T.T., Qiu, M.: A multiple priority queueing genetic algorithm for task scheduling on heterogeneous computing systems. In: 2012 IEEE 14th International Conference on High Performance Computing and Communications
16. Neshat, M., Sargolzaei, M., Najaran, A., Adeli, A.: The new method of adaptive CPU scheduling using Fonseca and Fleming's genetic algorithm. J. Theor. Appl. Inform. Technol. **37**(1) (2012)
17. Patel, J., Solanki, A.K.: Performance enhancement of CPU scheduling by hybrid algorithms using genetic approach. Int. J. Adv. Res. Comput. Eng. Technol. **1**(4) (2012)
18. Moin, N.H., Chung Sin, O., Omar, M.: Hybrid genetic algorithm with multiparents crossover for job shop scheduling problems. Math. Probl. Eng. **2015**(210680), 12 (2015)
19. Umbarkar, A.J.: Dual population genetic algorithm for solving constrained optimization problems. I.J. Intell. Syst. Appl. **02**, 34–40 (2015)
20. Yan-Fang, Y., Yue, Y.: An improved genetic algorithm to the job shop scheduling problem. J. Chem. Pharm. Res. **7**(4), 322–325 (2015)
21. Butt, M.A., Akram, M.: A novel fuzzy decision-making system for CPU scheduling algorithm. Neural Comput. Appl. doi:10.1007/s 00521-015-1987-8
22. Bhadula, S.J., Rohilla, B., Nautiyal, B.: A genetic algorithm for scheduling jobs with burst time and priorities. IOSR J. Comput. Eng. **17**(4), 69–74 (2015). IOSR-JCE. e-ISSN: 2278-0661, p-ISSN: 2278-8727

Bio-Inspired Computation for Optimizing Scheduling

Mamta Madan

Abstract Profitability is an important factor for sustainability of an organization. Profitability is important but cash flow is also important for the basic obligations like taxes, payroll, etc. In this paper, we have worked on the optimization of resource-constrained scheduling with discounted cash flow (payment scheduling or RCPSPDCF). We have conceptualized bio-inspired computing algorithm namely Genetic Algorithm. Microsoft dependency injection is also being used. It can be further used for problems like resource optimization (Madan and Madan in GASolver-A solution to resource constrained project scheduling, 2013) [1], Time versus Cost optimization (Madan and Madan in Optimizing time cost trade off scheduling) [2].

Keywords Bio-inspired computation · Genetic algorithm · GASolver.core · Discounted cash flow · Chromosome

1 Introduction

To sustain an organization, it is very important that the cash flow should be available to the organization to maintain the good health. It is important for an organization to focus on profitability. We normally prioritize the cash flow of an organization for sustenance [3]. Cash flow is important for an organization when the customer pays high amount of interest [4]. This is the real situation for many organizations. The problem is more accelerated in environments where uncertainty is more [5]. Sometimes, people do not pay on time, and hence, the timing of payments can be a problem in short-term financial decisions [6]. Thus in this paper, we have worked towards the optimization of cash flow of an organization while maintaining the resources and constraints with the bio-inspired computing algorithm–Genetic Algorithm.

M. Madan (✉)
VIPS, New Delhi, India
e-mail: mamta.vips@gmail.com

B.K. Panigrahi et al. (eds.), *Nature Inspired Computing*, Advances in Intelligent Systems and Computing 652, https://doi.org/10.1007/978-981-10-6747-1_8

Problem Statement of RCPSPDCF

It is a problem of optimizing the NPV of a project while maintaining resources and other constraints if any.

2 Bio-Inspired Computation

Genetic Algorithms (GAs) are algorithms which work on the principle that living organisms are adaptive in nature. Genetic Algorithm basically works on the Darwin theory of the fittest. It uses the concept of using random information in the algorithm. In each iteration, a new set of genome is created from randomly used fittest genomes. Genetic Algorithm is working as an optimization tool and hence tends to improve the performance with generations.

It majorly comprises of two steps: (1) it improves in each generation (2) reaching the optimum itself. The crucial part in this is the improvement which occurs during each generation. Genetic Algorithm (GA) [7–9] is one of an important method of optimization. It is also known as a technique which is biologically inspired by nature. Thus with the use of Genetic Algorithm, we move towards better solutions across generations [10–13].

3 Solution to Payment Scheduling Using Bio-Inspired Genetic Algorithm

To understand *Payment Scheduling Problem* with Genetic Algorithm, we have addressed the following issues:

a. Establishing relationships among the tasks using task precedence graph (TPG).
b. Chromosome identification.
c. Coding selection, crossover and mutation.
d. Devising an objective function to calculate the optimal cost.
e. Analysis of the test applied.

(a) Establishing Relationships Among the Tasks Using TPG

The various tasks can be explained with the help of TPG. A TPG is a table consisting of a set of tasks with their order of precedence. Using this table, we can arrange priorities for the task to be managed (Table 1).

Table 1 Precedence table

	Task 1	Task 2	Task 3
Task 1	x	x	x′
Task 2	x′	x	x′
Task 3	x	x	x

We can set the order of precedence of tasks from this table. Where x = Boolean 0 and x' = Boolean 1.

(b) Chromosome Identification

The most important issue in GA is to decide the structure for a chromosome. We have identified a chromosome consisting of employees and tasks. The chromosome structure is shown below which explains that employee A can only work on Task 2 and 4 as it contains a Boolean 1, whereas employee A cannot work on Task T1 and T3 as it contains a Boolean 0 (Table 2).

(c) Genetic Algorithm Operators

Genetic Algorithm survives on three important operators namely selection, crossover and mutation. Selection is a process in which we select those genomes from a list which should be able to reproduce further in next generation of GA. After calculating the fitness of the genomes, the genomes which will be able to survive in the next generation is selected. After the selection operator, crossover is performed that works on the concept of biological reproduction. We inherit certain genes from our parents. We can create two new offspring using crossover. It is accompanied by mutation operator. Mutation is performed to introduce randomness in the results. After applying mutation, the fitness of the genomes is again calculated and the most fitted genomes are accepted.

(d) Devising Fitness Function

Genetic Algorithm survives on the strength of fitness function. As we know, NPV is very important part of any project. Our objective was to generate a valid schedule which can have maximum NPV, i.e. the goal of Payment Scheduling Problem is to find the optimal schedule that maximizes NPV. The objective function for NPV is designed as follows:

$$\text{NPV} = \text{Cash Inflow} - \text{Cash Outflow} + \text{Bonus/Penalty}.$$

$$\text{Fitness Function} = \text{Value of objective Function}$$

Or

$$\text{Objective Function} = \text{NPV}$$

Cash Inflows

It consists of payments at milestone events. It consists of payments made at three different events. Firstly, payments made in the beginning (beg payment), then

Table 2 Chromosome structure

	Task 1	Task 2	Task 3	Task 4
Emp A	0	1	0	1
Emp B	1	0	1	0
Emp C	1	0	0	1
Emp D	0	0	1	1

payments at the intermediate stage (intermediate payment) and finally, payments made at the end (end payment). We may denote cash inflows by costin.

$$\text{Cost}_{\text{in}} = \text{beg payment} + \text{intermediate payment} + \text{end payment}$$

Cash Outflows

Cash outflow is the total expenses incurred during the execution of the project which includes expenses met for direct cost and indirect cost also.

It is calculated as cashout = dcost + icost.

Bonus and Penalty

We may include a factor of bonus and penalty. We may earn a bonus once the project finishes before time, and vice versa for penalty.

(e) Analysis of the Test

We have developed a tool which is implemented in .net. Microsoft unity injection is used in the tool which makes the tool versatile enough to handle other scheduling problems as well. We executed an optimal schedule with valid resource constraints and concluded that the NPV starts getting maximized with the above-mentioned fitness function explained in d section. Those results are shared in the form of case studies below. The first case study illustrates when the cash outflow starts decreasing, NPV starts increasing following the devised objective/fitness function. The second case study explains when the number of payment points is increased, the value of NPV starts increasing.

(a) Case Study 1

Find an optimized Schedule which will have maximum NPV.

As we know, it is very important to maximize NPV which is essential for the success of the project. Table 5 shows the results of a valid schedule with their cash outflows and NPV. We can see from Table 3 that NPV is increasing as the generations are growing with Genetic Algorithm. The project manager can choose the desired scenario as per his/her requirement. This case study validates the objective function devised for NPV and concludes that if we reduce the cash outflow for an organization, we may expect an increase in the value of NPV (Fig. 1).

(b) Case Study 2

Find a schedule that maximizes NPV when the numbers of payment events are more.

Table 3 Payment scheduling —NPV maximization

Generation	Cash outflow	NPV
1	3,241,570	2,603,844
2	3,225,760	2,649,529
8	3,186,235	2,695,640
13	3,095,610	2,793,706
26	3,011,395	2,824,001
30	2,986,395	2,874,559
36	2,986,395	2,875,804

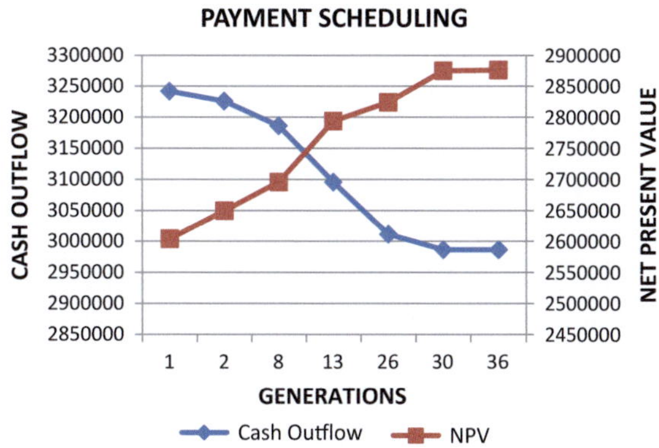

Fig. 1 Payment scheduling —NPV maximization

Table 4 Cash inflow

Cash	Time of payment
18,000	0
2,590,000	15
3,250,000	40
500,000	50

Table 5 Payment scheduling —NPV maximization (more payment points)

Generation	Cash outflow	NPV
1	3,142,420	2,813,447
4	3,105,570	2,830,557
24	2,967,500	2,946,680
50	2,966,395	2,948,739

The aim of the second case study is also to maximize NPV but the additional condition is that we have increased the number of payment events (Table 4).

Table 5 shows the results of NPV maximization with more number of payment points. We can see from the result that the value of NPV is more as compared to the first test case. Figure 2 shows the analysis of the same through the graph. The graph

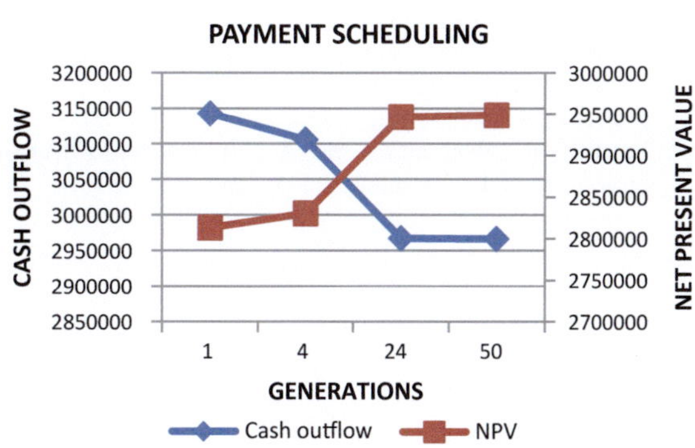

Fig. 2 Payment scheduling —NPV maximization (more payment points)

and the table below validates that if we increase more payment points, the value of NPV will increase.

4 Conclusion

We have focused on the maximization of net present value (NPV) keeping optimization of resources using the concept of bio-inspired computing Genetic Algorithm. We implemented it in .net and named it as GASolver.core. We have also implemented in .net all the three important operators of Genetic Algorithm. We also generated the schedules with values of NPV. To increase the NPV, we tested the project at different payment points and concluded that if we increase the number of payment points, the NPV increases. Thus, the project manager can see the results and choose the optimized schedule with maximum NPV as per his/her requirements. I feel it should be a contribution to the project managers, who are striving to attain an optimized schedule with a high value of NPV of the organization.

References

1. Madan, M., Madan, R.: GASolver—a solution to resource constrained project scheduling. IJACSA (2013)
2. Madan, M., Madan, R.: Optimizing time cost trade off scheduling. IJAIEM. ISSN 2319-4847
3. Emst, H.: New balance sheet for managing liquidity and growth. Harvard Bus. Rev. **62** (1984)
4. Milling, B.E.: Business Survival. Chilton Books, Reading, PA (1983)
5. Bourgeois, L.J., Eisenhardt, K.M.: Strategic decision processes in high velocity environments: four cases in the microcomputer industry. Manage. Sci. 816–835 (1988)
6. Sartoris W., Hill N.: Cash and working capital management: a generalized cash flow approach to short-term financial decisions. J. Finan. 349–359 (1983)
7. Chambers, L.D. (ed.): Practical Handbook of Genetic Algorithms: Complex Coding Systems. CRC Press, Boca Raton (1999)
8. Davis, L.: Handbook of Genetic Algorithms. Van Nostrand Reinhold, New York (1991)
9. Goldberg, D.: Genetic Algorithm, in search Optimization and Machine Learning
10. Wulianga, P., Chengenb W.: A multi-mode resource-constrained problem and its genetic algorithm based solution. Int. J. Project Manage. **27**(6), 600–609 (2009)
11. He, Z., Xu, Y.: Multi-mode project payment scheduling problems. Eur. J. Oper. Res. **189**
12. Ulusoya, G., Cebellib, S.: An equitable approach to the payment scheduling problem in project management. Eur. J. Oper. Res. **127**(2), 262–278 (2000)
13. Leyman, P., Vanhoucke, M.: A new scheduling technique for the resource–constrained project scheduling problem. Int. J. Prod. Res. (2014)

Segmentation of Mammograms Using a Novel Intuitionistic Possibilistic Fuzzy *C*-Mean Clustering Algorithm

Chiranji Lal Chowdhary and D.P. Acharjya

Abstract There is a partitioning of a data set X into *c*-clusters in clustering analysis. In 1984, fuzzy *c*-mean clustering was proposed. Later, fuzzy *c*-mean was used for the segmentation of medical images. Many researchers work to improve the fuzzy *c*-mean models. In our paper, we proposed a novel intuitionistic possibilistic fuzzy *c*-mean algorithm. Possibilistic fuzzy *c*-mean and intuitionistic fuzzy *c*-mean are hybridized to overcome the problems of fuzzy *c*-mean. This proposed clustering approach holds the positive points of possibilistic fuzzy *c*-mean that will overcome the coincident cluster problem, reduces the noise and brings less sensitivity to an outlier. Another approach of intuitionistic fuzzy *c*-mean improves the basics of fuzzy *c*-mean by using intuitionistic fuzzy sets. Our proposed intuitionistic possibilistic fuzzy *c*-mean technique has been applied to the clustering of the mammogram images for breast cancer detector of abnormal images. The experiments result in high accuracy with clustering and breast cancer detection.

Keywords Intuitionistic fuzzy *c*-mean · Possibilistic *c*-mean · Membership degree · Non-membership degree · Hesitation degree

1 Introduction

Segmentation arises as the basic technique towards image processing analysis because this is an important building block in it and also divides the image into various parts (regions) with homogeneous features. In the segmentation process, the image is partitioned into various non-overlapping and meaningful homogeneous regions. For common images, the segmentation is based on unsupervised clustering techniques but it becomes challenging in case of medical imaging because of poor

C.L. Chowdhary (✉)
School of Information Technology and Engineering, VIT University, Vellore, India
e-mail: c.l.chowdhary@gmail.com

D.P. Acharjya
School of Computing Science and Engineering, VIT University, Vellore, India

B.K. Panigrahi et al. (eds.), *Nature Inspired Computing*, Advances in Intelligent Systems and Computing 652, https://doi.org/10.1007/978-981-10-6747-1_9

contrast and noise. A number of techniques were offered by different researchers, and we may assume thresholding technique as the easiest over the other techniques. Thresholding became more difficult in the case of distributed illuminations. It is better to use local thresholding over global in such cases, and thresholds are found for each subdivision of image to get a local variation. Many authors have proposed clustering technology in decision-making, problem-solving and image segmentation to threshold an image. Otsu [1] has used thresholding techniques for a class variance to maximize the class reparability. In the last one decade, fuzzy approach is used in medical images due to the presence of uncertainty issues present in the form of vagueness, boundaries and variations in grey levels.

The main role of clustering is to separate unlabelled data into discrete sets. Clustering is a major technique of unsupervised learning. Many clustering techniques such as conventional *k*-mean, fuzzy *c*-mean, artificial neural network and genetic algorithms were used by different researchers. It is challenging to find an optimal threshold in thresholding technique. The *k*-mean clustering approach limits each data in a particular cluster which cannot be acceptable in all applications. Fuzzy *c*-mean is mostly used in image segmentation and assigns each pixel to unlabelled fuzzy clusters to keep each pixel in all clusters with different degrees of membership. So, the membership of fuzzy *c*-mean cannot represent the degrees of belonging of the data. Fuzzy *c*-mean was successfully incorporated into the segmentation of medical images to overcome the uncertainty and unknown noise available in them. The problems in the fuzzy *c*-mean membership do not represent the degree of belongings of the data. This problem was solved by Krishnapuram and Keller [2] by proposing possibilistic *c*-means. Each element of the kth column can be any numbers between 0 and 1, as long as the least one of them is positive. Possibilistic *c*-mean was useful to identify outliers (noise points). In 1997, some researchers [3] suggested possibilistic fuzzy *c*-mean algorithm to generate membership and typicality values where clustering unlabelled data. Later in 2005, [4] came with possibilistic fuzzy *c*-mean algorithm which produces membership and possibility simultaneously with useful point models or cluster centres for each centre. Possibilistic fuzzy *c*-mean was useful for fuzzy rule-based system identification.

Carvalho [5] proposed an adaptive and non-adaptive fuzzy *c*-mean for symbolic interval data. This does a fuzzy partition and model for every cluster by optimizing an adequacy criterion on proper Euclidian distance between vectors of intervals. Ji et al. [6] worked with an adaptive method to find the weights of local spatial factors in the objective function for local spatial continuity. They applied its magnetic resonance imaging images and found significant success with the proposed possibilistic fuzzy *c*-mean method. This method was found more robust and efficient for many levels of noise and was able to achieve higher accuracy in the context of brain magnetic resonance imaging image segmentation. Fuzzy *c*-mean cannot achieve accurate results due to noisy conditions. So, [7] proposed exponential fuzzy *c*-mean to enhance membership issues and result in more meaningful membership degree over fuzzy *c*-mean. Wahid et al. [8] proposed a genetic algorithm-based clustering technique which exploits multiple views to generate different clustering solutions and then selects a combination of clusters to form a final clustering solution. With the use of research work on theory and application of intuitionistic fuzzy sets by Attansov [9], Chaira [10] proposed intuitionistic fuzzy *c*-mean technique. This method is useful in clustering different regions of the medical images and helps to find abnormalities in image. In intuitionistic fuzzy sets, there are membership degree, non-membership degree and hesitation degree. Hesitation is an another uncertainty parameter.

In our proposed algorithm, possibilistic FCM was integrated with intuitionistic fuzzy *c*-mean. Traditional clustering methods are unable to handle the cases of noisy data and outliers. So we have used possibilistic approach to overcome this condition for improving membership assignments. To improve the possibilistic *c*-mean algorithm, we have embedded intuitionistic fuzzy *c*-mean. Intuitionistic fuzzy *c*-mean algorithm on uncertainty issue and there hesitation degree is discussed while defining the membership function. The remaining part of the proposed paper is organized in the following sections: Sect. 2 describes the preliminaries carried out on the clustering approaches; Sect. 3 covers the construction of intuitionistic possibilistic fuzzy *c*-mean; Sect. 4 describes the result analysis; and finally, Sect. 5 concludes the paper.

2 Preliminaries of Clustering

Clustering approach is in concern with image segmentation issues and that will decide about that how the pixels of an image concern with each other in a proper way. A clustering algorithm will divide the set of pixels into clusters such that pixels contained by a given cluster claim high degree of similarity over the pixels belonged to different clusters. An extensive literature provides information that different clustering methods are applied in many research areas such as pattern recognition, data mining, big data, taxonomy, image processing and information retrieval. Clustering approaches found to be categorized into two methods as hierarchical and partitioning methods. Hierarchical methods are nested in sequence of partitions of the input data, and partitioning methods obtain a single partition of the input data in a fixed number of clusters. According to the traditional *k*-means clustering method [11], every data belong just to one cluster, but this cannot be convincing in few applications. Fuzzy *c*-mean (FCM) clustering is a fuzzy type of *k*-mean clustering [7, 12]. In FCM, there is a combination of fuzzy approach that is used to allow data to be added in all clusters with diverse degrees of membership.

The fuzzy clustering approach [7, 12] is partitioned into a set B in k clusters, and the set is having N members as $B = \{b_1, b_2, b_3, \ldots .b_N\}$. There may be a situation of uncertainty that the data b_l were consigned to many clusters with diverse degrees of membership u_{lm}. The belongingness of a data with a cluster is decided by paralleling its distance or dissimilarity d_{lm}^2 from the cluster centroid v_m. The measurements of distances are calculated with the help of Euclidean formula:

$$\mathrm{FCM} = \sum_{m=1}^{k} \sum_{l=1}^{N} u_{ij}^{p} d_{lm}^{2}, \; p \in (1, \infty), \sum_{m=1}^{k} u_{lm} = 1. \tag{1}$$

The role of fuzzifier parameter (p) is about mechanizing the influence of the membership degree over the objective function. The value of membership degree and centroid is expressed in (2) and (3) correspondingly:

$$u_{lm} = \frac{1}{\sum_{q=1}^{k} \left(\frac{d_{lm}^{2}}{d_{lq}^{2}} \right)^{\frac{1}{p-1}}} \tag{2}$$

$$v_m = \frac{\sum_{l=1}^{N} u_{lm}^{p} x_l}{\sum_{l=1}^{N} u_{lm}^{p}} \tag{3}$$

FCM clustering results are better over k-mean results but more sensitive to noise. One limitation is that the cluster-wise addition of all the membership degrees for every data to one leads the abnormal points to be members of clusters. By integrating the possibilistic approach with the fuzzy c-mean, the drawback of FCM can be resolved and that approach can be given the name of possibilistic fuzzy clustering (PFCM). The main equation for possibilistic fuzzy c-mean approach can be written as:

$$\mathrm{PFCM} = \sum_{m=1}^{k} \sum_{l=1}^{N} u_{lm}^{p} d_{lm}^{p} + \sum_{m=1}^{k} \lambda_m \left(\sum_{l=1}^{N} 1 - u_{lm} \right). \tag{4}$$

The membership degree function and positive number are as follows in (5) and (6):

$$u_{lm} = \frac{1}{1 + \left(\frac{d_{lm}^{2}}{\lambda_m} \right)^{\frac{1}{p-1}}}, \tag{5}$$

$$\lambda_m = W \frac{\sum_{l=1}^{N} u_{lm}^{p} d_{lm}^{2}}{\sum_{l=1}^{N} u_{lm}^{p}}, \tag{6}$$

In (6), W is an amendable weight which is typically set to one.

Equation (3) of FCM is used to achieve an optimum solution to update in the centroid. In case if all clusters are coincident clusters, Eq. (4) may be really minimized. The membership degree from Eq. (5) relies heavily on the gap between the data and specific cluster without any consideration of other clusters.

Another improved fuzzy clustering is based on intuitionistic fuzzy clustering algorithm. The conventional fuzzy c-mean function is modified by the use of intuitionistic fuzzy sets. The cluster centres are modified so that we can integrate intuitionistic properties with fuzzy c-mean method. Atanassov [9] proposed intuitionistic fuzzy sets and said about the existence of hesitation degree. According to him, it cannot be always true that summation of degree of membership and degree of non-membership is being 1. There may be a possibility of hesitation degree, and a hesitation degree is defined as 1 minus the sum of membership and non-membership degrees. The hesitation degree is given as follows:

$$\pi_A = \text{hesitation\_degree} = 1 - (\text{membership\_degree} + \text{non\_membership\_degree}) \tag{7}$$

Hesitation degree is initially calculated using Eq. (7), and the intuitionistic fuzzy membership values are obtained as follows:

$$u^*_{lm} = u_{lm} + \pi_{lm} \tag{8}$$

where $u^*_{lm}(u_{lm})$ denotes the intuitionistic fuzzy membership of the mth data in lth class. Replacing Eq. (8) in (3), the modified cluster centre will be:

$$v^*_m = \frac{\sum_{l=1}^{N} u^{*,p}_{lm} x_l}{\sum_{l=1}^{N} u^{*,p}_{lm}} \tag{9}$$

Using Eq. (9), the cluster centre is updated and simultaneously the membership matrix is updated. At each iteration, the cluster centre and the membership matrix are updated and the algorithm stops when the updated membership matrix and the previous matrix. Thus, the criterion function in conventional FCM is modified using intuitionistic fuzzy sets.

3 Construction of Proposed Intuitionistic Possibilistic Fuzzy Clustering

Several medical image segmentation systems suggested by different authors have used the conventional k-mean clustering approach for tumour detection. But it has the limitations such as inadequate detection of tumour, predominantly in case of malignant cases. Some other researchers have used fuzzy c-mean approach which can detect malignant tumour mass more precisely over k-mean. These clustering methods are unable to handle the cases of noisy data and outliers. Possibilistic approach was used to overcome such condition for improving membership assignments. We have proposed an integrated intuitionistic fuzzy c-mean system to improve the possibilistic c-mean algorithm. Such medical image segmentation system will be called as intuitionistic possibilistic fuzzy c-mean (IPFCM) clustering system, and this system is taking the advantages of both approaches. Construction of the proposed system is in four paces: initiative pre-processing, main

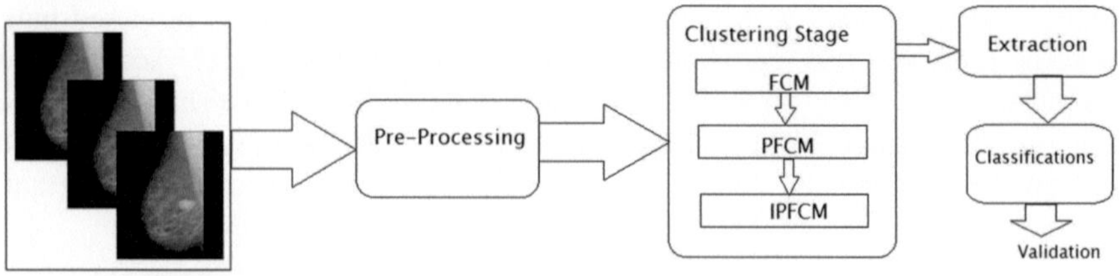

Fig. 1 Proposed intuitionistic possibilistic fuzzy clustering system

segmentation, i.e. clustering, statistical texture feature extraction and classification. The leading idea of our proposed work is based on segmentation part which does integration of possibilistic fuzzy *c*-mean with intuitionistic fuzzy *c*-mean and reduces the number of iterations to help in minimizing the execution time. The important portions of our IPFCM clustering method will be explained in the next paragraphs (Fig. 1).

Medical images are difficult to interpret, so the image is converted into the accessible form. This step involves removing unwanted parts which present in the background of the medical images. The main objective of this step is to improve the image quality by removing the unwanted areas. Disparate possibilistic clustering methods that try to minimize the membership degree of noisy data, the intuitionistic possibilistic fuzzy clustering (IPFCM) approach, assigns hesitation degree to them with membership and non-membership degree. Intuitionistic possibilistic fuzzy *c*-mean algorithm is applied to improving the detection duties of breast cancer detection system to assist a radiologist to some extent. After, medical images were enhanced using intuitionistic possibilistic fuzzy *c*-mean algorithm, choose intuitionistic fuzzy *c*-mean algorithm to separate between each cluster of pixels.

3.1 IPFCM Algorithm 1

Step 1. Initialization: Initialize B, k, d, u, v and the parameters used in the proposed algorithm.

Step 2. Evaluate the Eq. $\text{PFCM} = \sum_{m=1}^{k}\sum_{l=1}^{k} u_{lm}^{P} d_{lm}^{P} + \sum_{m=1}^{k} \lambda_m \left(\sum_{l=1}^{N} 1 - u_{lm} \right)$ by Eq. (4).

Sub-Step 2 (a). Find $u_{lm} = \frac{1}{1+\left(\frac{d_{lm}^2}{\lambda_m}\right)^{\frac{1}{P-1}}}$ by Eq. (5).

Sub-Step 2(b). Find $\lambda_m = W \frac{\sum_{l=1}^{N} u_{lm}^{P} d_{lm}^{2}}{\sum_{l=1}^{N} u_{lm}^{P}}$ by Eq. (6).

Step 3. Hesitation degree is initially calculated using Eq. (7)

Step 4. Intuitionistic fuzzy membership value is obtained as: $u_{lm}^{*} = u_{lm} + \pi_{lm}$, where $u_{lm}^{*}(u_{lm})$ denotes the intuitionistic fuzzy membership of the mth data in lth class.

Step 5. Replace Eq. in Step (4) in Sub-Section Eq. 2(b), the modified cluster center is will be: $\lambda_m = W \frac{\sum_{l=1}^{N} u_{lm}^{*,P} d_{lm}^{2}}{\sum_{l=1}^{N} u_{lm}^{*,P}}$ the cluster center is updated and simultaneously the membership matrix is updated.

Step 6. Determine the termination of iteration. Check convergence criterion. If convergence has been reached, stop the iteration, otherwise, go to Step 2.

4 Result Analysis

We have proposed algorithm on mammogram images. On common conditions and breast cancer images, we have compared different clustering algorithms. These clustering algorithms such as fuzzy *c*-mean, possibilistic fuzzy *c*-mean and intuitionistic fuzzy c-mean algorithms are compared with intuitionistic possibilistic fuzzy *c*-mean algorithm.

The importance of clustering is its ability to detect the tumour regions. Our proposed algorithm is having good results of detecting tumours over the other existing clustering algorithms (Fig. 2).

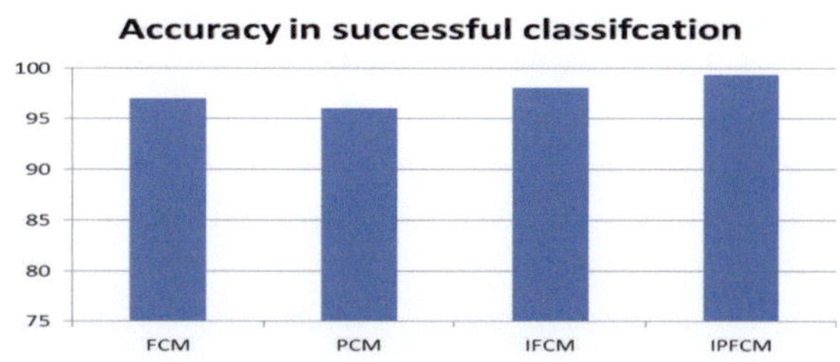

Fig. 2 Comparison between different clustering algorithms

5 Conclusions

Our proposed novel algorithm on intuitionistic possibilistic fuzzy clustering is hybridization of possibilistic fuzzy *c*-mean with intuitionistic fuzzy *c*-mean algorithm. We have tested our algorithm on breast cancer images (mammograms from MIAS dataset), and we have observed that efficiency of our approach is better over others.

References

1. Otsu, N.: A threshold selection method from gray level histograms. IEEE Trans. Syst. Man Cyber. **9**, 62–66 (1979)
2. Krishnapuram, R., Keller, J.M.: A possibilistic approach of clustering model. IEEE Trans. Fuzzy Syst. **1**, 98–110 (1993)
3. Pal, N.R., Pal, K., Bezdek, J. C.: A mixed c-means clustering model. Interrnational Conference Fuzzy Systems, Spain, pp. 11–21 (1997)
4. Pal, N.R., Pal, K., Keller, J. M., Bezdek, J.C.: A possibilistic fuzzy c-mean clustering algorithm. **13** (2005)
5. de Carvalho, F.D.A.: Fuzzy c-mean clustering for symbolic interval data. Pattern Recogn. Lett. (2006)
6. Ji, Z.X., Sun, Q.S., Xia, D.S.: A modified possibilistic fuzzy c-means clustering algorithm for bias MR images. Comput. Med. Imaging Graph. **35**, 383–397 (2011)
7. Treerattanapitak, K., Juruskulchai, C.: Outlier Detection with possibilistic exponential fuzzy clustering. 8th FSKD proceeding, pp. 453–457 (2011)
8. Wahid, A., Gao, X., Andreae, P.: Multi-view clustering of web documents using multi-objective genetic algorithm. IEEE Congress on Evolutionary Computation (2014)
9. Attanassov, K.T.: Intuitionistic fuzzy sets. Fuzzy Sets Syst. **20**, 87–96 (1986)
10. Chaira, T.: A novel intuitionistic fuzzy c-means clustering algorithm and its application to medical images. Appl. Soft. Comput. **11**, 1711–1717 (2011)
11. MacQueen, J.B.: Some methods for classification and analysis of multivariate observations. In: Proceedings of 5th Berkeley Symposium Mathematical Statistics and Probability. vol. 1, pp. 281–297 (1966)
12. Treerattanapitak, K., Juruskulchai, C.: Possibilistic exponential fuzzy clustering. J. Comput. Sci. Technol. **28**, 311–322 (2013)

Wireless Monitoring and Indoor Navigation of a Mobile Robot Using RFID

Prashant Agarwal, Aman Gupta, Gaurav Verma, Himanshu Verma, Ashish Sharma and Sandeep Banarwal

Abstract The advent of new technologies like ZigBee, RFID, Android, Arduino has revolutionized the era of embedded system design. Nowadays, every user is surrounded by smart devices (robots) which make their life easier and comfortable. It has also been predicted by the researchers that by 2020, there will be billions of embedded devices talking to each other as compared to human beings termed as Internet of things (IoT). This paper is concerned with the development of autonomous mobile robot used for wireless control and navigation. This robot is equipped with ZigBee (for wireless data transfer), RFID reader (for reading the RFID tags to change the robot direction), and Arduino (for calculating the shortest path and providing commands to robot after reaching a RFID tag). This mobile robot has wide variety of applications in indoor navigation. The basic functionality of the proposed design is simulated on a chart paper designed by us, and the complete design is implemented around Arduino microcontroller with required necessary interfaces.

Keywords RFID · ZigBee

P. Agarwal (✉) · A. Gupta · G. Verma · H. Verma · A. Sharma · S. Banarwal
Department of Electronics & Communication, Jaypee University,
A-10, Sector-62, Noida, UP, India
e-mail: prashant.agarwal92@gmail.com

A. Gupta
e-mail: aman.gggupta92@gmail.com

G. Verma
e-mail: gaurav.iitkg@gmail.com

H. Verma
e-mail: himanshutechdn@gmail.com

A. Sharma
e-mail: attach4ashish@gmail.com

S. Banarwal
e-mail: banrwals@gmail.com

B.K. Panigrahi et al. (eds.), *Nature Inspired Computing*, Advances in Intelligent Systems and Computing 652, https://doi.org/10.1007/978-981-10-6747-1_10

1 Introduction

Robotics, ZigBee, and RFID are new high technologies in the advancement of the new technology. Robotics is the field which requires the knowledge of many engineering fields like mechanical engineering for making the structure of robot, electronics engineering for making required circuits, information engineering for coding process, artificial intelligence. It is among one of the most popular fields in the present age. ZigBee wireless communication technology is a very new wireless technology with low cost, low power dissipation. ZigBee provides new features that improve the safety, security, and reliability of the system. Both energy and money can be saved by using it in the tools needs to gain control of our homes appliances [1–3]. Putting these techniques together, we designed a robot which will find a shortest path to destination and they follow that path to reach the destination, uses RFID tags to change its direction and ZigBee wireless network can be used to supervise and control [4] which resolve many problems like making possible communication between rescue robot and can also be helpful for long range surveillance, and it also makes the robot more active, more perfect, and stronger [5]. In this paper, we proposed a mobile robot that will reach to a specified location by using the coordinates provided by the shortest path algorithm and tracking the RFID tags to change its direction to left or right. The RFID reader is attached to the mobile robot and keeps on reading those tags that come in the path and will take the decision accordingly. The possible application of our paper can be extensive.

2 Proposed System Architecture

The goal of the proposed system is to prepare an autonomous robot system that will reach to a specified location and also being capable of wireless communication. The system consists of Arduino uno. Arduino is a hardware board designed around Atmega 328 Arduino uno is given the preference over all other processors as it possesses good operation speed and better data processing ability and easy programming makes our task easier to carry out a built-in system development [6–8]. Along all of these features, UNO comes with one port serial communication although you can use other pins for serial communication using software serial, and also it comes with sixteen MHz ceramic resonator, USB connection, power jack, ICSP header, and a reset button. It contains onboard burner so user has to only connect your computer with a USB cable to upload your program in microcontroller. We have used ZigBee for wireless communication and its interfacing with the controller is an important prospect. Xbee (ZigBee used for wireless communication) modules are inexpensive which comprise an antenna, transmitter/receiver, amplifier, and circuit that allows us to send and receive data between the Xbee and a microcontroller over predefined communication protocol [9–12] (Fig. 1).

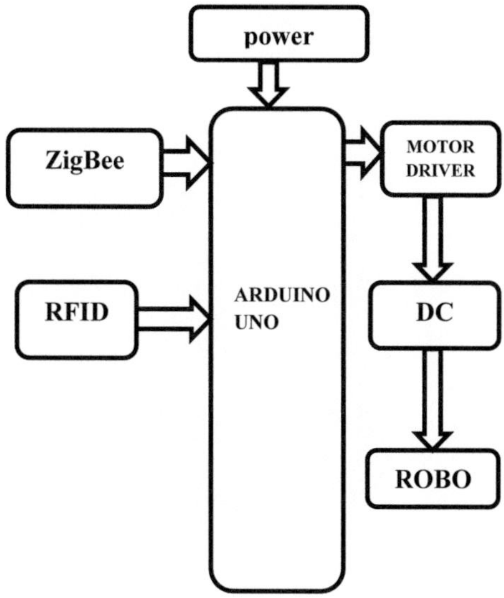

Fig. 1 Block diagram

A basic RFID System involves two mainstream sections Tag and a Reader. These passive tags are made from a very small tag chip normally a sort of integrated circuit (IC) [13–15]. We have tags in the form of apparel hang tags, labels, security tags, and a wide variety of industrial asset tags. The tag chip has designed with a memory to store the object's EPC and other variable and valuable information to make it readable and trackable by RFID readers.

Here, we have designed our matrix in which '1' represents the path and '3' represents the blockage. We have placed the tags on coordinates where there are multiple paths and in front of possible destinations (by possible destination we mean the places where user can send our robot). By this means, we can also keep track of our robot (Fig. 2).

$$
\begin{array}{l}
\{\{1\ ,\ 1\ ,\ 1\ ,\ 3\} \\
\ \{1\ ,\ 3\ ,\ 1\ ,\ 1\} \\
\ \{1\ ,\ 1\ ,\ 1\ ,\ 3\} \\
\ \{1\ ,\ 3\ ,\ 1\ ,\ 1\}\}
\end{array}
$$

A. *Wireless communication with ZigBee*

The Digi Xbee 802.15.4 modules are among one of the cheapest, user-friendly, and most reliable RF devices experienced. These modules can communicate from point to point or one point to a PC or in a network. ZigBee module is interfaced with Arduino for controlling application. The range of ZigBee is up to 100 m. Two ZigBee modules are used by us; one is connected to the PC and other to the

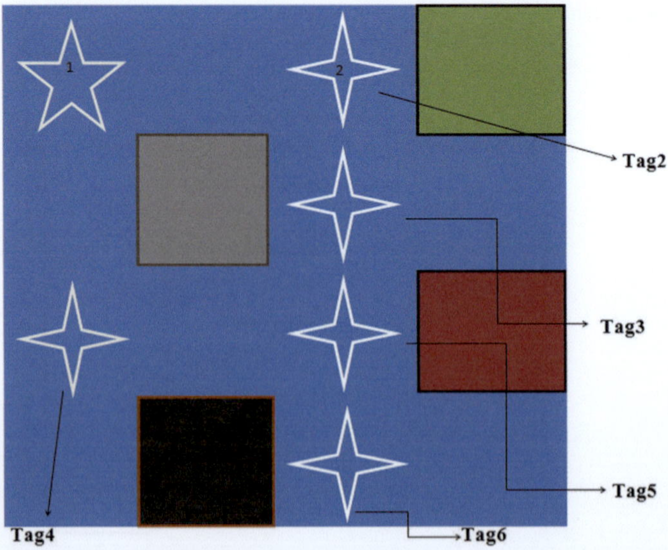

Fig. 2 Road map

microcontroller. XCTU software is used for serial communication through ZigBee. The destined coordinates were sent to the ZigBee module connected to the mobile robot by the help of serial communication. These coordinates were then transmitted to the microcontroller. The microcontroller by the help of our designed algorithm will try to move our mobile robot toward the desired coordinates.

3 Project Algorithm

We were finding our shortest path by the help of a short algorithm discussed below. It is somewhat similar to the Dijkstra's algorithm.

We designed a 4 × 4 matrix in which row defines horizontal path and column defines vertical path. If next point offered path it is defined by 1 and if blocked then defined by 3. Tags have been attached at all the points where there is either a turn or point which may be termed as destination points. First of all, we would take the initial and destination points from the user and then wirelessly send it to the robot through ZigBee. Once these points were obtained, the shortest path between these points was obtained by our self-made algorithm to navigate it to destination point.

Step 1 Get the initial and final coordinates from the user.

Step 2 Finding the coordinates of shortest path which robot will follow.

Step 3 The RFID reader will read the tag and accordingly assign the coordinates to that tag.

Step 4 If tag coordinate and destination coordinates are same then robot will stop and wait for next destination coordinate. If coordinates are not same then it will take next action depending on the procedure defined in Step 5.

Step 5 This is the most important and difficult step. To navigate the robot, we must know the heading of our robot and when and where to rotate our robot. For this, we continuously take current and previous tag position into consideration. Following cases will explain the procedure followed by the robot.

Case 1 If current tag and previous tag have same row coordinates and tc2 > tc1, where tc1 and tc2 are coordinates of column of previous and current tags, respectively.
Then, if next row coordinate obtained from shortest path (say *r*) is greater than tr2, the robot will turn right, if r is smaller than t2 then it will turn left and if r is same as tr2 then we have to check for column. On checking if next column coordinate obtained from shortest path(say *c*) is greater than column coordinate of current tag(say tc2) then robot will keep on moving straight until it finds a new tag and if ($c <$ tc2) then it will take 180° turn.

Case 2 If current tag and previous tag have same row coordinates and tc2 < tc1 and, if next row coordinate (say *r*) obtained from shortest path is less than tr2 then the robot will turn right. If ($r >$ t2) then it will turn left and if ($r =$ tr2) satisfies with ($c <$ tc2) (*c* is next column coordinate obtained from shortest path and tc2 is column coordinate of current tag) then robot will go straight until it finds new tag and if ($c <$ tc2) then it will take 180° turn.

Case 3 If current tag and previous tag have same column coordinates and (tr2 > tr1), where tr1 and tr2 are coordinates of row of previous and current tags, respectively, then if next column coordinate obtained from shortest path (say *c*) is greater than ($c >$ tc2) then the robot will turn left. If ($c <$ tc2) then robot will turn right and if ($c =$ tc2) satisfies with ($r >$ tr2) (*r* is next row coordinate obtained from shortest path and tr2 is row coordinate of current tag) then robot will go straight until it finds new tag and will take 180° turn if ($r <$ tr2).

Case 4 If current tag and previous tag have same column coordinates and (tr2 < tr1), then if next column coordinate (say *c*) obtained from shortest path is greater than tc2, the robot will turn right. If ($c < tc2$) then it will turn left and if ($c = tc2$) satisfies with ($r < tr2$) (r is next row coordinate obtained from shortest path and tr2 is row coordinate of current tag) then robot will go straight until it finds new tag and if ($r > tr2$) then it will take 180° turn.

Step 6 The robot will move forward until it finds new tag and if it reads new tag then again it will follow same procedure from Step 4 to Step 6.

4 Experimental Results

In this paper, we have designed autonomous mobile car using RFID and ZigBee. We have tested all possible paths but here I will show you some results.

Case 1: Destination is gray colored room (can be seen from Figs. 2 and 3).

Here our robot moves two blocks left from the start and then a block down to reach its destination.

Case 2: Destination is black colored room (can be seen from Fig. 4).

Here our robot moves two blocks left from the start and then three blocks down to reach its destination.

Case 3: Destination is red colored room (can be seen from Fig. 5).

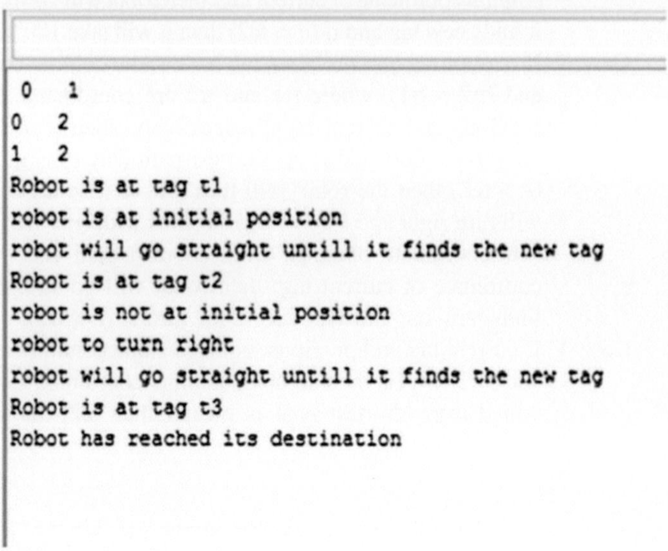

Fig. 3 Result for gray room

```
0  1
0  2
1  2
2  2
3  2
Robot is at tag t1
robot is at initial position
robot will go straight
robot will go straight untill it finds the new tag
Robot is at tag t2
robot is not at initial position
robot to turn right
robot will go straight untill it finds the new tag
Robot is at tag t3
robot will go straight
robot will go straight untill it finds the new tag
Robot is at tag t5
robot will go straight
robot will go straight untill it finds the new tag
Robot is at tag t6
Robot has reached its destination
```

Fig. 4 Result for black room

```
0  1
0  2
1  2
2  2
Robot is at tag t1
robot is at initial position
robot will go straight
robot will go straight untill it finds the new tag
Robot is at tag t2
robot is not at initial position
robot to turn right
robot will go straight untill it finds the new tag
Robot is at tag t3
robot will go straight
robot will go straight untill it finds the new tag
Robot is at tag t5
Robot has reached its destination
```

Fig. 5 Result for red room

5 Conclusion

This paper presents a novel method for wireless monitoring and control of a mobile robot that will reach to a specified location by using the coordinates provided by the shortest path algorithm and tracking the RFID tags to change its direction to left or right. The RFID reader is attached to the mobile robot and keeps on reading those tags that come in the path and will take the decision accordingly. Further, number of robots can be employed in an industrial environment, which can communicate with each other using ZigBee making a fully autonomous environment.

References

1. http://www.digi.com/support/forum/43558/xbee-s2-range-problem
2. http://zigbee.org/
3. http://www.wisegeek.org/what-is-a-baud-rate.htm
4. Wei, W., He, G., Wan, J.: Research on Zigbee wireless communication technology. National Natural Science Foundation of China (No. 51077079)
5. http://roborobotics.com/Robotics/Motors/robot-DC-motors.html
6. Chantharat, W., Pirak, C.: Image transmission over ZigBee network with transmit diversity. 2011 International Conference on Circuits, System and Simulation IPCSIT, IACSIT Press, Singapore, vol. 7 (2011)
7. http://arduino.cc/en/Main/ArduinoBoardUno
8. http://www.pocketgpsworld.com/howgpsworks.php
9. Sgorbissa, A., Zaccaria, R.: Integrated obstacle avoidance and path following through a feedback control law. Springer, Dordrecht (2013)
10. electronics.howstuffworks.com/gadgets/high-tech-gadgets/rfid.htm
11. Xiao, J.X., Lu, F.L.: An improvement of the shortest path algorithm based on Dijkstra algorithm. The 2nd International Conference on Computer and Automation Engineering (ICCAE), vol. 2 (2010)
12. Nakajima, M., Haruyama, S.: New indoor navigation system for visually impaired people using visible light communication. EURASIP J. Wireless Commun. Netw.
13. Zhang, Z., Jigang, W., Duan, X.: Practical algorithm for shortest path on transportation network. International Conference Computer and Information Application (ICCIA) (2010)
14. JayashreeOli, M., Sai Kumar, C., Akshitha, K.: RFID based autonomous mobile vehicle. Int. J. Adv. Comput. Theory Eng.
15. VenkataRamanaiah, B., Abdul Azi, M.: RFID based mobile robot in industries using ZiGBee

A Note on q-Bernoulli–Euler Polynomials

Subuhi Khan and Mumtaz Riyasat

Abstract In this article, a mixed family of q-Bernoulli–Euler polynomials is introduced by means of generating function, series definition, and determinantal definition. Further, the numbers related to the q-Bernoulli–Euler polynomials are considered, and the graph of the q-Bernoulli–Euler polynomials is also drawn for index $n = 3$ and $q = 1/2$.

Keywords q-Bernoulli polynomials · q-Euler polynomials · Determinantal definition

1 Introduction and Preliminaries

Recently, there is a significant increase of research activities in the area of q-calculus due to its applications in various fields such as mathematics, physics, and engineering. By using q-analysis and umbral calculus, many special polynomials have been studied; see for example [1–4].

We review certain definitions and concepts of q-calculus.

Throughout this work, we apply the following notations: N indicates the set of natural numbers, $N0$ indicates the set of nonnegative integers, R indicates set of all real numbers, and C denotes the set of complex numbers. We refer the readers to [5] for all the following q-standard notations.

The q-analogues of a complex number a and of the factorial function are defined by

$$[a]_q = \frac{1 - q^a}{1 - q}, \quad q \in \mathbb{C} - \{1\}; \quad a \in \mathbb{C}. \tag{1.1}$$

S. Khan · M. Riyasat (✉)
Department of Mathematics, Aligarh Muslim University, Aligarh, India
e-mail: mumtazrst@gmail.com

S. Khan
e-mail: subuhi2006@gmail.com

B.K. Panigrahi et al. (eds.), *Nature Inspired Computing*, Advances in Intelligent Systems and Computing 652, https://doi.org/10.1007/978-981-10-6747-1_11

$$[n]_q! = \prod_{k=1}^{n} [k]_q = [1]_q[2]_q \ldots [n]_q, \quad n \in N; \quad [0]_q! = 1; \; q \in C. \tag{1.2}$$

The Gauss q-polynomial coefficient $\binom{n}{k}_q$ is defined by

$$\binom{n}{k}_q = \frac{[n]_q!}{[k]_q![n-k]_q!} = \frac{\langle 1;q\rangle_n}{\langle 1;q\rangle_k \langle 1;q\rangle_{n-k}}, \quad k = 0, 1, \ldots, n, \tag{1.3}$$

where $\langle a;q\rangle_n$ are the q-shifted factorial.

The q-exponential function $e_q(x)$ is defined by

$$e_q(x) = \sum_{n=0}^{\infty} \frac{x^n}{[n]_q!} = \prod_{j=0}^{\infty} \frac{1}{(1-(1-q)q^j x)}, \quad 0<|q|<1; \; |x|<|1-q|^{-1}. \tag{1.4}$$

Al-Salaam, in [6], introduced the family of q-Appell polynomials $\{A_{n,q}(x)\}_{n\geq 0}$ and studied some of their properties. The n-degree polynomials $A_{n,q}(x)$ are called q-Appell provided they satisfy the following q-differential equation:

$$D_{q,x}\{A_{n,q}(x)\} = [n]_q A_{n-1,q}(x), \quad n = 0, 1, 2, \ldots; \; q \in C; \; 0<q<1. \tag{1.5}$$

The q-Appell polynomials $A_{n,q}(x)$ are also defined by means of the following generating function [6]:

$$A_q(t)e_q(xt) = \sum_{n=0}^{\infty} A_{n,q}(x) \frac{t^n}{[n]_q!}, \quad 0<q<1, \tag{1.6}$$

where

$$A_q(t) := \sum_{n=0}^{\infty} A_{n,q} \frac{t^n}{[n]_q!}, \quad A_{0,q} = 1; \; A_q(t) \neq 0. \tag{1.7}$$

Based on different selections for the function $A_q(t)$, different members belonging to the family of q-Appell polynomials can be obtained.

For $A_q(t) = \left(\frac{t}{e_q(t)-1}\right)$, the q-Appell polynomials $A_{n,q}(x)$ become the q-Bernoulli polynomials $B_{n,q}(x)$ [1, 7], which are defined by the generating function of the following form:

$$\left(\frac{t}{e_q(t)-1}\right) e_q(xt) = \sum_{n=0}^{\infty} B_{n,q}(x) \frac{t^n}{[n]_q!} \tag{1.8}$$

For $A_q(t) = \left(\frac{2}{e_q(t)+1}\right)$, the q-Appell polynomials $A_{n,q}(x)$ become the q-Euler polynomials $E_{n,q}(x)$ [1, 8], which are defined by the generating function of the following form:

$$\left(\frac{2}{e_q(t)+1}\right)e_q(xt) = \sum_{n=0}^{\infty} E_{n,q}(x)\frac{t^n}{[n]_q!}. \tag{1.9}$$

Taking $x = 0$ in the generating functions (1.10) and (1.11), we find that the q-Bernoulli numbers (qBN) $B_{n,q}$ [1] and q-Euler numbers (qEN) $E_{n,q}$ [1] are defined by the generating relations:

$$\left(\frac{t}{e_q(t)-1}\right) = \sum_{n=0}^{\infty} B_{n,q}(x)\frac{t^n}{[n]_q!}, \tag{1.10}$$

$$\left(\frac{2}{e_q(t)+1}\right) = \sum_{n=0}^{\infty} E_{n,q}(x)\frac{t^n}{[n]_q!} \tag{1.11}$$

respectively.

Consequently, from Eqs. (1.10), (1.11) and generating functions (1.8), (1.9), we have

$$B_{n,q} := B_{n,q}(0); \quad E_{n,q} := E_{n,q}(0). \tag{1.12}$$

The determinantal definition for the q-Appell polynomials is considered in [9]. Further, the determinantal definition for the q-Bernoulli polynomials $B_{n,q}(x)$ and q-Euler polynomials $E_{n,q}(x)$ are considered in [10]. The determinantal definition for a mixed family of q-Bernoulli and Euler polynomials can also be considered.

In this article, the q-Bernoulli and q-Euler polynomials are combined to introduce the family of q-Bernoulli–Euler polynomials by means of generating function, series definition, and determinantal definition. Further, the numbers related to the q-Bernoulli–Euler polynomials are considered, and the graph for these polynomials is also drawn for particular values of n and q.

2 q-Bernoulli–Euler Polynomials

The q-Bernoulli–Euler polynomials (qBEP) are introduced by means of generating function and series definition. In order to derive the generating function for the qBEP, we prove the following result:

Theorem 2.1 *The qBEP are defined by the following generating function*:

$$\frac{(2t)}{(e_q(t)-1)(e_q(t)+1)}e_q(xt)=\sum_{n=0}^{\infty}{}_BE_{n,q}(x)\frac{t^n}{[n]_q!},\quad 0<q<1. \tag{2.1}$$

Proof Expanding the q-exponential function $e_q(xt)$ in the l.h.s. of Eq. (1.9) and then replacing the powers of x, i.e., $x^0, x^1, x^2, \ldots, x^n$ by the corresponding polynomials $B_{0,q}(x), B_{1,q}(x), \ldots, B_{n,q}(x)$ in both sides of the resultant equation, we have

$$\left(\frac{2}{e_q(t)+1}\right)\left[1+B_{1,q}(x)\frac{t}{[1]_q!}+B_{2,q}(x)\frac{t^2}{[2]_q!}+\cdots+B_{n,q}(x)\frac{t^n}{[n]_q!}+\cdots\right]$$
$$=\sum_{n=0}^{\infty}E_{n,q}\{B_{1,q}(x)\}\frac{t^n}{[n]_q!}. \tag{2.2}$$

Summing up the series in l.h.s. and then using Eq. (1.8) and denoting the resultant qBEP in the r.h.s. by ${}_BE_{n,q}(x)=E_{n,q}\{B_{1,q}(x)\}=E_{n,q}\left\{x-\frac{1}{1+q}\right\}$, we are led to assertion (2.1).

Remark 2.1 We have derived the generating function (2.1) for the qBEP ${}_BE_{n,q}(x)$ by replacing the powers of x by the polynomials $B_{n,q}(x)$ (n = 0,1,...) in generating function (1.9) of the q-Euler polynomials $E_{n,q}(x)$. If we replace the powers of x by the polynomials $E_{n,q}(x)$ (n = 0,1,...) in generating function (1.8) of the q-Bernoulli polynomials $B_{n,q}(x)$, we get the same generating function. Thus, if we denote the resultant q-Euler–Bernoulli polynomials (qEBP) by ${}_EB_{n,q}(x)$, we have

$${}_BE_{n,q}(x)\equiv{}_EB_{n,q}(x). \tag{2.3}$$

Theorem 2.2 *The qBEP* ${}_BE_{n,q}(x)$ *are defined by the following series*:

$${}_BE_{n,q}(x)=\sum_{k=0}^{n}\binom{n}{k}_q E_{k,q}B_{n-k,q}(x). \tag{2.4}$$

Proof Using Eqs. (1.8) and (1.11) in the l.h.s. of generating function (2.1) and then using Cauchy's product rule in the l.h.s. of resultant equation, we find

$$\sum_{n=0}^{\infty}\sum_{k=0}^{n}\binom{n}{k}_q E_{k,q}B_{n-k,q}(x)\frac{t^n}{[n]_q!}=\sum_{n=0}^{\infty}{}_BE_{n,q}(x)\frac{t^n}{[n]_q!}. \tag{2.5}$$

Equating the coefficients of same powers of t in both sides of Eq. (2.5), we are led to assertion (2.4).

Next, we derive the determinantal definition for the qBEP ${}_BE_{n,q}(x)$. For this, we prove the following result:

Theorem 2.3 *The qBEP ${}_BE_{n,q}(x)$ of degree n are defined by*

$$ {}_BE_{0,q}(x) = 1, \tag{2.6}$$

$$ {}_BE_{n,q}(x) = (-1)^n \begin{vmatrix} 1 & B_{1,q}(x) & B_{1,q}(x) & \cdots & B_{n-1,q}(x) & B_{n,q}(x) \\ 1 & \frac{1}{2} & \frac{1}{2} & \cdots & \frac{1}{2} & \frac{1}{2} \\ 0 & 1 & \frac{1}{2}\binom{2}{1}_q & \cdots & \frac{1}{2}\binom{n-1}{1}_q & \frac{1}{2}\binom{n}{1}_q \\ 0 & 0 & 1 & \cdots & \frac{1}{2}\binom{n-1}{2}_q & \frac{1}{2}\binom{n}{2}_q \\ . & . & . & \cdots & . & . \\ . & . & . & \cdots & . & . \\ 0 & 0 & 0 & \cdots & 1 & \frac{1}{2}\binom{n}{n-1}_q \end{vmatrix}, $$

$$ n = 1, 2, \cdots, \tag{2.7}$$

where $B_{n,q}(x)$ $(n = 0,1,2,\ldots)$ are the q-Bernoulli polynomials.

Proof We recall the following determinantal definition of the q-Euler polynomials $E_{n,q}(x)$ [10]:

$$ E_{0,q}(x) = 1, \tag{2.8}$$

$$ E_{n,q}(x) = (-1)^n \begin{vmatrix} 1 & x & x^2 & \cdots & x^{n-1} & x^n \\ 1 & \frac{1}{2} & \frac{1}{2} & \cdots & \frac{1}{2} & \frac{1}{2} \\ 0 & 1 & \frac{1}{2}\binom{2}{1}_q & \cdots & \frac{1}{2}\binom{n-1}{1}_q & \frac{1}{2}\binom{n}{1}_q \\ 0 & 0 & 1 & \cdots & \frac{1}{2}\binom{n-1}{2}_q & \frac{1}{2}\binom{n}{2}_q \\ . & . & . & \cdots & . & . \\ . & . & . & \cdots & . & . \\ 0 & 0 & 0 & \cdots & 1 & \frac{1}{2}\binom{n}{n-1}_q \end{vmatrix}, \tag{2.9}$$

$$ n = 1, 2, \cdots. $$

Replacing the powers of x, i.e., $x^0, x^1, x^2, \ldots, x^n$ by the corresponding polynomials $B_{0,q}(x), B_{1,q}(x), \ldots, B_{n,q}(x)$ in both sides of Eqs. (2.8) and (2.9) and then using equation ${}_BE_{n,q}(x) = E_{n,q}, \{B_{1,q}(x)\}$ in l.h.s. of resultant equations for $n = 0,1,\ldots,$ we are led to assertions (2.6) and (2.7).

In the next section, we consider the numbers related to the q-Bernoulli–Euler polynomials.

3 Concluding Remarks

We consider the numbers related to the q-Bernoulli–Euler polynomials ${}_BE_{n,q}(x)$. Taking $x = 0$ in both sides of series definition (2.4) of the q-Bernoulli–Euler polynomials ${}_BE_{n,q}(x)$ and then using Eq. (1.12) in the r.h.s. and notation ${}_BE_{n,q} := {}_BE_{n,q}(0)$ in the l.h.s. of the resultant equation, we find the q-Bernoulli–Euler numbers denoted by ${}_BE_{n,q}$ are defined as:

$$ {}_BE_{n,q} = \sum_{k=0}^{n} \binom{n}{k}_q E_{k,q} B_{n-k,q}. \tag{3.1} $$

Next, we find the determinantal definition of the q-Bernoulli–Euler numbers ${}_BE_{n,q}$.

Taking $x = 0$ in both sides of Eqs. (2.6) and (2.7) and then using Eq. (1.12) in the r.h.s. and notation ${}_BE_{n,q} := {}_BE_{n,q}(0)$ in the l.h.s. of the resultant equations, we find that the q-Bernoulli–Euler numbers ${}_BE_{n,q}$ are defined by the following determinantal definition:

$$ {}_BE_{0,q} = 1, \tag{3.2} $$

$$ {}_BE_{0,q} = (-1)^n \begin{vmatrix} 1 & B_{1,q} & B_{2,q} & \cdots & B_{n-1,q} & B_{n,q} \\ 1 & \frac{1}{2} & \frac{1}{2} & \cdots & \frac{1}{2} & \frac{1}{2} \\ 0 & 1 & \frac{1}{2}\binom{2}{1}_q & \cdots & \frac{1}{2}\binom{n-1}{1}_q & \frac{1}{2}\binom{n}{1}_q \\ 0 & 0 & 1 & \cdots & \frac{1}{2}\binom{n-1}{2}_q & \frac{1}{2}\binom{n}{2}_q \\ . & . & . & \cdots & . & . \\ . & . & . & \cdots & . & . \\ 0 & 0 & 0 & \cdots & 1 & \frac{1}{2}\binom{n}{n-1}_q \end{vmatrix}, \tag{3.3} $$

$n = 1, 2, \cdots,$

where $B_{n,q}$ (n = 0,1,2,...) are the q-Bernoulli numbers.

Further, we proceed to draw the graph of ${}_BE_{n,q}(x)$. To draw the graphs of these polynomials, we consider the values of the first four $B_{n,q}$, $E_{n,q}$ [1], $B_{n,q}(x)$, and $E_{n,q}(x)$ [10]. We list the first four $B_{n,q}$, $E_{n,q}$ in Table 1 and first four $B_{n,q}(x)$ and $E_{n,q}(x)$ in Table 2.

Table 1 First four $B_{n,q}$ and $E_{n,q}$

n	0	1	2	3
Bn,q	1	$-(1+q)^{-1}$	$q^2([3]_q!)^{-1}$	$(1-q)q^3([2]q)^{-1}([4]_q)^{-1}$
En,q	1	$-\frac{1}{2}$	$\frac{1}{4}(-1+q)$	$\frac{1}{8}(-1+2q+2q^2-q^3)$

Table 2 First four $B_{n,q}(x)$ and $E_{n,q}(x)$

n	0	1	2	3
$B_{n,q}(x)$	1	$x - \frac{1}{1+q}$	$x^2 - \frac{[2]_q}{1+q}x + \frac{q^2}{[3]_q[2]_q}$	$x^3 - \frac{[3]_q x^2}{1+q} + \frac{q^2 x}{[2]_q} + \frac{(1-q)q^3}{[2]_q[4]_q}$
$E_{n,q}(x)$	1	$x - \frac{1}{2}$	$x^2 - \frac{[2]_q}{2}x + \frac{1}{4}(-1+q)$	$x^3 - \frac{[3]_q}{2}x^2 + \frac{[3]_q}{4}(-1+q)x + \frac{1}{8}(-1+2q+2q^2-q^3)$

Finally, we consider the values of ${}_BE_{n,q}(x)$ for $n = 3$ and $q = 1/2$. Therefore, taking $n = 3$ and $q = 1/2$ in series definition (2.4) and then using the expressions of first four $E_{n,q}$ and $B_{n,q}(x)$ in the resultant equation and then simplifying, we find

$$ {}_BE_{3,1/2}(x) = x^3 - \frac{49}{24}x^3 + \frac{79}{96}x + \frac{379}{2880}. \tag{3.4} $$

In view of Eq. (3.4), we get the following graph:

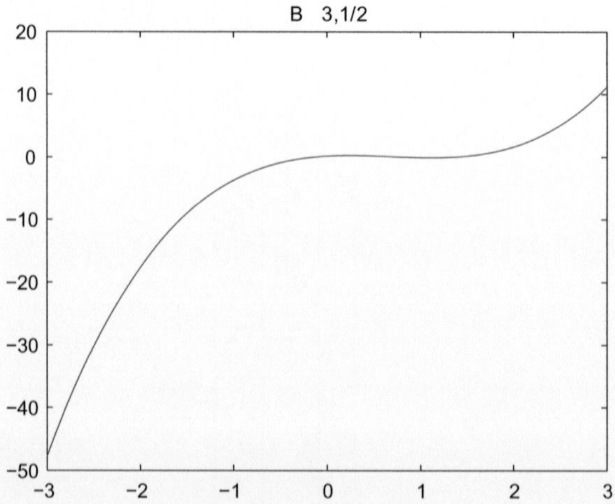

In view of relation (2.3), we remark that the results for the qEBP ${}_EB_{n,q}(x)$ will be same as the results established for the qBEP ${}_BE_{n,q}(x)$.

References

1. Ernst, T.: q-Bernoulli and q-Euler polynomials, an umbral approach. Int. J. Diff. Equ. **1**(1), 31–80 (2006). 0973-6069
2. Ernst, T.: Examples of q-orthogonal polynomials. U.U.M.D. Report 2008:24
3. Ernst, T.: A Comprehensive Treatment of q-Calculus, pp. xvi + 491. Birkhäuser/Springer Basel AG, Basel (2012)
4. Loureiro, A.F., Maroni, P.: Around q-Appell polynomials sequences. Ramanujan J. **26**(3), 311–321 (2011)
5. Andrews, G.E., Askey, R., Roy, R.: 71th Special Functions of Encyclopedia of Mathematics and Its Applications. Cambridge University Press, Cambridge (1999)
6. Al-Salam, W.A.: q-Appell polynomials. Ann. Mat. Pura Appl. **4**(17), 31–45 (1967)
7. Al-Salam, W.A.: q-Bernoulli numbers and polynomials. Math. Nachr. **17**, 239–260 (1959)
8. Mahmudov, N.I.: On a class of q-Bernoulli and q-Euler polynomials. Adv. Differ. Equ. **108**, 11 (2013)
9. Keleshteri, M.E., Mahmudov, N.I.: A study on q-Appell polynomials from determinantal point of view. Appl. Math. Comput. **260**, 351–369 (2015)
10. Khan, S., Riyasat, M.: 2-iterated q-Appell polynomials from determinantal point of view (preprint)

An Approach for Iris Segmentation in Constrained Environments

Ritesh Vyas, Tirupathiraju Kanumuri and Gyanendra Sheoran

Abstract Iris recognition has become a popular technique for differentiating individuals on the basis of their iris texture with high accuracy. One of the decisive steps of iris recognition is iris segmentation because it notably affects the accuracy of feature extraction and matching steps. Most state-of-the-art algorithms use circular Hough transform (CHT) for segmenting the iris from an eye image. But, CHT does not work efficiently for eye images having less contrast. Therefore, a new approach is proposed here for isolating and normalizing the iris region, which is more robust than CHT. Experiments are performed on IITD iris database. The proposed algorithm works better than the traditional CHT.

Keywords Iris recognition · Iris segmentation · Circular Hough transform · Normalization

1 Introduction

Biometrics generally refers to technologies that measure and analyze human body characteristics, such as DNA, fingerprints, eye retinas and irises, voice patterns, facial patterns, and hand measurements, for authentication purposes. Biometric authentication is becoming popular in various fields like public security systems, financial transaction activities, and law enforcement.

Among all physical traits of human body, iris is best suited for biometric identification because of its unique and permanent features [1]. Iris also has an

R. Vyas (✉) · T. Kanumuri · G. Sheoran
National Institute of Technology Delhi, Delhi, India
e-mail: ritesh.vyas@nitdelhi.ac.in

T. Kanumuri
e-mail: ktraju@nitdelhi.ac.in

G. Sheoran
e-mail: gsheoran@nitdelhi.ac.in

B.K. Panigrahi et al. (eds.), *Nature Inspired Computing*, Advances in Intelligent Systems and Computing 652, https://doi.org/10.1007/978-981-10-6747-1_12

advantage that it is always protected against damage and wears by a highly sensitive membrane. Different parts of the eye are depicted in Fig. 1.

Iris recognition system generally consists of the following four modules: eye image acquisition, iris segmentation, feature extraction and matching, and recognition (Fig. 2). Among these modules, iris segmentation is very crucial in maintaining the system performance. It includes separating the iris region from the eye image and normalizing the circular iris into rectangular shape so that further feature extraction can be applied to it.

Hough transform is generally used to detect circular shapes in any image, so it can be used to localize the iris in eye image [1], although it is not so robust (refer to Sect. 4). However, before using Hough transform, the specular reflections should be removed; otherwise, they can cause false circular regions to be detected in the eye image. While for localizing the iris in eye images captured in unconstrained environment, there are methods like circu-differential accumulator (CDA) [2] and contrast limited adaptive histogram equalization (CLAHE) [3].

State-of-the-art iris segmentation algorithm uses Hough transform for isolating iris from an eye image. But Hough transform approach has high time complexity as well as high storage and computation requirement. Hough transform is not so robust also. Proposed work uses one morphological operation, i.e., contrast stretching for enhancing the eye image. After that, it uses the matrix fit approach for removing the reflections as well as for finding the center coordinates. Thereafter, radial scanning is applied on the isolated circular iris region to convert it into the normalized

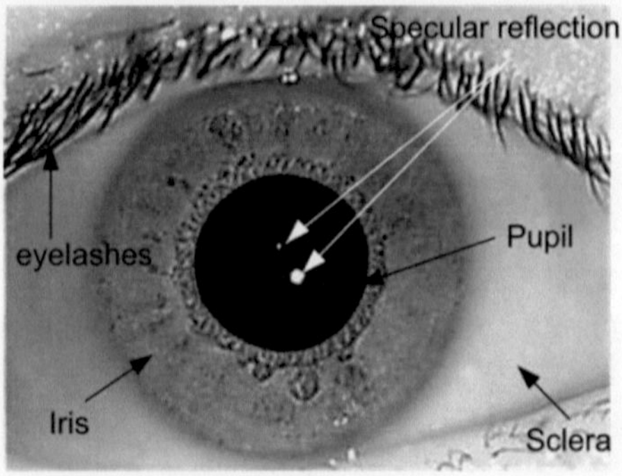

Fig. 1 Different parts of an eye image

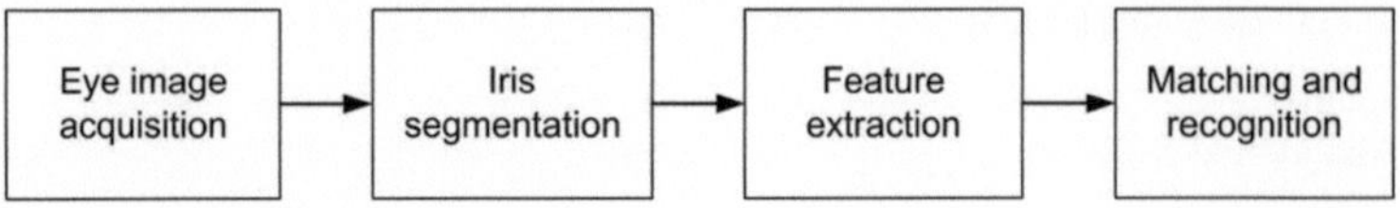

Fig. 2 Iris recognition process

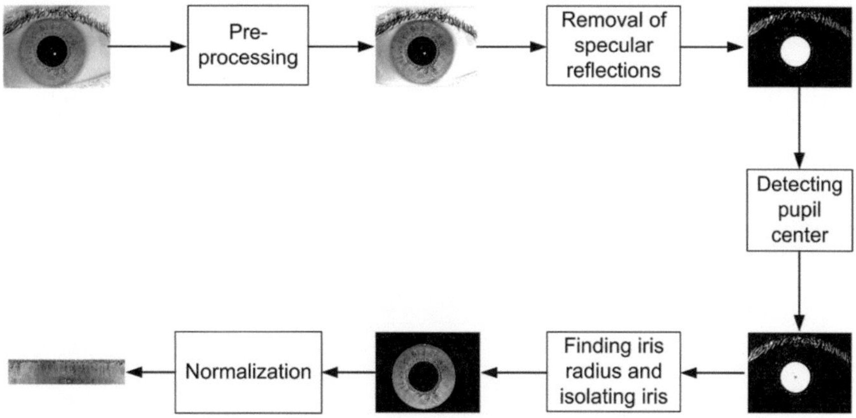

Fig. 3 Proposed iris segmentation method

rectangular shape (Fig. 3). This normalized template can further be used for feature extraction and matching steps of iris recognition algorithm.

So, rest of the paper is organized in the following way: Sect. 2 describes the preprocessing of the eye image. While Sect. 3 explains the removal of reflections, detection of pupil center, and normalization of iris, Sect. 4 gives experimental setup and results. Finally, Sect. 5 summarizes the work.

2 Preprocessing

Some eye images have very less difference between intensity values of sclera and iris region in an eye image. Due to this, iris segmentation becomes a quite tedious process. To avoid such situation, image enhancement is to be done. In the proposed work, contrast stretching has been used for this purpose.

2.1 Contrast Stretching

Contrast stretching is an image enhancement technique that focuses on improving the contrast of the image by stretching the range of intensity values it contains to span a desired range of values. Basically, it applies a linear scaling function to the image pixel values.

Before applying contrast stretching to the eye image, the histogram of the image is first analyzed. Then, two pixel values, c and d, are selected as the 5th and 95th percentile in the histogram, i.e., 5% of the pixels in the histogram will have values lower than c and 5% of the pixel will have values higher than d. Now, a and b are

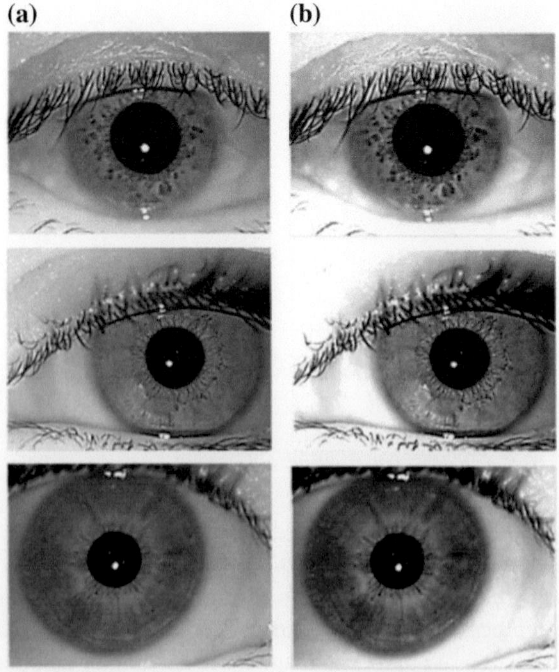

Fig. 4 Illustration of contrast stretching process **a** input images, **b** enhanced images

defined as the upper and lower pixel value limits over which the image is to be normalized. Generally, a and b are the minimum and maximum pixel values that the concerned image type allows.

So, each pixel P of the input eye image is scaled using the following function:

$$P_{\text{out}} = (P_{\text{in}} - c)\left(\frac{b-a}{d-c}\right) + a \quad (1)$$

In the experiments of the proposed algorithm, values of a and b are 0 and 255, respectively, and values of c and d are chosen to be 40 and 200. Results of contrast stretching are illustrated in Fig. 4.

3 Overview of the Proposed Approach

3.1 Removal of Specular Reflections

Specular reflections generally appear as holes in the acquired image (Fig. 1). A hole can be defined as a region of lighter pixels surrounded by the dark pixels. It is important to suppress these holes in the eye image; otherwise, they can cause

(a)

$$\begin{bmatrix} 1 & 1 & 1 \\ 1 & 0 & 1 \\ 1 & 1 & 1 \end{bmatrix} \begin{bmatrix} 1 & 1 & 1 & 1 & 1 \\ 1 & 0 & 0 & 0 & 1 \\ 1 & 0 & 0 & 0 & 1 \\ 1 & 0 & 0 & 0 & 1 \\ 1 & 1 & 1 & 1 & 1 \end{bmatrix}$$

(b)

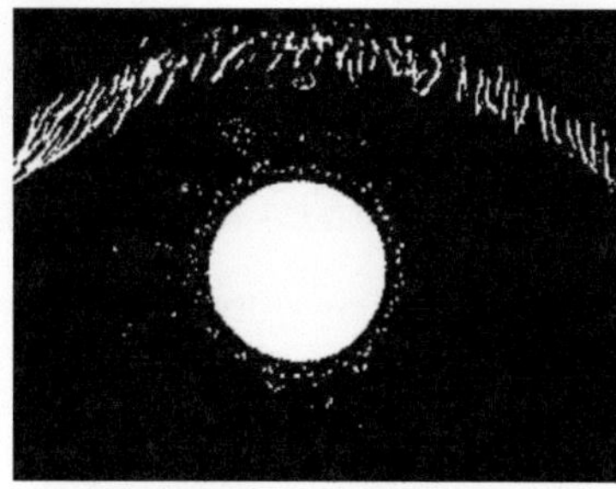

Fig. 5 **a** Scanning windows, **b** binary eye image with reflection removed

spurious edges inside the pupil [1]. In this work, a new approach is used for the removal of reflections.

First, the binary version of eye image is passed through windows of size 3 × 3, 5 × 5 (Fig. 5a) and so on, until a window is found that exactly fits on the reflection hole present in the pupil region. After getting the fit matrix, the pixels lying in the hole region are made brighter to form the continuity of the pupil as shown in Fig. 5b.

3.2 Finding Pupil Center and Iris Radius

Since a continuous pupil has already been formed in the eye image, it is easy to find out the center coordinates of the pupil by scanning the complete image through windows of sizes 3 × 3, 5 × 5 and so on, and having all elements equal to 1, until a window is found that exactly fits the circular pupil. Center pixel of the fit matrix (x_0 and y_0) will provide the coordinates of the center of the pupil (refer to Fig. 6a).

For finding the **iris radius**, the distance of every edge point of the eye image from the center point found in the preceding step is calculated as per the following distance formula:

$$\sqrt{(x - x_0)^2 + (y - y_0)^2} \tag{2}$$

The distance having maximum number of votes (i.e., repeated maximum number of times) is known as the radius of the iris. After getting iris radius, iris region can be easily differentiated as shown in Fig. 6b.

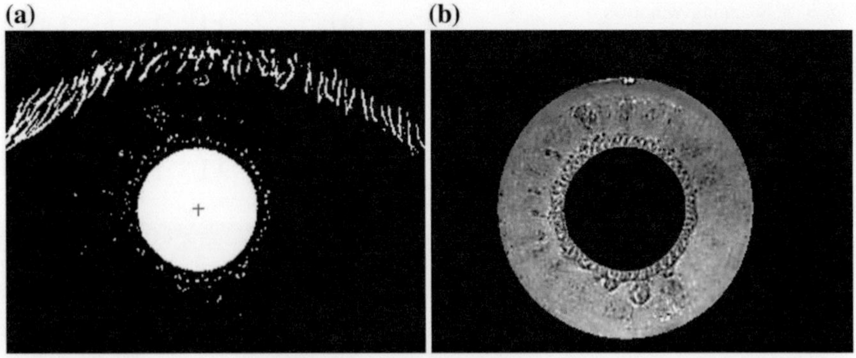

Fig. 6 **a** Binary eye image with pupil center and **b** isolated iris region

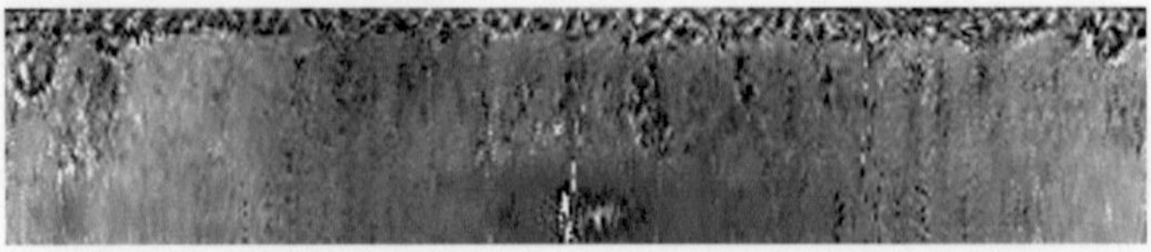

Fig. 7 Normalized iris template

3.3 Normalization

In order to allow comparisons, once the iris region is successfully segmented from an eye image, the next stage is to transform the iris region so that it has fixed dimensions. For this purpose, following strategy is adopted:

First, for every particular angle from 1° to 360°, the pixel coordinates are found from the segmented iris image, and then corresponding to those pixel coordinates, the intensity values are placed in a rectangular matrix in single row. In the proposed work, the segmented iris region is normalized into a rectangular template of constant dimensions 74×360 pixels. The example normalized iris template is shown in Fig. 7.

4 Experimental Setup and Results

The proposed technique is tested on IIT Delhi iris database [4]. The IIT Delhi iris database consists of the iris images collected from the students and staff at IIT Delhi, India. The currently available database is from 224 users, all the images are

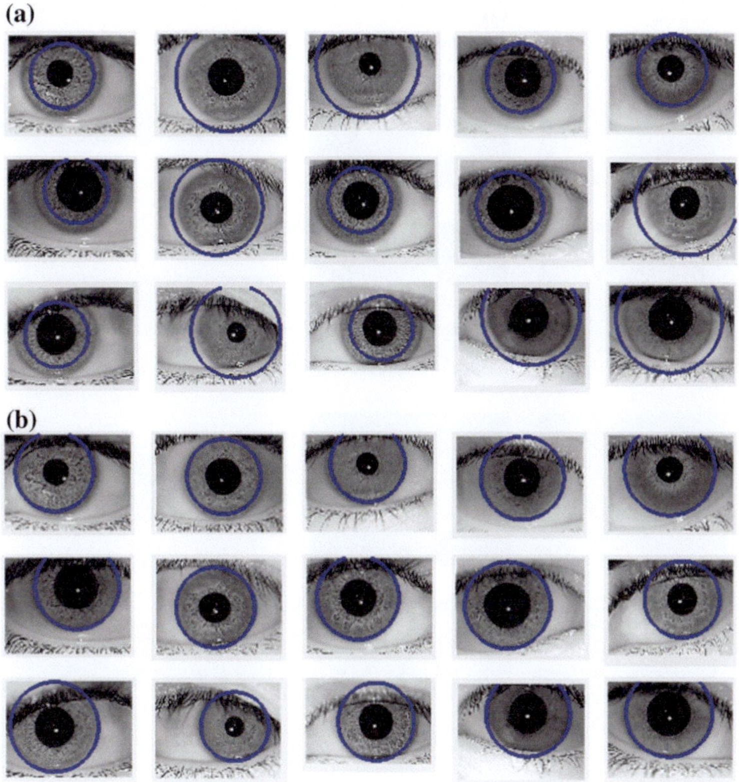

Fig. 8 **a** Iris segmentation results using CHT, **b** iris segmentation results using the proposed technique

in bitmap (*.bmp) format. All the subjects in the database are in the age group 14–55 years comprising of 176 males and 48 females. The resolution of these images is 320 × 240 pixels and all these images were acquired in the indoor environment [5–9].

The proposed technique is compared here with the traditional circular Hough transform (CHT) technique (refer to Fig. 8). It is clear from the figure that Hough transform is not so robust to noise, i.e., in the presence of eyelashes and eyelids; it may lead to poor results. And also, Hough transform requires large storage and computation.

Segmented and normalized irises for some of the eye images from the database have been shown in Fig. 9.

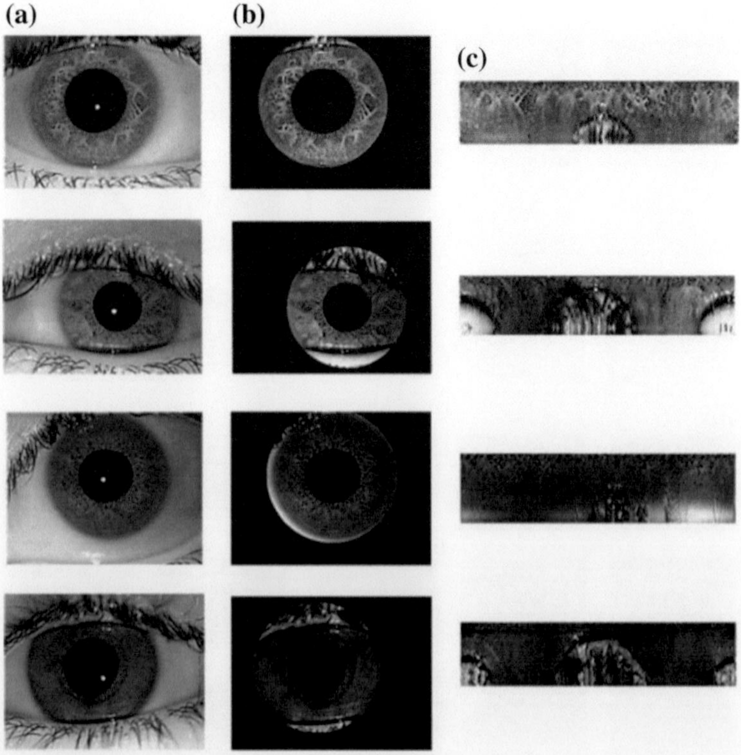

Fig. 9 Iris segmentation results of the proposed approach **a** input images, **b** isolated irises, and **c** normalized irises

5 Conclusion

Experiments are performed on IITD iris database using circular Hough transform (CHT) and the proposed technique. CHT is showing the accuracy of approximately 50% while the accuracy of the proposed technique is approximately 85% in segmenting the iris from the eye image. Then, the circular iris is converted to normalized template which can further be used for feature extraction and matching steps of iris recognition algorithm.

References

1. Jan, F., Usman, I., Agha, S.: Reliable iris localization using Hough transform, histogram-bisection, and eccentricity. Sig. Process. **93**, 230–241 (2013)
2. Jan, F., Usman, I.: Iris segmentation for visible wavelength and near infrared eye images. Optik-Int. J. Light Electron Opt. **125**, 4274–4282 (2014)

3. Farihan, A., Raffei, M., Asmuni, H., Hassan, R., Othman, R.M.: A low lighting or contrast ratio visible iris recognition using iso-contrast limited adaptive histogram equalization. Knowl.-Based Sys. **74**, 40–48 (2015)
4. Kumar, A., Passi, A.: Comparison and combination of iris matchers for reliable personal authentication. Pattern Recognit. **43**, 1016–1026 (2010)
5. Rai, H., Yadav, A.: Expert systems with applications iris recognition using combined support vector machine and hamming distance approach. Expert Syst. Appl. **41**, 588–593 (2014)
6. Sahmoud, S.A., Abuhaiba, I.S.: Efficient iris segmentation method in unconstrained environments. Pattern Recognit. **46**, 3174–3185 (2013)
7. Radman, A., Jumari, K., Zainal, N.: Fast and reliable iris segmentation algorithm. IET Image Process. **7**, 42–49 (2013)
8. Liu, J., Sun, Z., Tan, T.: Distance metric learning for recognizing low-resolution iris images. Neuro-comput. **144**, 484–492 (2014)
9. The Wavelet Tutorial. http://web.iitd.ac.in/sumeet/WaveletTutorial.pdf

Detection of Chronic Kidney Disease: A NN-GA-Based Approach

Sirshendu Hore, Sankhadeep Chatterjee, Rahul Kr. Shaw, Nilanjan Dey and Jitendra Virmani

Abstract In the present work, a genetic algorithm (GA) trained neural network (NN)-based model has been proposed to detect chronic kidney disease (CKD) which has become one of the newest threats to the developing and undeveloped countries. Studies and surveys in different parts of India have suggested that CKD is becoming a major concern day by day. The financial burden of the treatment and future consequences of CKD could be unaffordable to many, if not detected at an earlier stage. Motivated by this, the NN-GA model has been proposed which significantly overcomes the problem of using local search-based learning algorithms to train NNs. The input weight vector of the NN is gradually optimized by using GA to train the NN. The model has been compared with well-known classifiers like Random Forest, Multilayer Perception Feedforward Network (MLP-FFN), and also with NN. The performance of the classifiers has been measured in terms of accuracy, precision, recall, and F-Measure. The experimental results suggest that NN-GA-based model is capable of detecting CKD more efficiently than any other existing model.

Keywords Chronic kidney disease · Neural network · Random forest · Genetic algorithm

S. Hore (✉) · R.K. Shaw
Department of Computer Science & Engineering, HETC, Hooghly, India
e-mail: shirshendu.hore@hetc.ac.in

R.K. Shaw
e-mail: rahulshaw498@gmail.com

S. Chatterjee
Department of Computer Science & Engineering,
University of Calcutta, Kolkata, India
e-mail: sankha3531@gmail.com

N. Dey
Department of Computer Science & Engineering, BCET, Durgapur, India
e-mail: neelanjandey@gmail.com

J. Virmani
Department of EIED, Thapar University, Patiala, India
e-mail: jitendra.virnami@thapar.edu

B.K. Panigrahi et al. (eds.), *Nature Inspired Computing*, Advances in Intelligent Systems and Computing 652, https://doi.org/10.1007/978-981-10-6747-1_13

1 Introduction

Chronic diseases have become the newest threat to the developing nations. According to World Health Organization (WHO), the number of chronic disease cases has increased rapidly in developing countries and is becoming a major concern all over the world [1]. Most of the preventive measures have mainly focused on certain areas like diabetes mellitus, hypertension, cardiovascular disease (CVD). Though, the increase in the number of CKD and its consequences has emerged as another such chronic disease. The problem has become more challenging in the absence of a well-accepted method for predicting CKD, which in the future can lead to an end-stage renal failure (ESRD). Clinical decision-making is challenging due to the heterogeneity of kidney diseases, variable rates of disease progression, etc., [2]. In the absence of a proper database, the accurate study of CKD in India has faced serious problems. Though some local studies have been reported like [3], the study has covered the north Indian states and was mainly based on the serum creatinine alone (>1.8 mg/dl, the upper limit of normal for the laboratory) collected from 4,972 subjects. The authors have concluded that the prevalence of ESRD in India will be 785 person per million (pmp), and the incidence of ESRD will be 160 pmp. Another study [4], which has mainly covered the central Indian states have reported an average crude and age-adjusted incidence rates of ESRD of 151 and 232 pmp, respectively. Besides the population-based studies, few studies have been found which are mainly based on the patients of a particular hospital [5–7]. These studies have revealed that almost 30% of CKD have diabetes as the major cause. A study of patients from 48 different hospitals all over the India has revealed that prevalence of stage 3 CKD and beyond stage 3 is 0.8% (approximately) [8]. The studies from different parts of India have revealed that CKD is going to be one of the major concerns for the nation in the near future. Moreover, the financial burden of the treatment of such diseases could be unaffordable to many. Thus, a proper and early detection of CKD is extremely important to overcome the upcoming threat. Motivated by this, the authors have proposed a GA trained NN model to tackle the task.

Neural Networks [9] have been found to be suitable for several real-life applications [10–13]. Chiu et al. [14] proposed an intelligent model for detection of CKD using NNs. Back-propagation network (BPN), generalized feed forward neural networks (GRNN), and modular neural network (MNN) have been used to develop the model. In the present work, the authors have proposed GA-based hybrid models of all three NN-based models said earlier. The existing literatures [14] on this task do not have a vivid description of how the GA has been used with NN-based models. In the proposed work, the working procedure of GA to train the NN has been discussed in detail. In NN, different learning algorithms like variable metric, back-propagation, and gradient descent are used to gradually adjust the weights to converge the output to a better result, but these local search methods have a high possibility of getting trapped in local optima and a global search strategy is required. In the present work, initial input weight vector of NN has been gradually optimized using GA to improve the performance of NN. The performance of NN-GA has been compared with well-known Multilayer Perception Feedforward Network (MLP-FFN) [15], NN (trained with scaled conjugate descent learning algorithm) [16], and Random Forest classifiers [17]. The performances are measured in terms of accuracy, precision, recall, and *F*-Measure.

2 Experimental Methodology

The experiment is conducted on the dataset [18] obtained from UCI machine learning repository. The experiments are performed by using Random Forest and real coded NN (trained with scaled conjugate gradient descent algorithm), NN-GA classifiers. The basic flow of experiment consists of preprocessing, training phase to build the classification model, and test phase to test the model. After obtaining the experimental results, we measure the performance of the algorithms using several statistical performance measures like accuracy, precision, recall, and F-Measure which are obtained from the confusion matrix [19].

The genetic algorithm-based optimization of input weight vector has been implemented by following GA-NN algorithm which is shown in the flowchart depicted in Fig. 1b. The different parameters used as inputs have been depicted in Table 1.

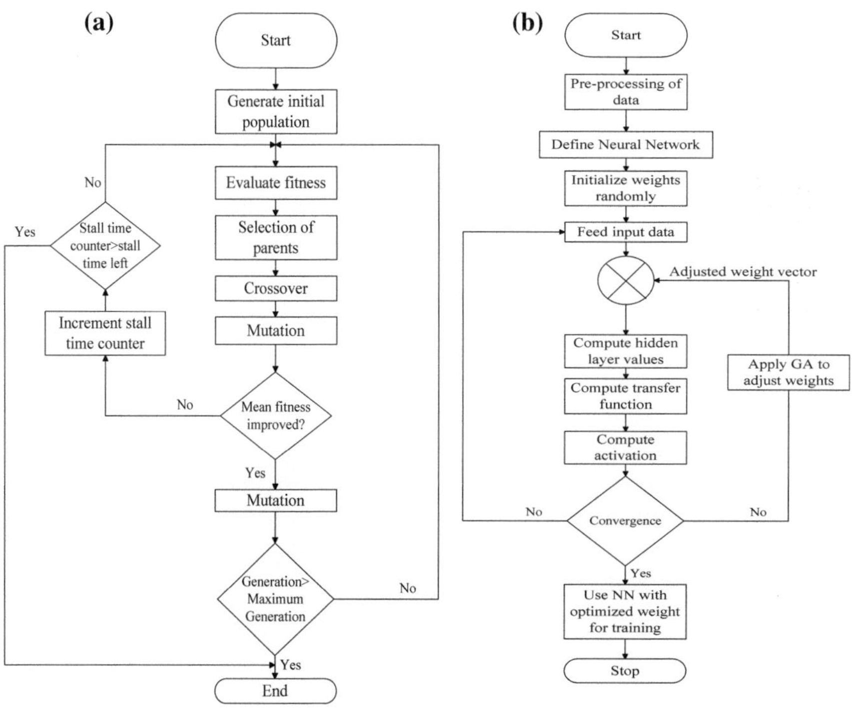

Fig. 1 **a** The genetic algorithm which has been followed to optimize the input weight vector, **b** Flowchart of NN training using genetic algorithm

Table 1 Genetic algorithm setup for input weight vector optimization

Maximum number of generation	1000
Population size	500
Crossover probability	0.2
Mutation	Gaussian
Crossover	Single-point crossover
Selection	Roulette
Stall time limit	75 s

3 Dataset Descriptions

The present work is carried out on the dataset [Early stage of Indians Chronic Kidney Disease (CKD)] obtained from UCI machine learning repository. The detection of CKD is based on 23 attributes which are described in Table 2. The dataset has 400 data instances of which 250 are positive CKD and 150 are negative CKD. The dataset has missing values, though the quantity is nominal (5% approximately).

Table 2 Attributes and corresponding descriptions of the dataset

Attribute	Description
1. Blood pressure (numerical)	Measured in mm/Hg
2. Specific gravity (nominal)	Range (1.005, 1.010, 1.015, 1.020, 1.025)
3. Albumin (nominal)	Range (0, 1, 2, 3, 4, 5)
4. Sugar (nominal)	Range (0, 1, 2, 3, 4, 5)
5. Red blood cells (nominal)	Range (normal, abnormal)
6. Pus cell (nominal)	Range (normal, abnormal)
7. Pus cell clumps (nominal)	Range (present, not present)
8. Bacteria (nominal)	Range (present, not present)
9. Blood glucose random (numerical)	Measured in mg/dl
10. Blood urea (numerical)	Measured in mg/dl
11. Serum creatinine (numerical)	Measured in mg/dl
12. Sodium (numerical)	Measured in mEq/L
13. Potassium (numerical)	Measured in mEq/L
14. Hemoglobin (numerical)	Measured in gm
15. Packed cell volume (numerical)	–
16. White blood cell count (numerical)	Measured in cells/cmm
17. Red blood cell count (numerical)	Measured in millions/cmm
18. Hypertension (nominal)	Range (yes, no)
19. Diabetes mellitus (nominal)	Range (yes, no)
20. Coronary artery disease (nominal)	Range (yes, no)
21. Appetite (nominal)	Range (good, poor)
22. Pedal edema (nominal)	Range (yes, no)
23. Anemia (nominal)	Range (yes, no)

4 Results and Discussion

The experiments are performed by following the setup described in Sect. 2. The results are tabulated in Table 3. First column depicts the result for neural network. Neural network has performed well with an accuracy of 98.33% and precision of 95.74%, recall of 100%, and *F*-Measure 97.82%. In the next column, the performance measure of Random Forest classifier has been shown. Random Forest has performed moderately with an accuracy of 92.54%, precision 85.71%, recall 96%, and *F*-Measure 90.56%. MLP-FFN performed well as expected compared to NN, and the experimental results have revealed its accuracy, precision, recall, and *F*-Measure to be 99.5, 99.2, 100, and 99.6%, respectively. The performance of NN has been improved significantly when GA is used to train it, and the experimental results have shown that it has an perfect accuracy, precision, recall, and *F*-Measure; all of them 100%, respectively.

Figure 2 depicts a comparative analysis of different classifiers with NN-GA in terms of accuracy, precision, recall, and *F*-Measure. The experimental results and the comparative chart (Fig. 2) suggest the superiority of NN-GA for predicting the chronic kidney disease with a significant improvement over the existing and traditional classifiers.

Table 3 Experimental results of NN-GA along with other classifiers

	NN	Random forest	MLP-FFN	NN-GA
Accuracy	98.33	92.54	99.5	100
Precision	95.74	85.71	99.2	100
Recall	100	96	100	100
F-Measure	97.82	90.56	99.6	100

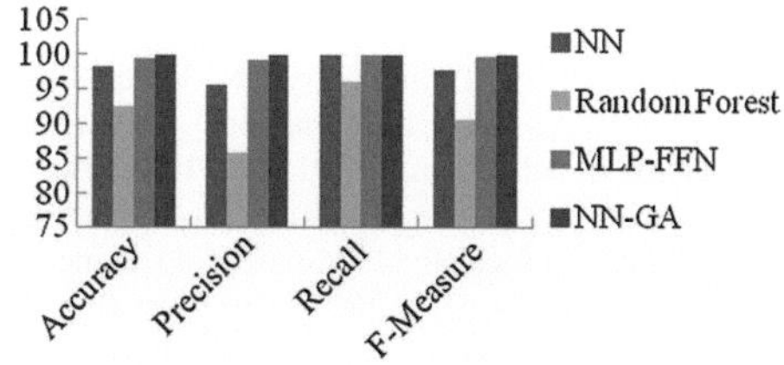

Fig. 2 Comparative analysis of different classifiers with NN-GA in terms of accuracy, precision, recall, and *F*-Measure

5 Conclusion

In this article, a genetic algorithm trained neural network has been proposed to efficiently detect chronic kidney disease (CKD) at an earlier stage. The local search-based learning algorithms may be trapped in local optima, the problem has been overcome using GA to train the neural network which actually tries to minimize the root-mean-squared error involved during the training phase. The performance of NN-GA-based model has been compared with NN, MLP-FFN, and Random Forest classifiers in terms of accuracy, precision, recall, and *F*-Measure. The results have suggested that NN-GA has outperformed other existing classifiers and is able to detect CKD with more efficiency. The future research may be focused on studying other such optimization techniques to train NNs to effectively improve the performance of NNs in real-life applications.

References

1. World Health Organization: Preventing Chronic Disease: A Vital Investment. WHO, Geneva (2005)
2. Keane, W.F., Zhang, Z., Lyle, P.A., et al.: Risk scores for predicting outcomes in patients with type 2 diabetes and nephropathy: the RENAAL study. Clin. J. Am. Soc. Nephrol. **1**(4), 761–767 (2006)
3. Agarwal, S.K., Dash, S.C., Irshad, M., et al.: Prevalence of chronic renal failure in adults in Delhi, India. Nephrol. Dial. Transplant. **20**, 1638–1642 (2005)
4. Modi, G.K., Jha, V.: The incidence of end-stage renal disease in India: a population-based study. Kidney Int. **70**, 2131–2133 (2006)
5. Sakhuja, V., Jha, V., Ghosh, A.K., Ahmed, S., Saha, T.K.: Chronic renal failure in India. Nephrol. Dial. Transplant. **9**, 871–872 (1994)
6. Mittal, S., Kher, V., Gulati, S., Agarwal, L.K., Arora, P.: Chronic renal failure in India. Ren. Fail. **19**, 753–770 (1997)
7. Mani, M.K.: Chronic renal failure in India. Nephrol. Dial. Transplant. **8**, 684–689 (1993)
8. Dash, S.C., Agarwal, S.K.: Incidence of chronic kidney disease in India. Nephrol. Dial. Transplant. **21**, 232–233 (2006)
9. Jain, A.K., Mao, J., Mohiuddin, K.M.: Artificial neural networks: a tutorial. Computer 31–44 (1996)
10. Chatterjee, S., Chakraborty, R., Hore, S.: A quality prediction method of weight lifting activity. In: An IET International Conference on Proceedings of the Michael Faraday IET International Summit—2015 (MFIIS-2015). 12–13 Sept 2015 in Kolkata, India (in press)
11. Virmani, J., Kumar, V., Kalra, N., Khandelwal, N.: Neural network ensemble based CAD system for focal liver lesions using B-mode ultrasound. J. Digit. Imaging **27**(4), 520–537 (2014). doi:10.1007/s10278-014-9685-0
12. Virmani, J., Kumar, V., Kalra, N., Khandelwal, N.: A comparative study of computer-aided classification systems for focal hepatic lesions from B-mode ultrasound. J. Med. Eng. Technol. **37**(4), 292–306 (2013)
13. Virmani, J., Kumar, V., Kalra, N., Khandelwal, N.: Prediction of cirrhosis based on singular value decomposition of gray level co-occurence matrix and a neural network classifier. In: Proceedings of the IEEE International Conference on Development in E-Systems Engineering, DeSe-2011, Dubai, pp. 146–151 (2011) (Published on IEEE Xplore)

14. Chiu, R.K., Chen, R.Y., Wang, S.-A., Chang, Y.-C., Chen, L.C.: Intelligent systems developed for the early detection of chronic kidney disease. In: Advances in Artificial Neural Systems, p. 1 (2013)
15. Hornik, K.: Multilayer feedforward networks are universal approximators. Neural Netw. **2**, 359–366 (1989)
16. Møller, Martin Fodslette: A scaled conjugate gradient algorithm for fast supervised learning. Neural Netw. **6**(4), 525–533 (1993)
17. Kulkarni, V.Y., Sinha, P.K.: Random forest classifiers: a survey and future research directions. Int. J. Adv. Comput. **36**(1), 1144–1153 (2013)
18. Lichman, M.: UCI machine learning repository (http://archive.ics.uci.edu/ml). University of California, School of Information and Computer Science, Irvine, CA (2013)
19. Stehman, S.V.: Selecting and interpreting measures of thematic classification accuracy. Remote Sens. Environ. **62**(1), 77–89 (1997)

An Optimal Tree-Based Routing Protocol Using Particle Swarm Optimization

Radhika Sohan, Nitin Mittal, Urvinder Singh and Balwinder Singh Sohi

Abstract Wireless sensor networks (WSNs) contain many sensor nodes which are deployed in the various geographical areas to perform various tasks like monitoring, data aggregation and data processing. For performing all these operations, energy is highly consumed, thus sensor nodes begin to die soon and also creates energy holes in some of the geographical locations. All the sensor nodes are powered by battery, and it is quite difficult to replace the battery, and so energy consumption is prime objective to increase the network lifetime. Clustering and tree-based routing like LEACH, PEDAP, TBC and TREEPSI solves most of the energy consumption problem as it saves energy during a lot of operations in WSNs. In this paper, we propose an optimal tree-based routing protocol (OTBRP) that is efficient in terms of stability period (time period before first node dead) and therefore offers good network lifetime. The parameters like first node dead, half node dead and last node dead are considered for the measurement of network lifetime. In order to evaluate the performance of OTBRP, the comparison is made with the GSTEB and PEGASIS. Simulation results show that there is a gain of approx. 200 and 150% in stability period in comparison with PEGASIS and GSTEB, respectively.

Keywords Tree branching · GSTEB · OTBRP · Network lifetime · Residual energy · WSNs

R. Sohan · N. Mittal (✉) · B.S. Sohi
Department of Electronics and Communication Engineering,
Chandigarh University, Mohali, Punjab, India
e-mail: mittal.nitin84@gmail.com

R. Sohan
e-mail: radhikasohan@gmail.com

U. Singh
Department of Electronics and Communication Engineering,
Thapar University, Patiala, Punjab, India
e-mail: urvinder@thapar.edu

B.K. Panigrahi et al. (eds.), *Nature Inspired Computing*, Advances in Intelligent Systems and Computing 652, https://doi.org/10.1007/978-981-10-6747-1_14

1 Introduction

Wireless sensor networks (WSNs) have influenced many researchers because of its enormous uses in various fields like environmental monitoring, disaster relief systems health applications, surveillance, habitat monitoring, industrial applications and many more [1, 2]. A WSN contains relatively huge number of small sensor nodes that are randomly or manually deployed in the sensor field. Sensor node consists of sensing unit, processor, communicating devices having power unit. The sensor nodes are efficient in sensing the target area, after that processes the data and transfers that data to the sink which is located far away. The main limitation of WSNs is limited power supply. Moreover, in many applications, it is a challenging task to replace batteries so energy consumption is foremost needed in these networks [3–5].

2 Background and Motivation

WSNs mainly send the sensed information to base station (BS) that aggregates part or all of the information. A bottleneck challenge is to create energy efficient communication with low cost on-node processing and self-organizing connectivity. Low power consumption is the main factor for ensuring long operations for energy constrained systems [6]. Hierarchical routing protocols are also termed as cluster-based routing, asserted in WSNs. These routing techniques are having special advantages in terms of scalability and efficient communication. Clustering solves the problem of energy consumption up to some extent [7, 8]. In clustering, the sensor nodes form a group called clusters and the cluster member with the highest energy is chosen as cluster head (CH), only CHs are allowed to communicate with BS [9]. In the chain-based approach like in PEGASIS, all the nodes are arranged in the chain-type fashion, one node associates with other node next to it and data fusion is done [10]. In the recent past, the routing was emphasized with clustering, but nowadays tree-based routing is more popular because of its inherent property of efficient routing by using different tree branching techniques. Tree-based clustering (TBC) is also considered to be an improvement to LEACH protocol [11]. It forms several clusters likewise in LEACH, and every cluster has cluster members as well as CH. PEDAP [12] makes use of minimum spanning tree, and it is a tree-based routing protocol. Minimum spanning tree leads to loop-free topology which costs minimum for the transmitting of data. A tree-based power saving routing protocol [13] considers the maximum capacity of a node to have s number of children and the maximum tree depth as parameters to control the tree construction. In tree-based efficient protocol for sensor information (TREEPSI) protocol, a root node is chosen before data transmission [14]. General self-organizing tree branching energy balancing protocol (GSTEB) [15] aims to achieve prolong network lifetime for distinct applications in WSN environment.

3 OTBRP Routing Protocol

WSN consists of spatially distributed autonomous sensor nodes, and these nodes are have limited battery life and storage capacity [16]. Many protocols are introduced to work efficiently against the high energy consumption of nodes which in return increases the network lifetime. In this work, an optimal tree-based routing protocol (OTBRP) for WSN is proposed in order to increase the stability period of network.

3.1 Communication Model

The radio model used in OTBRP is shown in Fig. 1. Both the multi-path fading (d^4 power loss) and the free space (d^2 power loss) models are used on the basis of distance between transmitter and receiver. If the distance is more than the threshold distance then multi-path (mp) model is used, otherwise, free space (fs) model is used.

For transmitting k number of bits, the energy consumed will be:

$$E_{\mathrm{TX}}(k,d) = E_{\mathrm{elec}} \cdot k + E_{\mathrm{amp}}(k \cdot d), \tag{1}$$

where E_{elec} is energy consumed in electronic circuit to transmit the bit.

If $d < do$, then

$$E_{\mathrm{TX}}(k,d) = k \cdot E_{\mathrm{elec}} + k \cdot \varepsilon_{\mathrm{fs}} \cdot d^2. \tag{2}$$

And if $d > do$, then

$$E_{\mathrm{TX}}(k,d) = k \cdot E_{\mathrm{elec}} + k \cdot \varepsilon_{\mathrm{amp}} \cdot d^4. \tag{3}$$

Here threshold

$$do = (\varepsilon_{\mathrm{fs}}/\varepsilon_{\mathrm{amp}})^{1/2}, \tag{4}$$

where $\varepsilon_{\mathrm{fs}}$ is the amplifier energy consumption to transmit at a smaller distance and $\varepsilon_{\mathrm{amp}}$ is the amplifier energy consumption to transmit at a larger distance.

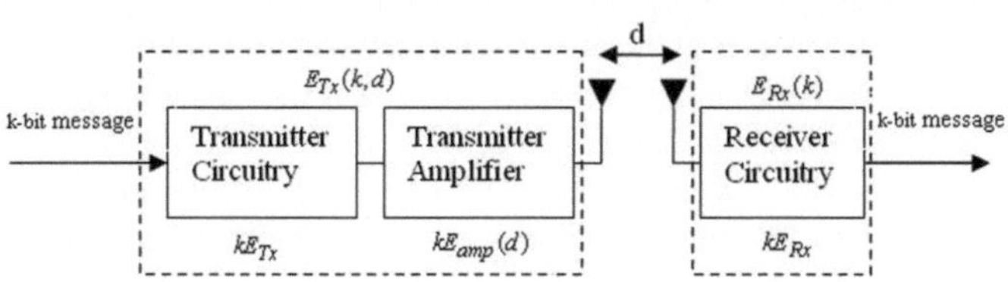

Fig. 1 Energy dissipation radio model

To receive k number of bits, the radio spends energy

$$E_{\mathrm{TX}}(k,d) = E_{\mathrm{elec}} \cdot k. \tag{5}$$

3.2 Proposed Fitness Function

Let us assume network consists of N sensor nodes which are divided into K number of branches, the number of candidate parent node (PN) is denoted by M generally greater than K, and there can be C_M^K ways of clustering.

Fitness function for parent node selection is defined as:

$$f = \alpha f_1 + \beta f_2 + \gamma f_3. \tag{8}$$

Here $\alpha, \beta, \gamma \,€\, [0,1], \alpha + \beta + \gamma = 1$.

In the fitness function, f_1 is the reciprocal of the total sum of the energy of the present round PN and sum of energy of all the sensor nodes in the network, f_2 is the maximum of the Euclidean distance average, how much distance is found from every cluster sensor nodes to this PN and f_3 is the distance ratio of the average distance from the PN to the BS and the Euclidean distance from the BS to the centre of the network.

$$f_1(p_j) = \frac{\sum_{i=1}^{N} E(nj)}{\sum_{i=1}^{N} E(PNP_{j,k})} \tag{9}$$

$$f_2(p_j) = \max_{\forall k = 1,2,3\ldots N} \frac{\sum_{\forall ni \in Cpj,k}^{N} d(ni, PNP_{j,k})}{BP_{j,k}} \tag{10}$$

$$f_3(p_j) = \frac{\sum_{i=1}^{N} d(\mathrm{BS}, \mathrm{PNP}_{j.k})}{K * d(\mathrm{BS}, \mathrm{NC})}. \tag{11}$$

3.3 OTBRP Protocol Phases and Operation

OTBRP is a tree-based routing protocol. The aim of OTBRP is to attain a prolong network lifetime for various applications. In every round, BS assigns itself as root node and broadcasts its ID and coordinates to all sensors. The operation of OTBRP is divided into four phases as follows (Fig. 2):

Initial Phase: In the initial phase, the network parameters are initialized. BS broadcasts a packet to all the sensor nodes to inform them of beginning time, time slot length and the number of nodes.

Fig. 2 OTBRP operation

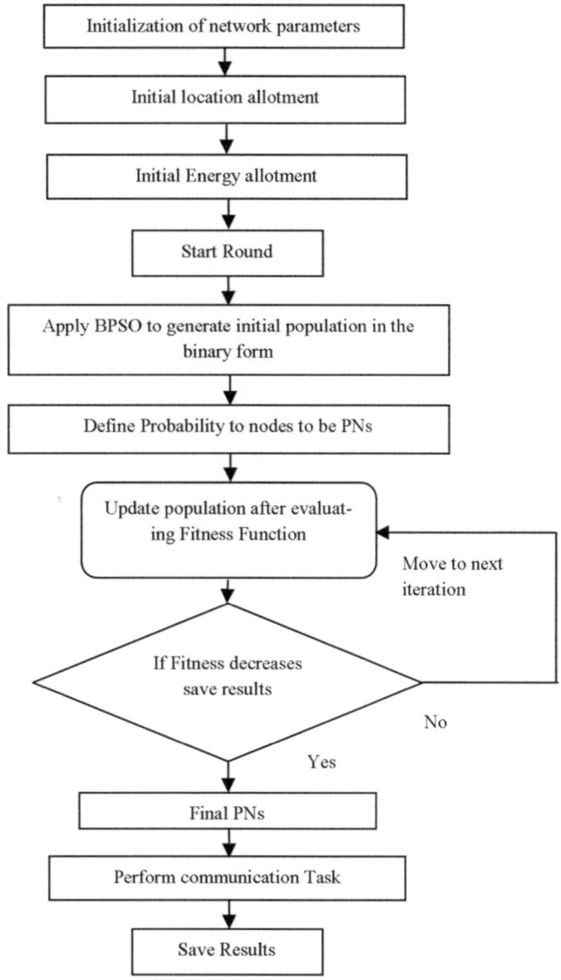

Tree Constructing Phase: In the tree constructing phase, sensor nodes are selected as parent nodes with some predefined parameters termed as fitness function (described in Sect. 3.2) using BPSO. It starts with the initial population in the binary form on the basis of probability of nodes to become parent nodes. The number of parent nodes varies in each round.

Data Transmitting Phase: Every node selects its parent by considering energy as well as distance optimal values. There may be many leaf nodes sharing one parent node in the same time slot. If all the leaf nodes try to send the data to the parent node at the same time, the data messages may interfere and cause routing overhead and thus decrease throughput. By applying code division multiple access (CDMA) or frequency division multiple access (FDMA), these access techniques are efficiently meant to avoid collisions.

Information Exchange Phase: In the initial phase, BS can collect the energy and coordinate information of all the sensor nodes. For each round, BS builds the routing tree and network schedule by using coordinates and energy information. The BS exchange information by sending DATA-PKT to sensor nodes and in return receives CTRL-PKT from them.

4 Simulation Results

The performance of OTBRP protocol is explored in terms of network lifetime and stability period (the time internal or the rounds before the first node dead) against the GSTEB and PEGASIS protocols. The performance evaluation of OTBRP is done on 10 different WSN networks. To make a fair comparison between the protocols, characteristics of the network are used for the proposed protocol are made identical and are described in Table 1.

Figure 3a, b show the average results of 10 simulations of PEGASIS, GSTEB and OTBRP both for setup 1 and setup 2, respectively. These figures clearly show OTBRP is better than the two protocols for first node dead (FND) and half node dead (HND). Due to large instability period, last node dead (LND) is better for GSTEB. Network lifetime is increased by using OTBRP protocol, and thus, less amount of energy is consumed per round. Tables 2 and 3 present the number of rounds taken for FND, HND and LND together with stability and instability periods

Table 1 Network parameters used in MATLAB simulation for OTBRP

Parameter	Setup 1	Setup 2
Number of nodes, N	100	150
Network size	100 m × 100 m	
Location of BS	(50, 175)	
Initial energy of normal node, E_0	0.25 J	
Number of CH nodes, K	5% of nodes	
Radio electronics energy, $E_{Tx} = E_{Rx}$	50 nJ/bit	
Energy for data aggregation, E_{DA}	5 nJ/bit	
Radio amplifier energy, ε_{friss_amp}	100 pJ/bit/m^2	
Radio amplifier energy, $\varepsilon_{two\_ray\_amp}$	0.0013 pJ/bit/m^4	

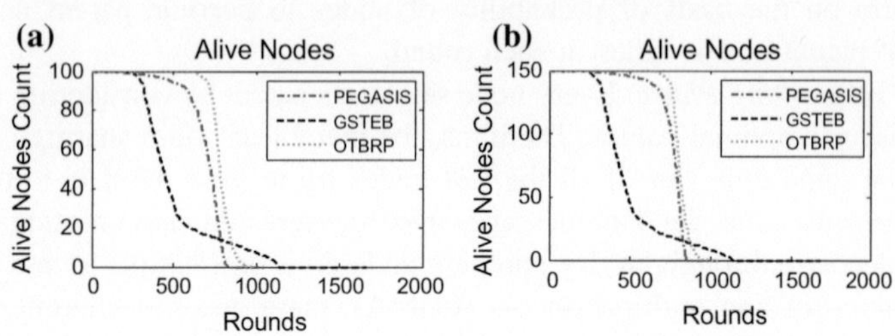

Fig. 3 Number of alive nodes per round using OTBRP for **a** setup 1 and **b** setup 2

Table 2 Comparison of network lifetime of protocols together with stability and instability periods (setup 1)

Protocol	FND	HND	LND	Stability period	Instability period
PEGASIS	215.2	718.2	804.3	215.2	589.1
GSTEB	**277**	436.1	**1131.1**	277	854.1
OTBRP	**641.9**	**771.9**	931	**641.9**	**289.1**

Table 3 Comparison of network lifetime of protocols together with stability and instability periods (setup 2)

Protocol	FND	HND	LND	Stability period	Instability period
PEGASIS	192.7	700.8	758	192.7	565.3
GSTEB	265.8	428.2	**1133.7**	265.8	867.9
OTBRP	**661.8**	**799**	953	**661.8**	**291.2**

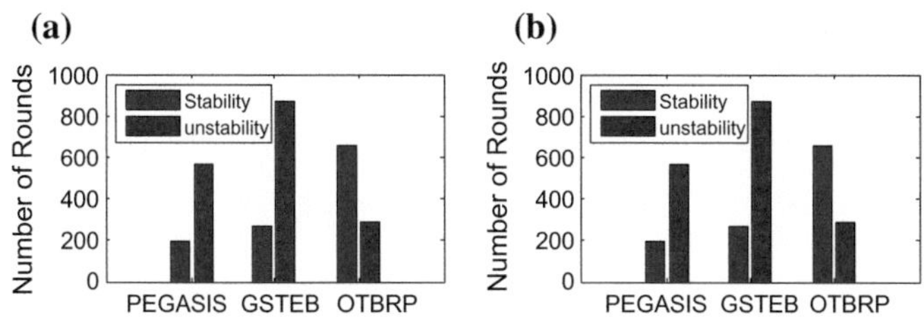

Fig. 4 Performance results for GSTEB, OTBRP and PEGASIS for **a** setup 1 and **b** setup 2

of PEGASIS, GSTEB and OTBRP protocols for setup1 and setup 2, respectively. The use of PN selection using residual energy helps to get longer stability and smaller instability periods as shown in Fig. 4.

5 Conclusion and Future Work

In WSNs, the major design issues in the research of routing protocols are energy consumption and network lifetime. In tree-based routing protocols, parent node selection is an NP-hard problem. Therefore, nature-inspired optimization algorithms may be applied to tackle parent node selection in WSN. In this work, we have proposed OTBRP, in that parent nodes are selected using BPSO on the basis of residual energy of nodes, distance between parent node and root node, and the distance between parent node and child node. Simulation results show that the application of BPSO optimization technique in the GSTEB improves the energy efficiency and prolongs the stability period of the network. Future work can be done to decrease the routing overhead and transmission delay. Though load balancing is not a major problem in OTBRP but still one can work on it.

References

1. Akyildiz, I.F., Su, W., Sankarasubramaniam, Y., Cayirci, E.: Wireless sensor networks: a survey. Comput. Netw. **38**(4), 393–422 (2002)
2. Yick, J., Mukherjee, B., Ghosal, D.: Wireless sensor network survey. Comput. Netw. **52**, 2292–2330 (2008)
3. Giuseppe, A., Conti, M., Francesco, M.D., Passarella, A.: Energy conservation in wireless sensor networks: a survey. Ad Hoc Netw. **7**, 537–568 (2009)
4. Chong, C.Y., Kumar, S.P.: Sensor networks: evolution, opportunities, and challenges. Proc. IEEE **91**(8), 1247–1256 (2003)
5. Edoardo, R., Emanuele, L., Andrea, A.: Energetic sustainability of routing algorithms for energy-harvesting wireless sensor networks. Comput. Commun. **30**, 2976–2986 (2007)
6. Pantazis, N.A., Nikolidakis, S.A., Vergados, D.D.: Energy-efficient routing protocols in wireless sensor networks: a survey. IEEE Commun. Surv. Tutorials **15**(2), 551–591 (2013)
7. Heinzelman, W.B., Chandrakasan, A.P., Balakrishnan, H.: An application-specific protocol architecture for wireless microsensor networks. IEEE Trans. Wireless Commun. **1**(4), 660–670 (2002)
8. Mittal, N., Singh, U.: Distance-based residual energy-efficient stable election protocol for WSNs. Arab. J. Sci. Eng. **40**, 1637–1646 (2015)
9. Abdullah, M., Ehsan, A.: Routing protocols for wireless sensor networks: classifications and challenges. J. Electr. Commun. Eng. Res. **2**(2), 05–15 (2014)
10. Lindsey, S., Raghavendra, C.: Pegasis: power-efficient gathering in sensor information systems. In: Proceedings of IEEE Aerospace Conference, vol. 3, pp. 1125–1130 (2002)
11. Kim, K.T., Youn, H.Y.: Tree-based clustering (TBC) for energy efficient wireless sensor networks. Proc. AINA **2010**, 680–685 (2010)
12. Tan, H.O., Korpeoglu, I.: Power efficient data gathering and aggregation protocol in wireless sensor networks. SIGMOD Rec. **32**(4), 66–71 (2003)
13. AL-Momani, I., Saadeh, M., AL-Akhras, M., Jawawdeh, H.A: A tree-based power saving routing protocol for wireless sensor networks. Int. J. Comput. Commun. **2**(5) (2011)
14. Satapathy, S.S., Sarma, N.: TREEPSI: tree based energy efficient protocol for sensor information. In: Wireless and Optical Communications Networks 2006 IFIP International Conference (2006)
15. Han, Z., Wu, J., Zhang, J., Liu, L., Tian, K.: A general self-organized tree based energy balance routing protocol for wireless sensor network. IEEE Trans. Nucl. Sci. **61**(2) (2014)
16. Kim, T., Yang, J.: Neighbor table based shortcut tree routing in ZigBee wireless networks. Proc. IEEE Trans. Parallel Distrib. Syst. **25**(3), 706–716 (2014)

Sybil Attack Prevention Algorithm for Body Area Networks

Rohit Kumar Ahlawat, Amita Malik and Archana Sadhu

Abstract Advancement in wireless network technologies, such as wearable and implantable biosensors, along with present developments in the embedded computing area is enabling the design, progress and implementation of body area networks. Security in BANs is a big issue. In this paper, a new security algorithm for body area networks named Sybil attack prevention algorithm for body area networks (SAPA-BAN) is proposed. This algorithm protects the BANs from Sybil attack. It provides the confidentiality and integrity to the data or critical information about the patient's health sent by a BAN to the coordinating centre/emergency services. This algorithm is energy efficient and reliable also because it operates on less energy. SAPA-BAN performs better in terms of throughput, packet delivery ratio, end-to-end delay, hops count and overhead. A comparative analysis of SAPA-BAN with respect to LSA is performed on the basis of above said parameters.

Keywords Body area networks · Sybil attack · Cluster head · Security · Non-key

1 Introduction

The increasing use of wireless technologies and the advances in electronics have empowered the development of body area networks (BAN) [1]. A BAN consists of number of sensor nodes that are placed on/around human body or implanted in human body to measure physiological parameters like blood pressure, heart rate,

R.K. Ahlawat (✉) · A. Malik
Deenbandhu Chhotu Ram University of Science and Technology Murthal, Sonepat, Haryana, India
e-mail: ahlawatrohit8@gmail.com

A. Malik
e-mail: amitamalik.cse@dcrustm.org

A. Sadhu
PM College of Engineering and Technology, Sonepat, India
e-mail: asandhu43@gmail.com

B.K. Panigrahi et al. (eds.), *Nature Inspired Computing*, Advances in Intelligent Systems and Computing 652, https://doi.org/10.1007/978-981-10-6747-1_15

electroencephalogram (EEG), electrocardiogram (ECG), respiration rate about patient's health [2].

In BAN, a central node is decided which acts as link between other sensor nodes and monitoring place like hospital. Sensor nodes regularly send status report about physiological parameters of patient's health to the remote node or PDA, and that remote or PDA forwards that information to the remote base station that can be a hospital, emergency service, doctor, etc. BANs can also connect to other wireless links like Wi-fi and cellular networks. Sensor nodes of BAN act as a drug delivery system. In BAN, the actuator node is used which can communicate with other nodes or BANs via wireless connections that is also known as drug delivery system. When a sudden drop of glucose is detected, then the actuator starts the injection of predetermined dose of insulin [3].

BAN is a communication standard for device using low power; i.e. it uses low-power sensors. BAN differs from wireless sensor network (WSN) in various features like security, energy efficiency. In BAN, information about the patient's health can be transferred by three types of communication: (i) intra-body communication, (ii) extra-body communication, (iii) inter-body communication. The intra-body communication is used between sensors and actuators; i.e. when different sensor nodes communicate with each other within a BAN, then it is called intra-BAN communication. The extra-body communication is used between BAN and other networks; i.e. when a BAN communicates with other networks to transfer the information, then it is called extra-BAN communication, and the inter-body communication is used between different BANs; i.e. when a BAN communicates with other BAN, then it is called inter-BAN communication [4].

Security is a big issue for BANs. Some security threats in BANs [5, 6] are given below:

- Eavesdropping/interception
- Interruption/communication jamming
- Modification of data
- Repudiation
- Unauthorized access
- Spoofed, altered or replayed routing information
- Black hole attack
- Selective forwarding attack
- Sinkhole attack
- Wormhole attack
- Acknowledgement spoofing
- Node replication
- Sybil attack
- Rushing attack
- Jellyfish attack
- Flooding

2 Related Work

Considerable work has been done on security in BANs. Different researchers have proposed different techniques and solutions for this problem. The security techniques used for BANs can be of four types [4]. These are as follows:

A. Symmetric key-based security protocols for BAN
B. Asymmetric key-based security protocols for BAN
C. Hybrid key-based security protocols for BAN
D. Non-key-based security protocols for BAN

In first technique, protocols use same key for encryption and decryption. BARI [7], TuLP [8], PSKA [9], etc., are the security protocols for BANs, which use symmetric key cryptography technique. In second technique, protocols use different keys for encryption and decryption. Encryption is done using public key, and decryption is done using private key. ECSA [10] and AAL [11] use asymmetric key-based cryptography for security. The protocols of third technique are based on hybrid key cryptography technique. This cryptography is either a combination of symmetric and asymmetric or uses the concept of two keys like preloaded key and master key. PMAC [12] is an example of hybrid key cryptography. And in last technique, protocols do not use key for security; i.e. encryption and decryption are not used in the protocols of this technique. IDS [13] and SVM [14] are examples of non-key-based security technique.

3 SAPA-BAN

As we have discussed in Sect. 2, there are four categories by which we can provide security to the BANs. In first three techniques, we use key for encryption and decryption of data, but in fourth category, we do not use any type of key for security. In this scheme, we use some non-key-based technique to secure the BANs from security threats. The proposed scheme in this paper is a non-key-based scheme named as SAPA-BAN. It stands for Sybil attack prevention algorithm for body area networks. This scheme protects the BANs from Sybil attack. Before discussing the algorithm in detail, we will discuss Sybil attack.

There are many security threats as discussed in Sect. 1 that can be harmful for any BAN. Sybil attack is also one of them. In Sybil attack, the attacker disturbs the network by creating many false identities and forges the path. When sender sends the data to the destination, then the sender cannot differentiate the destination and the Sybil attacker immediately. When transmission starts, attacker forges the path, and as a result, the sender starts sending data to the Sybil attacker instead of original destination. By this, data does not go to the specific destination [15]. In case of BAN, as we have discussed in Sect. 1, sensor nodes send critical and non-critical information about the patient's health to the base station or we can say to the emergency services such as hospital, doctor. It is very important that data should reach at the destination in a secure way because if anybody hacks and modifies the data about the patient's health, then it can be dangerous for the life of patient. So to avoid this situation, we proposed SAPA-BAN. Now, let us discuss SAPA-BAN, and it is working in detail.

3.1 Components of SAPA-BAN

Components are the main parts that are used in any system. The SAPA-BAN has three main components, which are BANs, cluster heads and base station or coordinating centre. Sybil node is an attacker that is also a component of SAPA-BAN. BANs are mobile so they change their regions time to time. There is a cluster head in each region, which aggregates the data coming from different BANs of its region, and then this cluster head forwards this data to the coordinating centre or base station, which can be any hospital or emergency services. The components of SAPA-BAN are shown in Fig. 1.

3.2 Algorithm for SAPA-BAN

The algorithm for SAPA-BAN is working in three different stages. Each has its own process. These three stages are as follows: initialization stage, Sybil attack detection stage and protection from Sybil attack stage.

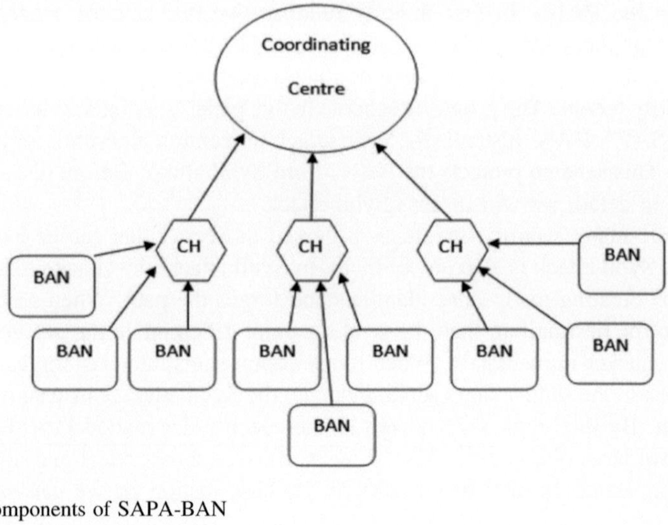

Fig. 1 Components of SAPA-BAN

(1) Stage 1 (Initialization stage)
(2) Stage 2 (Sybil attack detection stage)
(3) Stage 3 (Sybil attack prevention stage)

Now, we will understand each stage one by one in detail.

(1) Stage 1 (initialization stage)

The first stage of SAPA-BAN algorithm is initialization stage. In this stage, we initialize our network. Let n be the number of BANs, x_i is the ID of BAN.

$$i = 1, 2, 3, \ldots, n, n = \text{no. of BANs}$$
$$x_i = \text{ID of BAN}$$
$$m = \text{malicious node}$$
$$x_m = \text{ID of malicious node (minimum)}$$
$$x_m < x_i$$

BANs are mobile so they start to move from one region to another. BANs communicate with the cluster head of that region. During path selection procedure, each BAN broadcasts its neighbour list and chooses the shortest path using distance vector.

(2) Stage 2 (Sybil attack detection stage)

The second stage of SAPA-BAN is Sybil attack detection stage. In this stage Sybil node attacks on the BANs. There is a malicious node say x_m in the network. This malicious node generates the Sybil node x_s in such a way that the ID of Sybil node is less than ID of BAN.

$$x_s < x_i$$

In this scheme, we assume that the no. of BANs communicate with Sybil node is less than or equal to no. of total BANs; i.e.

$$n' \leq n$$
$$n' = \text{no.of BANs communicate with Sybil node}$$
$$n = \text{no. of total BANs}$$

During path selection process, each BAN broadcasts its neighbour list. As identity of the Sybil node is the smallest in the network, it can bypass the lowest ID clustering scheme by becoming the mediator time and again. To detect the Sybil attack, the base station first checks the identity of the malicious node. If the base station detects the forged path, it re-initiates the path election process.

(3) Stage 3 (protection from Sybil attack)

The next and final stage of SAPA-BAN is protection from Sybil attack. In this stage, we protect the BANs from Sybil attack detected in Stage 2. When base station detects any forged path, then it re-initiates the path selection process. During path re-selection process each BAN broadcasts its neighbour list excluding that malicious that generates Sybil node. The BANs select the shortest path using distance vector and delete the malicious node form its neighbour list. After getting this new neighbour list excluding malicious node, the BANs send data to the nearest cluster head.

4 Performance Evaluation

Here, performance evaluation of SAPA-BAN is divided into three parts.

A. Simulation scenario
B. Simulation parameters
C. Result analysis

4.1 Simulation Scenario

We used network simulator NS-2 for the implementation of SAPA-BAN. In NS-2, we use Tcl script to create simulation scenario. It is just like C# [16–18]. In scenario of BAN, we used cluster heads, BANs, Sybil node. SAPA-BAN is compared with an existing lightweight security algorithm for BANs (Table 1).

4.2 Simulation Parameters

In this section, we will discuss various simulation parameters on the basis of which we analyze the performance of SAPA-BAN. These simulation parameters are as follows:

- **Throughput**:
  Throughput is a measure of how many units of information a network can process in a given amount of time.
- **Packet delivery ratio**:

Table 1 Parameters of simulation scenario

Simulation parameter	Range of values
No. of BAN	11
No. of CH	6
No. of Sybil node	1
Simulation time (s)	200
Channel type	Wireless
Area	1000 * 800
MAC type	MAC/802_11

It is the ratio of the number of delivered data packet to the destination. This illustrates the level of delivered data to the destination.

$$= \sum \text{Number of packet receive} / \sum \text{Number of packet send}$$

- **End-to-end delay**:
  The average time taken by a data packet to arrive at the destination is called end-to-end delay. It also includes the delay caused by route discovery process and the queue in data packet transmission.

$$= \sum (\text{arrive time} - \text{send time}) / \sum \text{Number of connections}$$

- **Overhead**:
  Overhead is the number of packets that are required for data transmission.
- **Hops count**:
  Hops count is the number of intermediates that are used by a sender to send the data to destination.

4.3 Result Analysis

We analyze the performance of SAPA-BAN w.r.t. lightweight security algorithm (LSA) on parameters like throughput, packet delivery ratio and end-to-end delay is shown in Figs. 2, 3, 4, 5 and 6.

Figure 2 shows the comparison between throughput of SAPA-BAN and LSA. Throughput of SAPA-BAN is high; i.e. it transfers more data in a given time than LSA because LSA is a complex algorithm so it does not give high throughput.

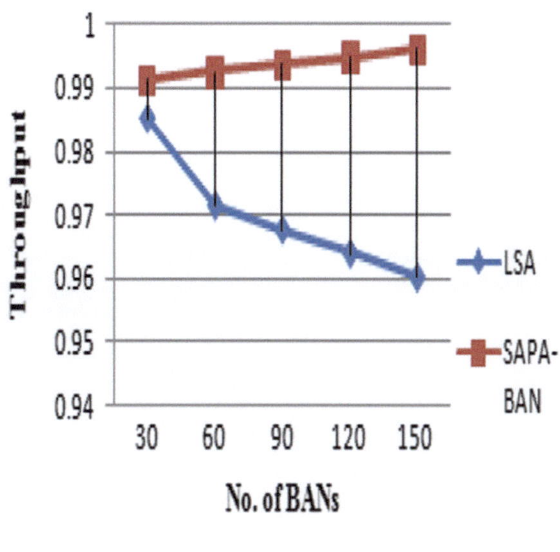

Fig. 2 Comparison of throughput

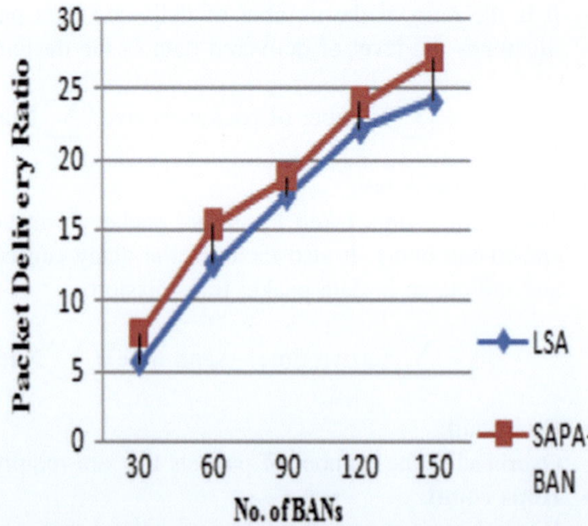

Fig. 3 Comparion of packet delivery ratio

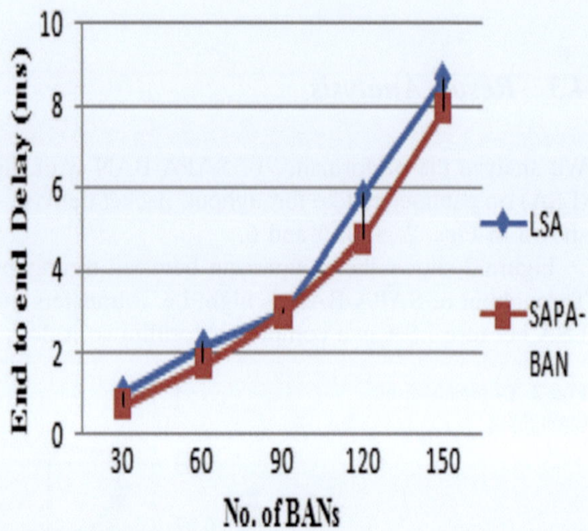

Fig. 4 Comparison of end-to-end delay

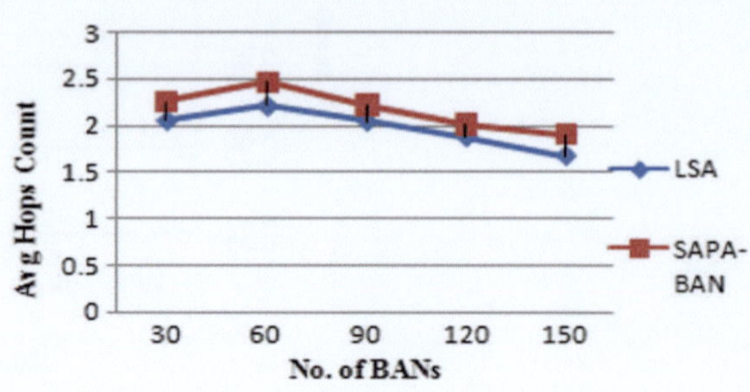

Fig. 5 Comparison of average hops count

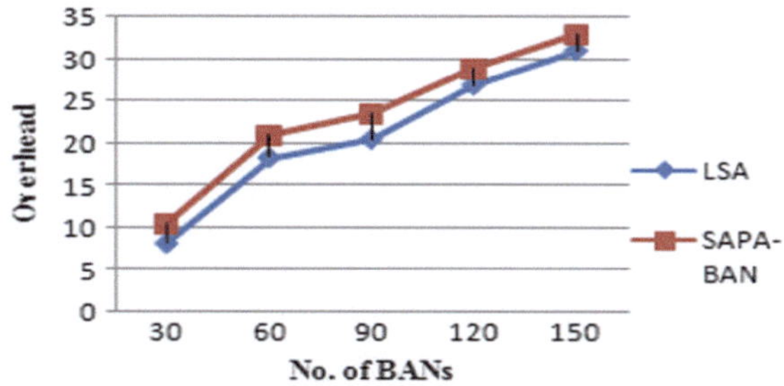

Fig. 6 Comparison of overhead

Figure 3 shows the comparison between packet delivery ratio of SAPA-BAN and LSA. The packet delivery ratio of SAPA-BAN is high; i.e. it sends more packet to the destination as compared to LSA.

Figure 4 shows the comparison between end-to-end delay of SAPA-BAN and LSA. It is less in case of SAPA-BAN, because path re-selection is used and that does not take more time. But in LSA, the end-to-end delay is higher than SAPA-BAN.

Figure 5 shows the comparison of hop counts between SAPA-BAN and LSA. In SAPA-BAN, hop count is little more as compared to the LSA. When Sybil attack is detected, then data is sent via other path so hops count increases in this scheme.

Figure 6 shows the comparison between overhead of SAPA-BAN and LSA. The overhead of SAPA-BAN is slightly higher than overhead of LSA, because data is sent to cluster head in a secure way. When Sybil attack is detected on BAN, then to prevent it data is sent via other nearest sensor node or BAN. Then data is sent to destination via that other node or BAN. So overhead is increasing in this scheme.

5 Conclusion and Future Scope

In this paper, a Sybil attack prevention algorithm for body area networks for security of BANs from Sybil attack is proposed. It is a non-key-based algorithm, which means key is not used in this scheme so encryption and decryption are not used here. SAPA-BAN provides confidentiality and integrity to the data sent by BAN. Various parameters like throughput, packet delivery ratio, end-to-end delay, hops count and overhead are used for analyzing the simulated result of SAPA-BAN as compared to LSA using NS-2 simulator. End-to-end delay is reduced in SAPA-BAN. Other discussed parameters are also computed, which give better results for SAPA-BAN. It is energy efficient also because there is no extra load and energy required for any component of SAPA-BAN. Body area network has three-tiered architecture, and for each tier, a strong security technique is required. For future work we can enhance and use it on other tiers to make it protect from Sybil attack. The proposed work can be implemented in more realistic environment, and its performance can be checked. SAPA-BAN is energy efficient and can also be applied on other tiers of BAN.

References

1. Aziz, O., Lo, B., Darzi, A., Yang, G.-Z.: Body Sensor Network. EBook (2006)
2. Ullah, S., Higgins, H., Islam, S.M.R., Khan, P., Kwak, K.S.: On phy and mac performance in body sensor networks. EURASIP J. Wirel. Commun. Netw. **47**, 777–780 (2009)
3. Park, S., Jayaraman, S.: Enhancing the quality of life through wearable technology. IEEE Eng. Med. Biol. Mag. **22**(3), 41–48 (2003)
4. Ajit, Malik, A.: Security in body area network: a survey. Int. J. Enhanced Res. Manag. Comput. Appl. **3**(5). ISSN: 2319-7471 (2014)
5. Jang, C.-S., Lee, D.-G., Han, J.-W.: A proposal of security framework for wireless body area network. In: International Conference on Security Technology (2008)
6. Segovia, M., Grampín, E., Baliosian, J.: Analysis of the Applicability of Wireless Sensor Networks Attacks to Body Area Networks. Bodynets (2013)
7. Raazi, S.M.K.R., Lee, H.: Bari: a distributed key management approach for wireless body area networks. In: International Conference On Computational Intelligence and Security. IEEE (2009)
8. Gong, Z., Hartel, P., Nikova, S., et al.: TuLP: a family of lightweight message authentication codes for body sensor networks. J. Comput. Sci. Technol. **29**(1), 53 (2014). doi:10.1007/s11390-013-1411-8
9. Venkatasubramanian, K.K., Banerjee, A., Gupta, S.K.S.: PSKA: usable and secure key agreement scheme for body area networks. IEEE Trans. Inf. Technol. Biomed. **14**(1) (2010)
10. Sangari, S., Manickam, M.L.: Security and privacy in wireless body area network. Ind. Streams Res. J. **4**(8) (2014). ISSN 2230-7850
11. He, D., Zeadally, S.: Authentication protocol for an ambient assisted living system. IEEE Commun. Mag. (2015). 0163-6804/15/$25.00 © 2015 IEEE
12. Ullah, S., Imran, M., Alnuem, M.: A hybrid and secure priority-guaranteed MAC protocol for wireless body area network, Hindawi Publishing Corporation. Int. J. Distrib. Sens. Netw. 2014(481761), 7 p
13. Sundararajan, T.V.P., Shanmugam, A.: A novel intrusion detection system for wireless body area network in health care monitoring. J. Comput. Sci. **6**(11), 1355–1361 (2010). ISSN 1549-3636 © 2010 Science Publications
14. Agarwal, S., Divya, Pandey, G.N.: SVM Based Context Awareness Using Body Area Sensor Network for Pervasive Healthcare Monitoring, IITM'10, 28–30 Dec 2010, Allahabad, UP, India. Copyright 2010 ACM 978-1-4503-0408-5/10/12
15. https://en.wikipedia.org/wiki/Sybil_attack
16. Introductiontons2simulat or http://www.springer.com/engineering/signals/book/978-0-387-71759-3
17. The Network Simulator: ns-2. http://www.isi.edu/nsnam/ns
18. Introduction to Network Simulator NS2 by Teerawat Issariyakul, Ekram Hossain

Surface Acoustic Wave E-nose Sensor Based Pattern Generation and Recognition of Toxic Gases Using Artificial Neural Network Techniques

M. Sreelatha and G.M. Nasira

Abstract SAW E-nose sensor is one of the chemical sensor detectors to sense and detect the toxic vapors or gases. This paper proposes an approach to process the SAW sensor data and to predict the type of chemical warfare agents (CWA). Artificial neural network (ANN) approach is one of the pattern recognition technique for processing the signal produced by SAW E-nose. We have applied Principal component analysis (PCA) technique to normalize the data sets of SAW sensors. Here, we have designed a system to predict the toxic vapors like ammonia, acetone, ethylene, and ethanol. This pattern recognition system also classifies the humidity of the toxic vapors. Sensor arrays were used for predicting different types of toxic vapor as a result. The results were obtained through MATLAB tool with sensor data set converted from analog to digital data type.

Keywords Surface acoustic wave (SAW) · Chemical warfare agents (CWA) · Artificial neural network (ANN) · Principal component analysis (PCA)

1 Introduction

Pattern recognition for gas sensor data is a challenging task. The environment contains various toxic gases which result in devilish damage to the mankind and environment. Toxic gases generate diabolical detriment in war field when it scatters over in war. Discovering new innovative gas sensors in the field of defense to prevent toxic gases from the environment which is the most promising task in the present scenario. Designing a sensor with single gas identification will not serve the fully needy purpose of toxic vapor identification when the environment contains

M. Sreelatha (✉)
Bharathiar University, Coimbatore, India
e-mail: sreelatharaghuraman@yahoo.co.in

G.M. Nasira
Department of Computer Science, Chikkanna Government Arts College, Tiruppur, India
e-mail: nasiragm99@yahoo.com

B.K. Panigrahi et al. (eds.), *Nature Inspired Computing*, Advances in Intelligent Systems and Computing 652, https://doi.org/10.1007/978-981-10-6747-1_16

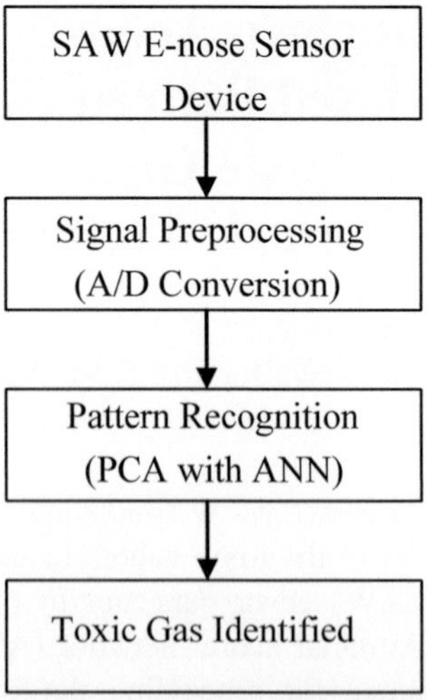

Fig. 1 Schematic representation of pattern recognition system

a mixture of toxic gases. Selective detection of gases using single gas sensor is a challenge due to the problem of cross sensitivity from various interferants. Here, we used SAW E-nose sensors to detect chemical warfare agents (CWA) [1]. The SAW sensor contains an array of four detectors called TeO_2, SnO_2, TiO_2, and ZnO have been developed for the detection of four compounds of CWA [2]. Each simulant vapor gives a specific characteristic pattern for E-nose. The generated patterns of E-nose showed great discrimination of the target vapors both in the absence and the presence of interferant vapors [3]. Principal component analysis (PCA) can be used to reduce data set extracted from E-nose. Artificial neural networks were utilized successfully for pattern recognition of stimulants of chemical warfare agents over the specified concentration range of 50, 100, 150, 200 ppm (piles per million). The output of the SAW sensor which is in a signal format was processed and converted, and the pattern was recognized using PCA and ANN to identify the toxic gas as shown in Fig. 1.

2 Sensor Technologies

In olden days, sensors were developed as mono sensors, which can identify a single chemical or vapor, but in the modern world, a large volume of sensors with multi-sensor arrays were discovered to detect more than one vapor from a mixture of gases. The multi-sensor arrays are made up of multiple detector or various chemically polymer coated films on a base to identify multiple vapors simultaneously [4]. Such sensor shows an immediate interaction with the sensor array presented in base structure when the vapor scatters across the environment or sensors. Such sensors are mainly used in defense department to identify various chemical warfare agents at war field. The selection of sensor among various sensors present in the modern world is broadly as odor sensors, tasting sensors, biosensors, constitutes the piezoelectric crystal sensors (surface acoustic wave sensors), and conducting organic polymer sensors.

The selection of a particular sensor among a large volume of the sensor is difficult. Though it is difficult, here, we choose the SAW E-nose sensor for the specific experiment to produce better identification of vapors in a mixture of chemicals.

2.1 SAW Sensor

Surface acoustic wave device is used to vapor identification and recognition. Electronic nose is a device which reflects the human olfactory response. SAW E-nose is based on fast chromatography which encompasses the separation of components from a mixture of vapors. The response of SAW E-nose comprises the voltage induced frequency shifts, such as analog signal called radar plots.

Figure 2 shows the schematic representation of SAW sensor. SAW E-nose composed of a piezoelectric substrate as a base with an input IDT and an output IDT (inter digital transducer) placed on the piezo electric base, and various polymer coated sensor arrays are placed between the transducers. Technically, the area presents between input IDT and output IDT is called delay line and always an AC signal is passed over the input IDT.

When a gas molecule sits on the substrate or base, while passing continues voltage between two IDT's, then the electronic field generates stress in the substrate due to the piezoelectric effect which generates an acoustic wave signal at various frequencies normally more than 100 MHz. Frequencies may differ due to the mass

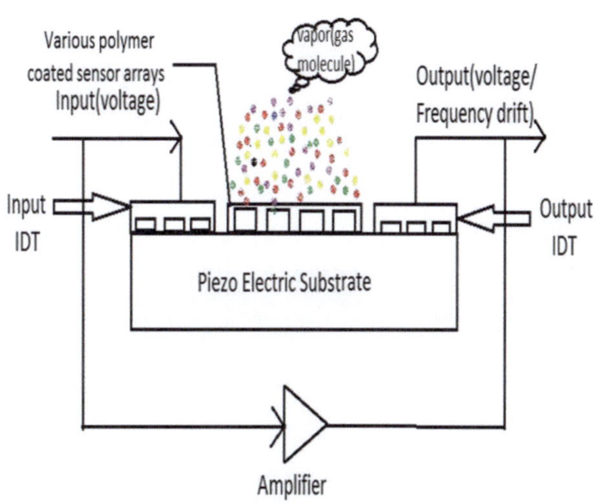

Fig. 2 Schematic representation of SAW sensor

of gas. The sensor measures the voltage change or the frequency drifts due to the presence of certain chemicals. Through the resistance across the sensor gets changes, this could be measured as a voltage drop or frequency drifts by checking with normal conditions.

Normally, the response of sensor is analog signal. To process the sensor data, it is necessary to convert the analog signal into digital signal. This is known as signal preprocessing [5]. For this purpose, A/D converter is used. A/D converter gets analog signal and converts it into digital signal and produced the result in an array of different vapor. The array of vector depends on various polymer films called detector. This overall process is called signal preprocessing. Figure 3a represents analog signal produced by gas sensor, and Fig. 3b represents the digital data produced by A/D converter which fed into computer, and all the different vector inputs are derived from the change in resistance of sensor. It can be combined and produced one or more normalized vector. Here, Principal component analysis (PCA) is used to perform the data set reduction called normalization of data. The ANN has

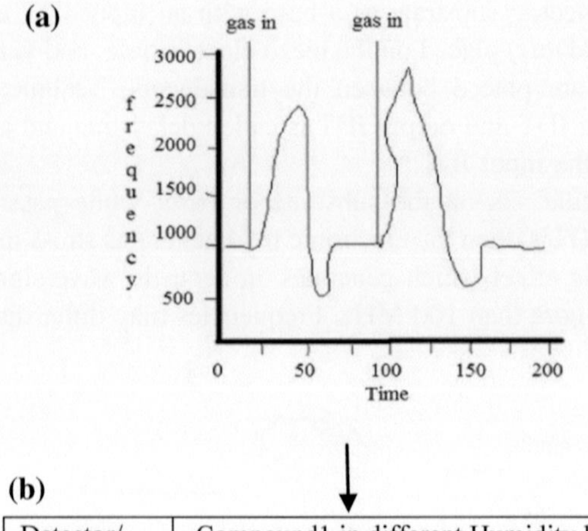

(b)

Detector/ Compound	Compound1 in different Humidity levels			
	100ppm	150ppm	200ppm	250ppm
Detector1	5.6983	7.5094	8.1297	9.5196
Detector2	6.8729	8.6387	9.7158	10.3485
Detector 3	4.8134	5.8566	6.7298	7.8158
Detector4	6.5488	7.1771	8.0478	9.9053

Fig. 3 **a** Analog signal, **b** digital data conversion produced by A/D converter

processing units called neurons. It is used to learn patterns and relationships among various vapors and trained to distinguish certain chemical vapors. The output generated is either 0 or 1.

Here, MATLAB tool has been used to code PCA and ANN.

2.2 *PCA—Principal Component Analysis*

PCA—Principal component analysis is a well-known linear pattern recognition technique used in feature reduction in a large amount of sensor signal data set. Applying PCA to an electronic nose sensor signal will yield an adroit result in single- and multi-gas odor detection system which is mainly used in dimensionality reduction. Figure 4 shows how dimensionality reduction performed for sensor's vector inputs to each compound detection.

Digital data input of Compound 1

Detector/ compound	Compound1 at different Humidity levels			
	50ppm	100ppm	150ppm	200ppm
Detector1	4.1948	11.4550	15.7152	17.6549
Detector2	5.8729	22.3181	32.6731	34.3086
Detector 3	7.1183	28.6860	42.9793	45.4821
Detector4	8.1086	32.7197	52.8041	56.0853

PCA algorithm applied

-0.0000	0	0	0
0	0.0293	0	0
0	0	0.7615	0
0	0	0	609.2847

(a) Extracted Feature vector of Compound 1

Digital data input of Compound 2

Detector/ compound	Compound2 at different Humidity levels			
	50ppm	100ppm	150ppm	200ppm
Detector1	1.4289	2.5887	3.3927	4.3061
Detector2	1.5709	3.0781	4.1672	4.8100
Detector3	1.5082	3.4691	5.4415	6.6490
Detector4	1.5692	4.0002	6.6446	7.8899

PCA algorithm applied

-0.0000	0	0	0
0	0.0001	0	0
0	0	0.0279	0
0	0	0	5.1322

(b) Extracted Feature vector of Compound 2

Digital data input of Compound 3

Detector/ compound	Compound3 at different Humidity levels			
	50ppm	100ppm	150ppm	200ppm
Detector1	1.5484	0.5089	0.6543	2.0600
Detector2	1.2520	0.8038	1.1563	2.4104
Detector3	1.3368	1.8166	1.9417	5.5032
Detector4	1.3937	1.4935	2.2425	3.2892

PCA algorithm applied

-0.0000	0	0	0
0	0.0001	0	0
0	0	0.0279	0
0	0	0	5.1322

(c) Extracted Feature vector of Compound 3

Digital data input of Compound 4

Detector/ compound	Compound4 at different Humidity levels			
	50ppm	100ppm	150ppm	200ppm
Detector1	10.3125	37.0372	51.6060	53.7244
Detector2	14.7100	57.6286	79.5828	82.5312
Detector3	17.1737	74.3753	101.2121	106.3502
Detector4	20.1934	82.9969	117.8478	123.435

PCA algorithm applied

-0.0000	0	0	0
0	0.0001	0	0
0	0	0.0014	0
0	0	0	2.1626

(d) Extracted Feature vector of Compound 4

Fig. 4 **a** Extracted feature vector of Compound 1, **b** extracted feature vector of Compound 2, **c** extracted feature vector of Compound 3, **d** extracted feature vector of Compound 4

Figure 4a represents Principal component extraction of compound 1. Figure 4b represents Principal component extraction of compound 2. Figure 4c represents Principal component extraction of compound 3. Figure 4d represents Principal component extraction of compound 4.

The Principal components for large set of sensor signal are described as a diagonal vector matrix which contains variance at diagonal places which are known as first Principal component PC1. Further, Principal vector matrix formed by applying next set of sensor signal which is known as second Principal component PC2, as such more number of Principal components are formed by arranging in a decreasing order which is explained in the below methodology to implement PCA.

2.2.1 PCA Methodology for Normalization of Sensor Data

1. Extract the input in a vector array
2. Find the mean for each row and column. Then, deduct the corresponding mean value from each element present in each row and column as follows:

$$x_1 = x - \ddot{x}, \quad y_1 = y - \bar{y}$$

   where $\ddot{x}$, $\bar{y}$ are the mean, and it is deducted from each value present in each row and column values.
3. Find the covariance matrix by using this formula:

$$\text{Covariance matrix} = \left(\sum (x - \ddot{x})(y - \bar{y})\right) / (n - 1)$$

4. Extract the eigenvector and eigenvalues from the covariance matrix and arrange it in a decreasing order by placing the first highest eigenvalue first and second highest eigenvalue second and so on.
5. Eigenvector with maximum eigenvalue is taken to form the feature vector, which is nothing the elements present in diagonal places; it is called diagonal matrix or feature vector.
6. Principle component can be obtained by doing the transpose of feature vector.

The feature vector as shown in Fig. 4a–d has been given as input to the artificial neural network structure to train with four inputs of each vapor (16) to get preferred one output. After training, ANN has been tested with the new input to get the expected output.

2.3 Artificial Neural Networks (ANN) Implementations for Pattern Identification

The Artificial neural network is developed by a system of interconnected components called "neurons". In wireless gas sensor, artificial neural networks use highly interconnected neurons to recognize the specific patterns for each toxic gas from large volume of toxic gases present in the environment [6]. Figure 5 shows the basic network structure of ANN.

The feature vector produced by PCA can be fed into the ANN and train the network to produce specified gas pattern which is shown in Fig. 6.

Figure 6 shows the network training window of ANN with feature vector input.

Figure 7a shows performance window generated by ANN training. The sample pattern of a particular vapor with time (ms) and frequency shift (Hz) is as shown in Fig. 8.

The output value produced by ANN is compared with the target value; if the difference between the produced value and target value is minimum, then the better performance is arrived. Comparisons of target and ANN value are shown in Table 1, and the error percentage of the ANN has been calculated by using below formula:

$$\text{Error percentage} = ((\text{Target Value} - \text{Ann Value})/\text{Target value}) * 100$$

Different training functions were executed with the same input data in ANN for producing comparison result among those functions. Table 2 shows comparison ANN results through various ANN training functions such as TRAINCGF, TRAINRP, TRAINLM, TRAINBFG [7, 8].

Fig. 5 Artificial neural network structure (16, 50, 25, 10, 1)

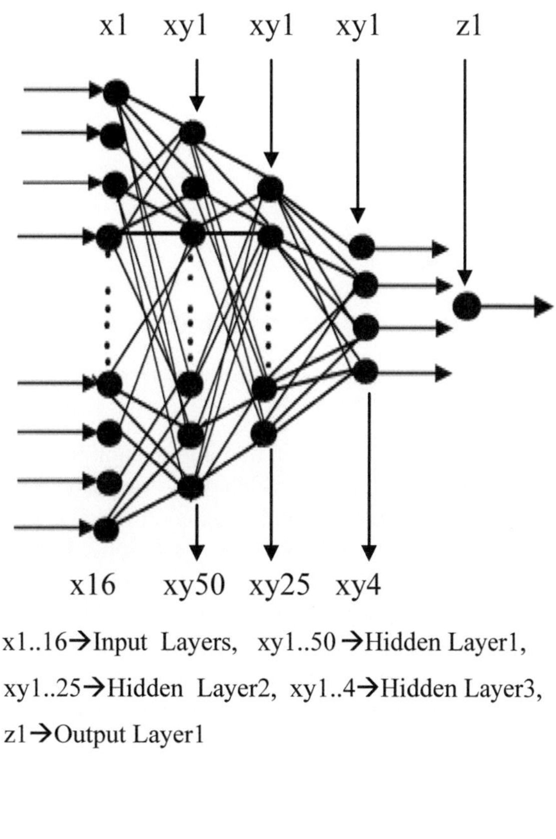

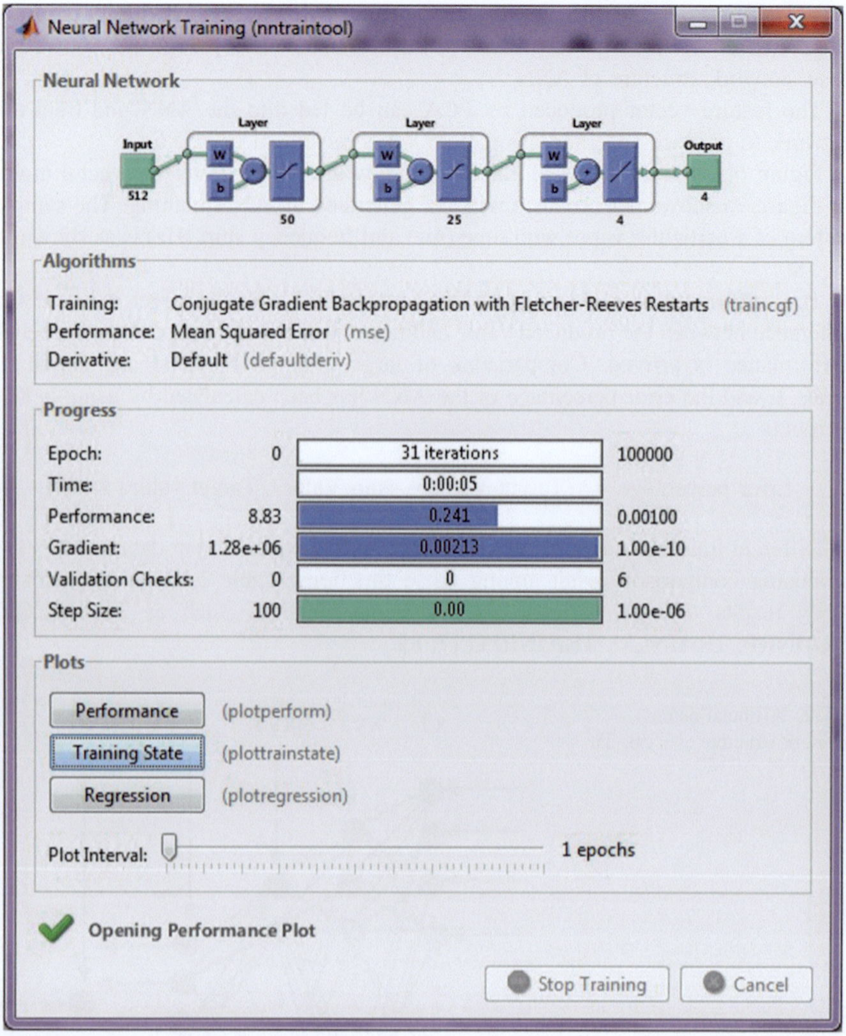

Fig. 6 Artificial neural network training window

TRAINLM is the default training function because it is very fast, but it requires a lot of memory to run. Such that we may gets an "out-of-memory" error. TRAINBFG is another training function which is slower but more memory efficient than TRAINLM and TRAINBFG. TRAINCGF is known as follows.

Conjugate gradient backpropagation with Fletcher–Reeves updates. The conjugate gradient algorithms are usually much faster than variable learning rate backpropagation, and are sometimes faster than TRAINRP, although the results vary from one problem to another. The conjugate gradient algorithms require only a little more storage than the simpler algorithms such as TRAINLM, etc., Therefore, these

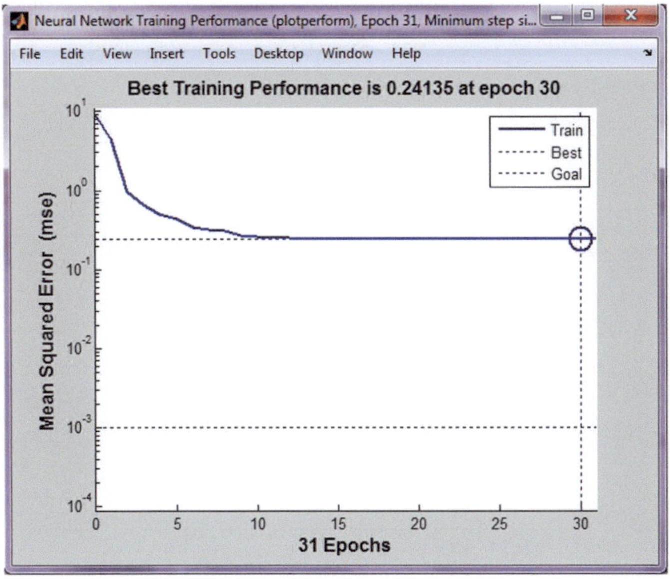

Fig. 7 Performance window

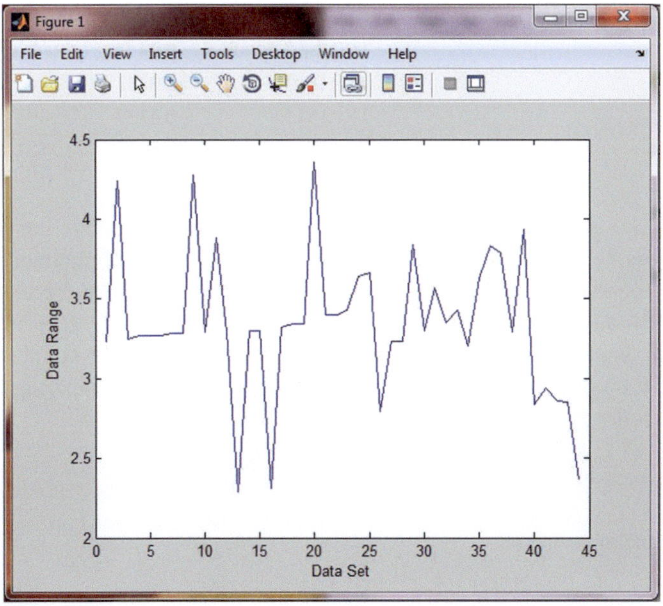

Fig. 8 Sample pattern of a gas/vapor

Table 1 Comparison of target and ANN and error %

Comparison of target and predicted values			
S. No.	Target value	ANN value	Error %
1	3.23	3.07	5.04
2	4.24	4.10	3.41
3	3.25	3.12	3.96
4	3.27	3.09	5.37
5	3.27	3.26	0.40
6	3.27	3.27	0.08
7	3.28	3.19	2.69
8	3.28	3.11	5.26
9	4.28	4.28	0.00
10	3.29	3.19	3.04
11	3.57	3.57	0.03
12	3.35	3.35	0.00
13	3.43	3.43	0.01
14	3.20	3.20	0.03
15	3.63	3.63	5.04
16	3.83	3.83	3.41

Table 2 Comparison of various training methods

S. No.	Training function	Type of error		
		MSE	MAE	SSE
1	TRAINCGF	0.2413	0.1021	0.200
2	TRAINRP	0.3281	0.2843	10.217
3	TRAINLM	0.4327	0.1492	13.526
4	TRAINBFG	0.5023	0.3521	49.621

algorithms are good for networks with a large number of weights generally converges in less iteration than TRAINRP although there is more computation required in each iteration. The performance comparison can be done by the execution of **MSE**, **MAE**, and **SSE**.

From the analysis of various values in the table and graph, we conclude that the TRAINCGF training function produces the better result when comparing with other training function, and the comparison graph has shown in Fig. 9.

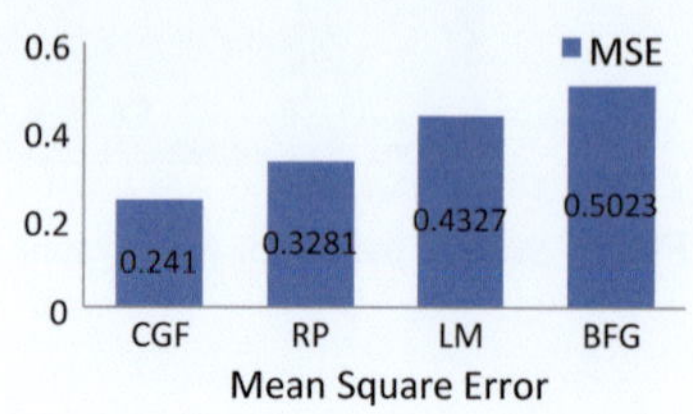

Fig. 9 Comparison graph of MSE

3 Conclusion

In this paper, we discussed various sensor technologies and a different pattern recognition system with various algorithms among those PCA, and ANN has produced the better result in describing the correct pattern identification of vapors with a selected set of data inputs in a timely manner.

References

1. Singh, H., Raj, V.B., Kumar, J., Mittala, U., Mishraa, M., Nimala, A.T., Sharma, M.U., Gupta, V.: Metal oxide SAW E-nose employing PCA and ANN for the identification of binary mixture of DMMP and methanol. Sens. Actuators B **200**, 147–156 (2014)
2. Lakshmi, B., Parish Venkat Kumar, K., Rao, N., Shahnazbanu, K.: Simulation of Artificial Noses for the Automated Detection and Classification of Organic Compounds, IJCSIT, vol 4, no 2 (2013). ISSN: 0975-9646
3. Lee, D.S., Lee, D.D., Ban, S.W., Lee, M., Kim, Y.T.: SnO_2 gas sensor array for combustible and explosive gas leakage recognition. IEEE Sens. J. **2**, 140149 (2002)
4. Zohora, S.E., Khan, A.M., Srivastava, A.K., Hundewale, N.: Chemical sensors employed in electronic noses: a review. IJSCE **3**(2) (2013). ISSN: 2231-2307
5. Nimal, A.T., Singh, M., Mittal, U., Yadava, R.D.S.: A comparative analysis of one-port Colpitt and two-port Pierce SAW oscillators for DMMP vapor sensing. Sens. Actuators B **114**, 316–325 (2006)
6. Fu, J., Li, G., Qin, Y., Freeman, W.J.: A pattern recognition method for electronic noses based on an olfactory neural network. Sens. Actuators B **125**, 489–497 (2007)
7. Kim, E., Lee, S., Kim, J.H., Kim, C., Byun, Y.T., Kim, H., Lee, T.: Pattern Recognition for Selective Odor Detection with Gas Sensor Arrays (2012). ISSN 1424-8220
8. Bermak, A., Belhouari, S.B., Shi, M., Martinez, D.: Pattern Recognition Techniques for Odor Discrimination in Gas Sensor Array, vol. X (2005). ISBN: 1-58883-056

Pico-Nym Cloud (PNC): A Method to Devise and Peruse Semantically Related Biological Patterns

Mukesh Kumar Jadon, Pushkal Agarwal and Atul Nag

Abstract Text mining works widely in the field of research techniques, which allow an individual to store text and its important terms in form of electronic document (.doc, .txt). Obliviously, one cannot remember such huge amount of text; moreover, the manual approach is more time-taking, unreliable, and accessible to that person only. Text mining techniques optimize this approach by extracting and storing this data. Computational comparison, file read, file write are more efficiently done. With the help of Pico-Nym Cloud (PNC), we generated more semantically similar, related, and significant patterns. The give, generate, and get sequence modeling is adopted. Over the other available Web applications, we present our application with improved stemming, relation, and average case consideration. This approach does not limit the displayed number of words as all the generated sets can be traversed with the GUI, with opted size of patterns. This PNC is highly applicable in bioinformatics, related information retrieval from document, sentimental analysis using social Web sites (Twitter and Facebook), query expansion (Google) and many more.

Keywords Text mining · Stemming · Cosine similarity · Tag cloud · Patterns

M.K. Jadon (✉) · P. Agarwal
Department of Computer Science and Engineering, The LNM Institute of Information Technology, Jaipur, India
e-mail: jadonmukesh30@gmail.com

P. Agarwal
e-mail: pushkalagarwal@gmail.com

A. Nag
Department of Bioinformatics, Sambalpur University Institute of Information Technology, Sambalpur, India
e-mail: nag.atul@gmail.com

B.K. Panigrahi et al. (eds.), *Nature Inspired Computing*, Advances in Intelligent Systems and Computing 652, https://doi.org/10.1007/978-981-10-6747-1_17

1 Introduction

Paradigms of text mining are worthwhile in retrieving text, especially in case of enormous data analysis. They crimp a large portion of data and the relevant result is scrutinized easily [1]. The text mining applications allow more intelligible visual assessment. "Text mining" is cited as study of patterns in a given text [2]. In 1999, Hearst said that although people were familiar with text mining and this was a frequently searched phrase on popular search engine at that time but only a few were working in this domain [2]. It is also said that text mining has emerged from machine learning and statistics. Carving out the niche of text and finding out the relevant similarity are the main cause of concern. The extraction of the cached similarities depends on the approach [3]. A better approach will end up with a quick and accurate result. The tag cloud in this scenario gives a quick summarization and a better way of visualization [4]. Color, size, and orientation of words are the concerned attributes of a tag cloud [5].

Bioinformatics largely utilizes the domain of text mining with tag cloud representation for its ability to summarize enormous amount of biologist's data [6]. Gene2WordCloud [6] and Wordle [7] are two web applications which generate the most occurring keywords and construct a word cloud out of it. The former is superior in case of bioinformatics study due to its more intellectual approach. Wordle visualizes the most occurring words from a given text or an URL. It satisfies the color, orientation, and compactness aspects in its tag clouds. However, it does not entertain the case sensitivity and the stemming relations. Thus, the repetition of words occurs irrespective of their same biological meaning. Gene2WordCloud hit a purple patch by overcoming this issue, and the term's frequency becomes more precise.

Representing all the words in a single tag cloud more signifies the number of instances of each word in the whole text. It does not furnish any idea about the relation of two occurring words. It does not justify with the average frequency terms either. As a matter of fact, frequently occurring words are commonly known in an analysis rather than the average occurring words. Hence, more emphasis should be given to the latter for an efficient analysis.

We delightedly introduce Pico-Nym Cloud (PNC), Pico refers to intense level, and Nym literally means name, from the Greek word "Onoma" which refers to name or word [8]. In this paper, we demonstrate the methods of extraction that are incorporated in Pico-Nym Cloud (PNC), along with the relevant tag clouds that display PubMed benchmark data set. These tag clouds appropriately relate the bottleneck biological terms; this makes Pico-Nym Cloud (PNC) advantageous in the field of bioinformatics. The approach in Pico-Nym Cloud (PNC) is comprised of basic preprocessing in text mining such as stemming algorithm, stop-word removal, frequency cutoff on the provided free text. The user interface is developed using the PHP and the CSS techniques. This takes the input query from the user and generates a certain number of patterns of given pattern length. Moreover, the generated patterns can be easily traversed using this user interface. The following discussion explains its approach.

2 Proposed Approach

The approach in Pico-Nym Cloud (PNC) is comprised of basic file operations, stemming algorithm, searching and sorting techniques, and some matrix manipulations on the provided free text. Later, the PHP and the CSS techniques fetch the processed data set and represent it as a tag cloud accordingly with a GUI. The following discussion explains its approach.

2.1 Preprocessing

This segment refines the free text to its maximum extent and avoids discrepancies for succeeding segments. Figure 1 shows the main preprocessing steps. We took PubMed benchmark data set as our free text for this purpose. The steps involve character by character traversal. Only lowercase alphabetic values were left after the completion of these steps. This also ensures the confinement of the lowercase domain. Stop words (a, an, the, etc.) are removed. Stop words generally create a mess and need to be filtered out. Lastly, stemming was done to improvise the given text. This eliminated the difference between root word and its derived words.

2.2 Method

After generating unique words in preprocessing part, we followed the under-mentioned method (Fig. 2) for the final result. For this, matrix manipulation is performed on moderately occurring unique words and a mathematical relation is deduced (Eq. 2). Based on PubMed benchmark data set, we plotted frequency versus words graph (Fig. 3) and drew the most relevant slope. By extrapolating, we got the average frequency range (i.e. 960–25) and the corresponding average case unique words.

Now, for $m \in M$ such that M is a set of all the given documents and $n \in N$ such that N is a set of all average case unique words, we generated a frequency matrix F of size $m \times n$. The element $f(i,j) \in F$ represents weighting factor frequency of

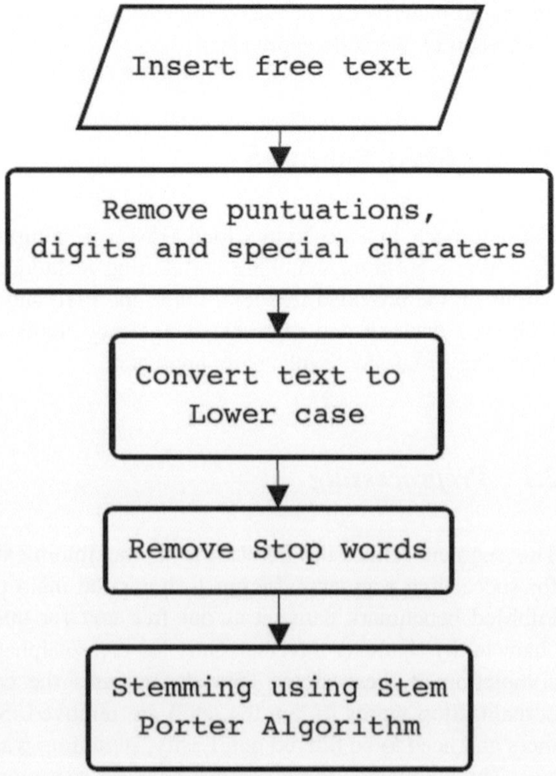

Fig. 1 Preprocessing

*j*th word in *i*th document for $0 < i \leq$ m and $0 < j \leq n$. With this frequency matrix *F*, we calculated $tf - idf(i, j) \in tf - idf$ (Eq. 1) [9], where $tf - idf$ (term frequency–inverse document frequency, weighting scheme) is a matrix of same size $m \times n$.

$$tf - idf(i,j) = f(i,j) \times \left\{ \log\left(\frac{m'}{|1+d|}\right) \right\}, \tag{1}$$

where $m' = |M|$ is the total number of given documents in data set, and *d* is the number of documents which actually contain the *j*th word, i.e., the count of documents having frequency of that word, greater than zero. The denominator in Eq. 1 is adjusted to 1 + |*d*| to avoid division by zero. We named this if—idf matrix as *W*-matrix such that $W = tf - idf$ and $w(i, j) \in W$ for $0 < i \leq m$ and $0 < j \leq n$.

Lastly, we calculated cosine similarity matrix $c(i,j) \in C$ (Eq. 2) for $n \in N$ words. Each $c(i, j)$ represents cosine relation [10] between *i*th and *j*th column vectors of *W*-matrix hence it acquired a dimension $n \times n$. Let $0<k\leq m \in M$, we took two column vectors say $w(k, i)$ and $w(k, j)$ of *W*-matrix and computed $c(i, j)$ traversing all rows of the same matrix with $k = 1–k = m$.

Fig. 2 Algorithm

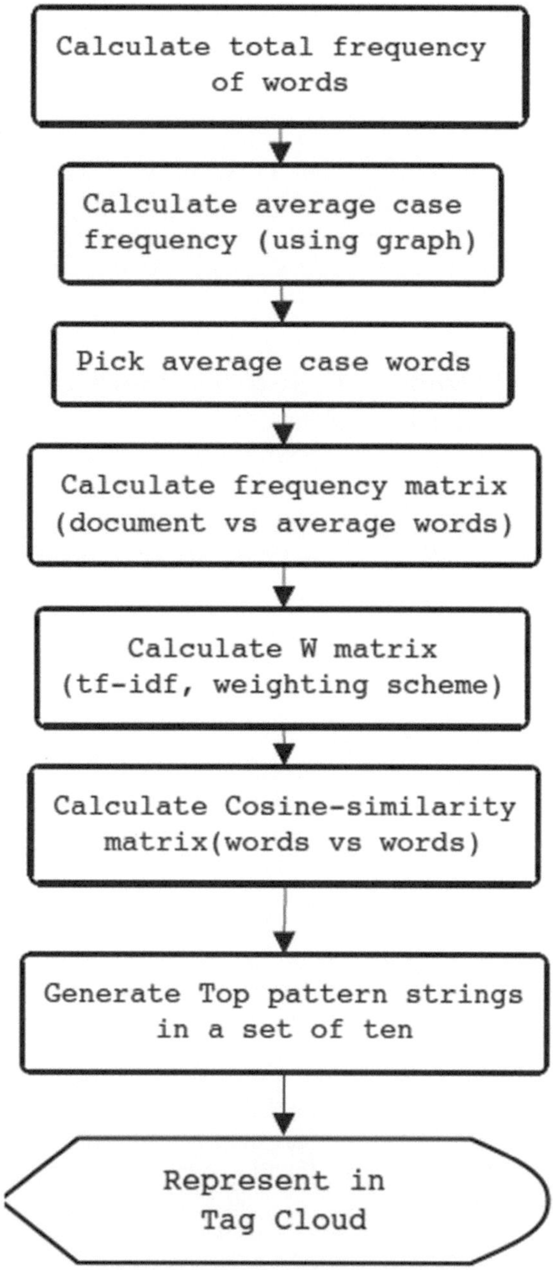

$$c(i,j) = \frac{\sum_{k=1}^{m} w(k,i) \times w(k,j)}{\sqrt{\sum_{k=1}^{m} (w(k,i))^2} \times \sqrt{\sum_{k=1}^{m} (w(k,j))^2}}. \quad (2)$$

Then we combined a pair of two *c*(*i*, *j*) having maximum cosine similarity value and created string patterns (maximum ten words per string) (Algorithm 1). Finally, PHP and CSS techniques were used for the generation of tag cloud. The largest and centrally located word is the first entry of the top pattern string, following which in spiral way are the succeeding nine words. The algorithm is written below.

2.3 Algorithm 1: To Create Patterns from the Cosine Similarity Matrix C

```
Input  : Training Data
Output: Cosine Similarity Matrix C, Word string set P
(maximum 10 words per string)
--------------------------------------------------------
1.  Let s∈ S such that S be a set of unique words in
    PubMed training dataset and d∈ D such that D be a
    the set of all given documents
2.  Create frequency matrix F
3.      Do for all
4.          Do for each s_j ∈ S, j=1,2,…,s
5.              Do for each d_i ∈ D, i=1,2,…,d
6.                  w_ij= Cal_tf-idf(F,i,j)
7.              EndDo
8.          EndDo
9.      EndDo
10.     Do for all
11.         Do for each s_j ∈ S, j=1,2,…,s-1
12.             Do for each s_k ∈ S, k=j+1,,…,s
13.               Do for each d_i ∈ D, i=1,2,…,d
14.                   c_ij= Cal_Cosine_Sim(W,i,j,k)
15.               EndDo
16.               max_similar=Find_Max_Cosine_Sim()
17.               If (stringcount < 10) Then
18.                   add  s_i and  s_k to p_z
19.                   increment stringcount by 1
20.               Else
21.                   increment z by 1 for next string
22.               EndIf
23.             EndDo
24.         EndDo
25.     EndDo
```

Fig. 3 Average area section

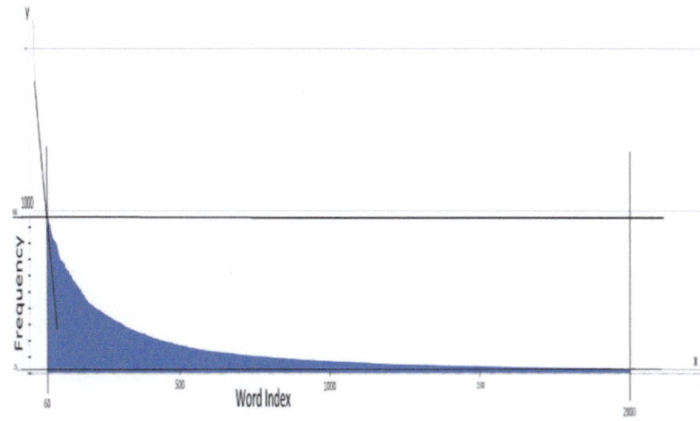

3 Experimental Analysis and Comparisons

Based on the proposed approach (Sect. 2), we asymptotically analyzed (Fig. 3) the text and used the average case words in the seceding method (Fig. 2). By cognitively creating the tag cloud from the final string patterns, we analyzed our result with respect to some of the familiar online word cloud generators (refer mentioned link). Table 1 shows some Pico-Nym Cloud (PNC)'s tag clouds.

The above results were generated on some portion of text ($\sim$65 K words). The following Table 2 shows some more tag clouds created by Pico-Nym Cloud (PNC). These tag clouds are free from any punctuation, digit, special character, uppercase alphabets, and general stop words. Since the cloud generation is possible with ten, twenty, thirty, and so on. In 10–30 words patterns, it is easy to analyze rather than a cluster of words where one have to carve out the niche of more than hundred words. The traversal through GUI is a user-friendly approach along with a display of related attributes and a jump to specific word pattern. The GUI is given below which allows a user to enter a text in form of text, provided words per document are specified along with choose destination folder option. For a better look font selection drop down menu is also provided.

4 Conclusion

We concluded that finding a correlation improves the representation of a tag cloud. Pico-Nym Cloud (PNC) would emerge as a feather in the cap of text mining and word cloud generator. Along with bioinformatics, the same approach can generate

Table 1 Comparison list

Popular online word cloud generator	Tag cloud generated by Pico-Nym cloud (PNC)
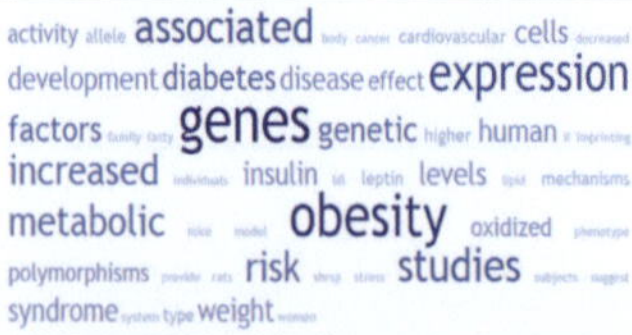 (1) http://tagcrowd.com/, Created by Daniel Steinbock	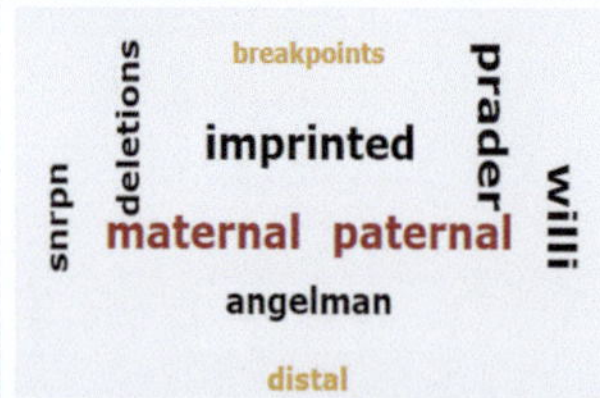
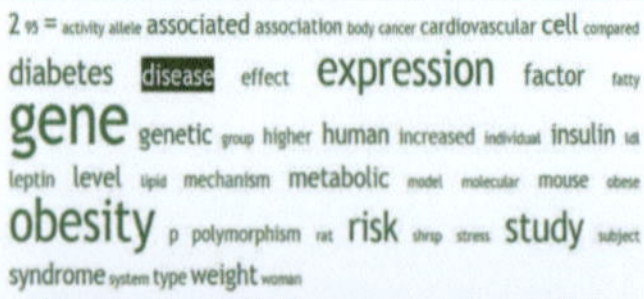 (2) http://wordsift.com/, Greg Wientjes production, Stanford University © 2010	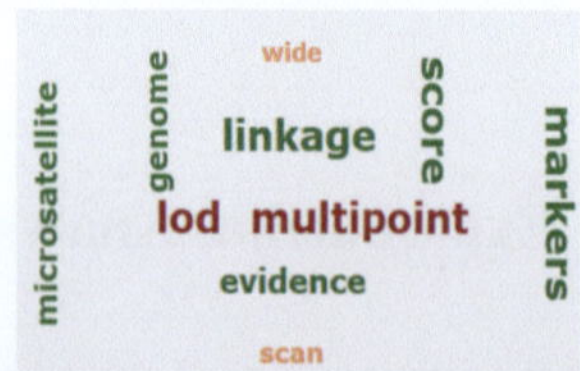
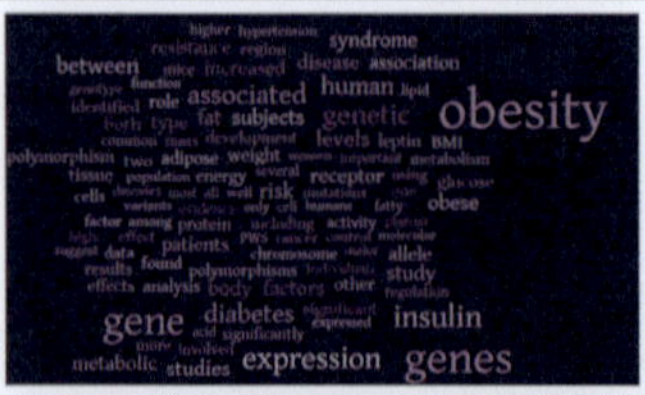 (3) http://worditout.com/ © 2015 Enideo	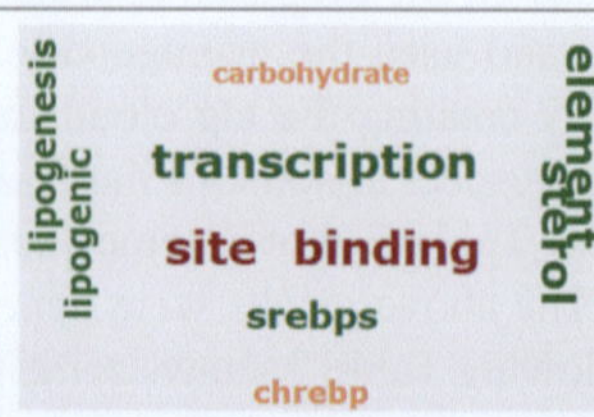
 (4) http://www.jasondavies.com/wordcloud/ Copyright © Jason Davies 2014	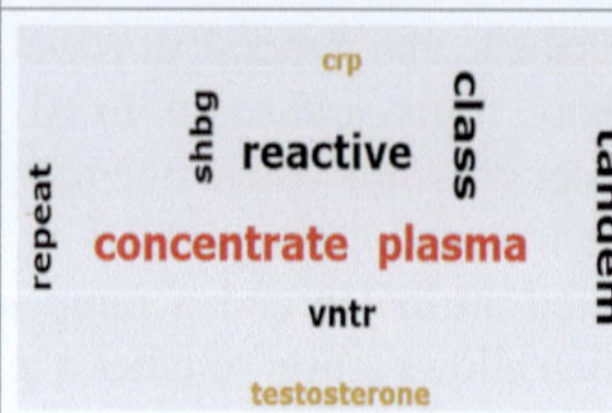
 (5) http://www.wordle.net/, © 2013 Jonathan Feinberg	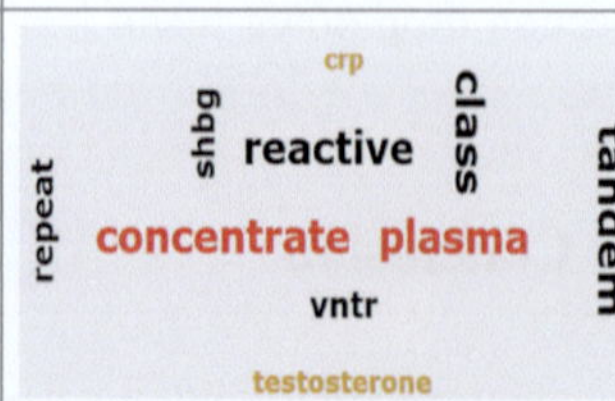
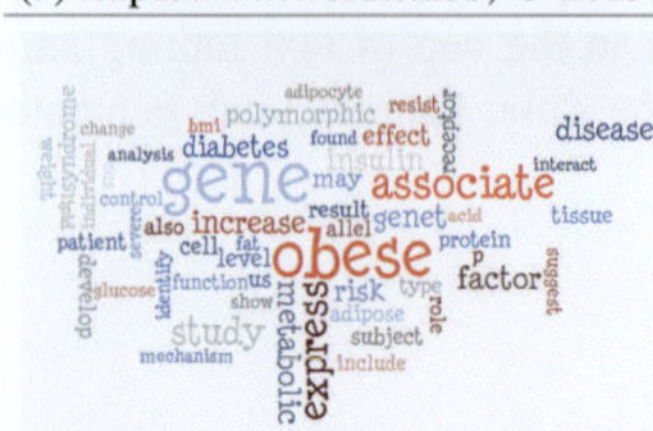 (6) www.maayanlab.net/G2W/, Gene2WordCloud by the Ma'ayan Laboratory	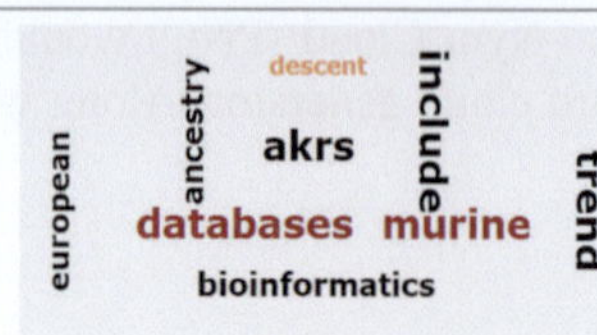

Table 2 Tag clouds

(1) Pattern size: 10; Total patterns generated: 65; Pattern number: 21

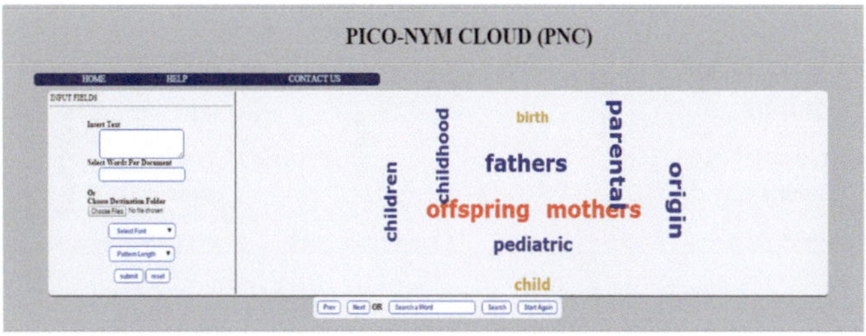

(2) Pattern size: 20; Total patterns generated: 29; Pattern number: 22

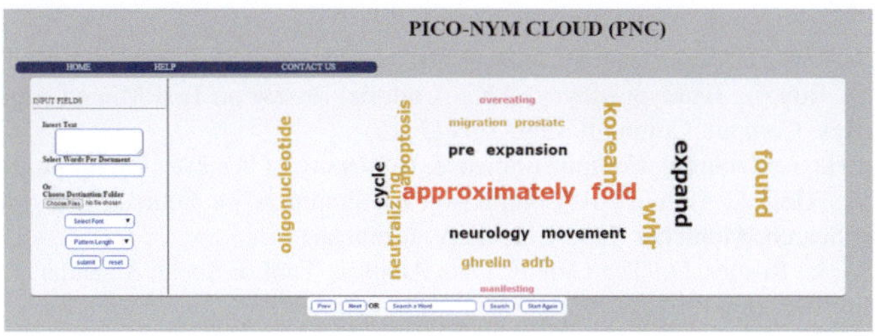

(3) Pattern size: 30; Total patterns generated: 12; Pattern number: 7

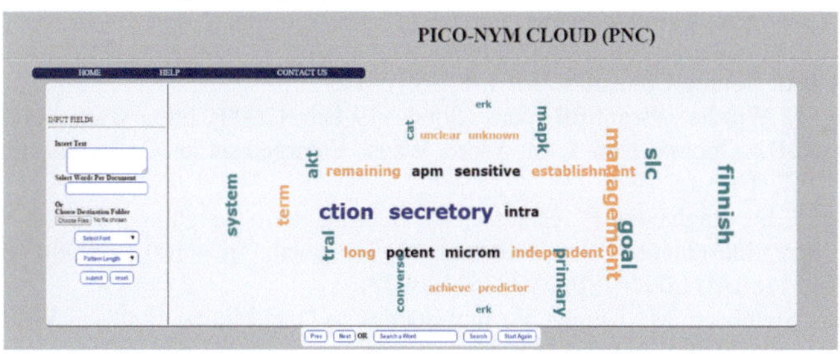

word cloud for text books, novels, or any free text and a reader would get the best-related term without even opening his book. These patterns would then be directly used for reading, teaching, notes making, and revision purposes. Finally, we have given some tag clouds in Table 3; these are generated by the text of this document itself. These are self-explanatory for correctness of the implemented approach of PNC.

Table 3 Pico-Nym cloud (PNC)'s word cloud

Authors' and institute's names. Pattern number 4.	Algorithm and implementations. Pattern number 15.
	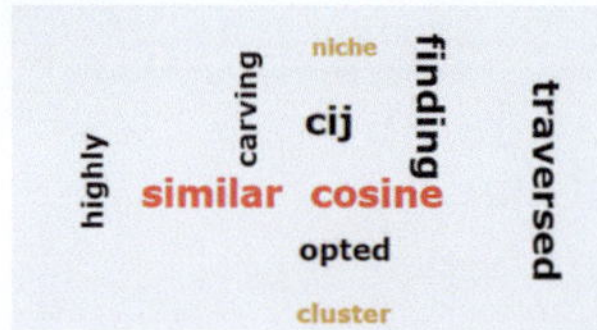

References

1. Ghosh, S., Roy, S., Bandyopadhyay, S.K.: A tutorial review on Text Mining Algorithms. Int. J. Adv. Res. Comput. Commun. Eng. **1**(4) (2012)
2. Witten, I.H.: Text mining. Computer Science, University of Waikato, Hamilton, New Zealand
3. Wiese, A., Ho, V., Hill, E.: A Comparison of Stemmers on Source Code Identifiers for Software Search. Montclair State University, Montclair
4. Hearst, M.A., Rosner, D.: Tag Clouds: Data Analysis Tool or Social Signaller, University of California, Berkeley (2012)
5. Manuela, W., Schrammel, J, Klein, M, Kristjánsdóttir, K., Unger, D., Tscheligi, M: FacetClouds: Exploring Tag Clouds for Multi-Dimensional Data, Cure—Center for Usability Research and Engineering, Vienna
6. Baroukh, et al.: Genes2WordCloud: a quick way to identify biological themes from gene lists and free text. Source Code Biol. Med. **6**, 15 (2011)
7. Feinberg, J.: Wordle—Beautiful Word Clouds, 19 Feb. (2009). http://www.wordle.net/create
8. Scheetz, G.H.: Onomasticon I. In: Word Ways. Enlarged as an Onomastic Onomasticon, pp. 165–167, 10 Aug. 1977
9. Manning, C.D., Raghavan, P., Schutze, H.: Scoring, term weighting, and the vector space model. In: Introduction to Information Retrieval, p. 100 (2008) doi:10.1017/CBO9780511809071.007 (ISBN 9780511809071)
10. Tan, P.N., Steinbach, M., Kumar, V.: Introduction to Data Mining. Addison-Wesley. Chapter 8, p 500 (2005) (ISBN 0-321-32136-7)

Assessment on VM Placement and VM Selection Strategies

Neeru Chauhan, Nitin Rakesh and Rakesh Matam

Abstract Cloud Computing is captivating many organizations and individuals because it provides a framework where the user can access diverse resources such as applications, storage capacity, network bandwidth, and many resources. Cloud users rent the resources that they need from the cloud provider. The optimum allocation of resources to the users in a dynamic environment is a major challenge for the cloud providers. Virtualization technology in Cloud enables allocation of resources to the end user applications in Cloud by hosting numerous Virtual Machines on a single host. There are number of approaches to decide the placement of Virtual Machines to the various hosts. As numbers of applications are submitted by the users, some of the hosts become overloaded and some become under loaded. As a result, some of the user applications hosted on a Virtual Machine of one host needs to be transferred to another Virtual Machine of another host. The migration of Virtual Machines from one host to another needs to be minimized to improve the response time, turnaround time for an end user application. This paper addresses the various VM placement and VM selection algorithms and their scope of improvement.

Keywords Resource allocation · VM placement · VM selection · VM migration

N. Chauhan (✉) · N. Rakesh
Department of Computer Science and Engineering, Amity School of Engineering and Technology, Amity University, Noida, Uttar Pradesh, India
e-mail: nchauhan@amity.edu

N. Rakesh
e-mail: nitin.rakesh@gmail.com

R. Matam
IIIT, Guwahati, India
e-mail: matamrakesh@gmail.com

B.K. Panigrahi et al. (eds.), *Nature Inspired Computing*, Advances in Intelligent Systems and Computing 652, https://doi.org/10.1007/978-981-10-6747-1_18

1 Introduction

The resources in Cloud Computing can be physical resources as well as virtual resources that the developer may demand from the cloud provider. Resources can be network bandwidth, CPU, memory, storage, and other issues including network delay, topology of network, etc. These resources are located in the data centers. The problems encountered in resource allocation system in Cloud Computing can be arranged in the following sequence. The first problem is the placement of heterogeneous hosts with varying capacities to the various Cloud data centers [1]. The second problem is the placement of Virtual Machines to the different hosts [2, 3]. The third problem is to check whether the hosts in data centers are overloaded or under loaded. The fourth problem is the selection of Virtual Machines for migration [4, 5]. This paper is organized as follows. In section second, we discussed the various VM placement algorithms with their objectives and scope of improvement. The VM selection algorithms with their objectives and scope of improvement are discussed in section third which also comprises the complexities of the various algorithms. Section fourth comprises the conclusion.

2 Comparison of VM Placement Algorithms

2.1 VM Placement Algorithms Objectives and Loopholes

In Cloud Computing, data centers contain all the resources whether they are physical or logical. There are number of data centers and number of variable capacity hosts. These heterogeneous hosts are allocated to the various data centers [6]. Then, Virtual Machines are allocated to the hosts. Then, applications of users are allocated to these various VMs. Table 1 shows various VM placement algorithms and the scope of improvement with these algorithms [7–13]. In the risk aware VM consolidation algorithm [8], the author focused on the dynamic allocation of resources to VMs so as to minimize the energy and SLA violations. The objectives of shadow routing algorithms for VM placement are reduction in the number of data centers used [9]. The objectives of rule-based mapping are maximizing compute performance and minimizing the energy consumption [10]. The goals of statistics-based approach for VM placement are better to load balancing [7]. Matrix transformation algorithm aims to reduce the number of host machines and optimum utilization of the resources of the used host machines [11]. In adaptive min–min scheduling, the author focuses on smallest average time of execution for the tasks [12]. The objectives of Virtual Machine splitting and assignment are less number of host machines and high performance [13]. There are some other heuristic-based algorithms for VM placement to the host machine. The heuristic-based VM placement algorithms can be categorized as offline and online algorithms (see Table 2). In offline algorithms, the user requests are known in advance. The examples of offline algorithms are Best Fit Decreasing,

Table 1 VM placement algorithms

S. No.	VM placement approach [7–13]	Scope of improvement
1	Risk aware VM consolidation algorithm	The rejection rate of end user requests is high, CPU capacity is the only parameter used which can be extended to network bandwidth, memory, and so on
2	Shadow routing	Mean service time parameter is needed, and it varies with the actual observed sample. A mechanism is required to predict the mean service time, the algorithm assumes one PM in a DC. It can be extended to multiple PMs
3	Rule-based mapping	The nature of application can be communicated to the mapper so that performance can be improved further
4	Statistics based	Cannot be used for dynamic environment
5	Matrix transformation	More number of resource rejections of the end users requests
6	Adaptive min–min scheduling	Complexity is high
7	Virtual Machines splitting and assignment	More VMs required when application is split into multiple tasks. Moreover, some applications are non-splitable

Table 2 Heuristic-based VM placement algorithms

S. No.	VM placement approach [14–17]	Scope of improvement
1	First Fit	Immediate rejections and resource allocation rejections high
2	Next Fit	Wastage of resources is more
3	Best Fit	Resource fragmentation
4	Worst Fit	High wastage of resources
5	First Fit Decreasing	More number of rejections of end user requests
6	Best Fit Decreasing	Utilization of resources and the rejection of resources are same
7	Best Fit Max	Resources are underutilized due to the reservation of resources
8	Round Robin	Context switching required, time quantum affects performance
9	Modified Best Fit Decreasing	Complexity is highest

First Fit Decreasing, and Modified Best Fit Decreasing. In online algorithms, the user requests are unpredictable and dynamic in nature. The examples of offline algorithms include First Fit, Best Fit, Worst Fit, Next Fit, Round Robin [14–17].

2.2 Performance Metrics for VM Placement Algorithms

A VM placement algorithm should be designed in a manner such that it can serve the requests of end user in a given by making use of less number of physical machines [11]. Virtual Machines should be placed such that most of the resources of the host machines are utilized [7, 18]. The VMs should be placed on the host machines such that the time required for the execution of tasks is less [12]. The algorithm should be able to satisfy all the end user requests [10].

3 VM Selection/Migration Algorithms

3.1 VM Selection Algorithms Objectives and Loopholes

The Virtual Machines are placed on the appropriate host machines. The applications of the end users are assigned to these Virtual Machines. Virtual Machines need to be selected for migration from one machine to another in a number of situations [19, 20]. The first reason is that the applications submitted by the users over the Cloud are dynamic in nature, and the resources required by a particular application may increase or decrease, and to fulfill those additional resource requirements, migration is required. Secondly, when the overall utilization of resources of a host exceeds a certain threshold value, some Virtual Machines need to be migrated from the host in order to maintain the utilization of the host below the upper utilization threshold. Table 3 shows some VM selection algorithms with their loophole.

VM migration can be categorized as hot migration, cold migration, and live storage migration. In hot migration, the Virtual Machine is not switched off but migrates from one Virtual Machine to another in power on state. In cold migration, the machine is switched off when it moves from one host machine to another.

Table 3 VM selection algorithms

S. No.	VM selection approach [4–6]	Scope of improvement (gap) in the approach
1	Minimization of migrations	Heterogeneous load of the applications is not taken into account, complex, high performance overhead
2	Single threshold	As the value of utilization threshold of VMs increases, the power consumption decreases but SLA violation, more VM migrations
3	Two phase minimization of migrations	SLA violations for an end user should be reduced to average SLA violations while reducing the number of VM migrations
4	Highest potential growth	More number of VM migrations compared to minimization of migrations
5	Random choice	More number of VM migrations

Table 4 Complexities of the various algorithms

S. No.	Nature of algorithm	Name of algorithm	Complexity
1	VM placement	Next Fit	$O(n)$
2	VM placement	First Fit	$O(n\log n)$
3	VM placement	Best Fit	$O(n\log n)$
4	VM placement	Next Fit Decreasing	$O(n\log n)$
5	VM placement	First Fit Decreasing	$O(n\log n)$
6	VM placement	Best Fit Decreasing	$O(n\log n)$
7	VM placement	Modified Best Fit Decreasing	$O(n, m)$
8	VM selection	Minimization of Migrations	$O(n, m)$

In live storage migration, the files or virtual disk of a running Virtual Machine is moved to new storage area without interrupting its services [14, 21]. The goal of all of the VM selection algorithms is to reduce the consumption of energy, less number of VM migrations, less number of SLA violations [4, 6]. An analysis showed that two phase minimization of migrations results in less number of VM migrations [5].

3.2 Performance Metrics of VM Selection Algorithms

A VM selection algorithm should be designed in such a way so that it results in less number of VM migrations. More number of VM migrations result in increase in turnaround time and response time for the end users [4–6]. The consumption of energy is directly proportional to the number of VM migrations. Less VM migrations result in less consumption of energy. A good VM selection algorithm should consume less energy [4–6]. When VMs are migrated from one host machine to the another, SLA agreements between the customer and cloud provider are violated. A good VM selection algorithm should result in less number of SLA violations [4–6]. Table 4 shows the complexities of the various algorithms of VM placement and selection in the worst case performance ratios [4, 16, 17].

4 Conclusion

This paper addresses the problems encountered while placing Virtual Machines on host machines and selecting the Virtual Machines for migration. The difficulty arises as we have to integrate VM placement algorithms with a VM selection algorithm in order to find an optimum allocation of resource. There is no single approach that combines VM placement and VM selection into one integrated approach so that the number of VM migrations is minimized. The end user application should have less turnaround time, response time, SLA violations, and rejection rate. Moreover, the complexities of the existing algorithms are very high.

References

1. Pan, Y., Hu, N.: Research on dependability of cloud computing systems. In: Proceedings of IEEE International Conference on Reliability, Maintainability and Safety (ICRMS), Guangzhou, China, Aug 2014, pp. 435–439 (2014)
2. Sridharan, M., et al.: Defragmentation of resources in virtual desktop clouds for cost-aware utility-optimal allocation. In: Proceedings of the Fourth IEEE International Conference on Utility and Cloud Computing(UCC), Victoria, NSW, Dec 2011, pp. 253–260 (2011)
3. Suarez, C.D.T., et al.: A heuristic algorithm for the offline one-dimensional bin packing problem inspired by the point Jacobi matrix iterative method. In: Proceedings of the Fifth IEEE Mexican International Conference on Artificial Intelligence (MICAI'06), Mexico City, Mexico, Nov 2006, pp. 281–286 (2006)
4. Buyya, R., Beloglazov, A., Abawajy, J.: Energy efficient management of data center resources for cloud computing: a vision, architectural elements, and open challenges. In: Proceedings of the 2010 International Conference on Parallel and Distributed Processing Techniques and Applications (PDPTA 2010), Las Vegas, USA, July 2010 (2010)
5. Taheri, M.M., Zamanifar, K.: 2-phase optimization method for energy aware scheduling of virtual machines in cloud data centers. In: Proceedings of 6th International IEEE Conference on Internet Technology and Secured Transactions(ICITST), Abu Dhabi, United Arab Emirates, Dec 2011, pp. 525–530 (2011)
6. Beloglazov, A., Abawajy, J., Buyya, R.: Energy-aware resource allocation heuristics for efficient management of data centers for cloud. Future Gener. Comput. Syst. **28**(5), 755–768 (2012). ISSN: 0167-739X
7. Zhang, Z., et al.: A VM-based resource management method using statistics. In: Proceedings of 18th IEEE International Conference on Parallel and Distributed Systems, Singapore, Dec 2012, pp. 788–793 (2012)
8. Jin, X., et al.: Risk management for virtual machines consolidation in data centers. In: Proceedings of 2013 IEEE Global Communications Conference (GLOBECOM), Atlanta, GA, Apr 2013, pp. 2872–2878 (2013)
9. Guo, Y., et al.: Shadow–routing based dynamic algorithms for virtual machine placement in a network cloud. In: Proceedings of 2013 IEEE INFOCOM, Turin, Apr 2013, pp. 620–628 (2013)
10. Kleineweber, C., et al.: Rule based mapping of virtual machines in clouds. In: Proceedings of 19th IEEE International Euromicro Conference on Parallel, Distributed and Network–based Processing (PDP), Ayia Napa, Feb 2011, pp. 527–534 (2011)
11. Sun, M., et al.: A matrix transformation algorithm for virtual machine placement in cloud. In: Proceedings of 12th IEEE International Conference on Trust, Security and Privacy in Computing and Communications (TrustCom), Melbourne, VIC, July 2013, pp. 1778–1783 (2013)
12. Li, J., Qiu, M., et al.: Adaptive resource allocation for preemptable jobs in cloud systems. In: Proceedings of 10th IEEE International Conference on Intelligent Systems Design and Applications (ISDA), Cairo, Nov–Dec 2010, pp. 31–36 (2010)
13. Liu, L., et al.: A novel performance preserving VM splitting and assignment scheme. In: Proceedings of IEEE International Conference on Communications (ICC), Sydney, NSW, June 2014, pp. 4215–4220 (2014)
14. Ezugwu, E.A., Buhari, M.S., Junaidu, B.S.: Virtual machine allocation cloud computing environment. Int. J. Cloud Appl. Comput. **3**(2), 47–60 (2013)
15. Buyya, R., Yeo, C.S., et al.: Cloud computing and emerging IT platforms: vision, hype, and reality for delivering computing as the 5th utility. Future Gener. Comput. Syst. **25**(6), 599–616. ISSN: 0167-739X (2009)
16. Grant, A.B., Eluwole, O.T.: Cloud resource management—virtual machines competing for limited resources. In: Proceedings of 55th International Symposium ELMAR, Zadar, Croatia, Sept 2013, pp. 269–274 (2013)

17. Bin Packing Problem Available: "http://www.or.deis.unibo.it/kp/Chapter8.pdf"
18. Diaz, F., et al.: Impact of over-reservation (ROR) and dropping polices on cloud resource allocation. In: Proceedings of IEEE Third International Conference on Cloud Computing Technology and Science (CloudCom), Athens, Nov–Dec 2011, pp. 470–476 (2011)
19. Beloglazov, A., Buyya, R.: Optimal online deterministic algorithms and adaptive heuristics for energy and performance efficient dynamic consolidation of virtual machines in cloud data center. Concurr. Comput.: Pract. Exp. **24**(13), 1397–1420 (2012). ISSN: 1532-0626
20. Anand, A., Lakshmi, J., et al.: Virtual machine placement optimization supporting performance SLAs. In: Proceedings of IEEE 5th International Conference on Cloud Computing Technology and Science (CloudCom), Bristol, Dec 2013, vol. 1, pp. 298–305 (2013)
21. Mills, K., Filliben, J., Dabrowski, C.: Comparing VM-placement algorithms for on-demand clouds. In: Third IEEE International Conference on Cloud Computing Technology and Science (CloudCom), Athens, Nov–Dec 2011, pp. 91–98 (2011)

Distributed Denial of Service Attack Detection Using Ant Bee Colony and Artificial Neural Network in Cloud Computing

Uzma Ali, Kranti K. Dewangan and Deepak K. Dewangan

Abstract Distributed Denial of Services (DDoS) attack is the one of the most dangerous threats in the cloud computing. A group of zombies tries to attack a single target so that the victim is not able to use the resources more, and it leads to shutting down the system. And the actual attacker is hard to trace. In the proposed method, we used a hybrid approach which is Artificial Bee Colony and Back Propagation Artificial Neural Network. The proposed method is used to detect the DDoS attack in cloud computing. Firstly, the Artificial Bee Colony selects the weights and thresholds on the basis of minimum mean square error. And these weights and thresholds are used to initialize Back Propagation Artificial Neural Network. And then the training is performed based on the Back Propagation technique. It increases the speed and accuracy of detecting the DDoS attack.

Keywords Cloud computing · Artificial Neural Network · Back Propagation · Artificial Bee Colony · Distributed Denial of Services Attack

1 Introduction

One of the fastest growing and most used technologies is cloud computing in the IT field [1]. The cloud computing has allowed there user to pay for only the services which they have used that is called as "Pay-as-you-go". The expense in cloud computing is less. The architecture is good in flexibility in the cloud computing [2].

U. Ali (✉) · K.K. Dewangan · D.K. Dewangan
ITM University, New Raipur, Chhattisgarh, India
e-mail: uzmaali1307@gmail.com

K.K. Dewangan
e-mail: krantid@itmuniversity.org

D.K. Dewangan
e-mail: deepakd@itmuniversity.org

B.K. Panigrahi et al. (eds.), *Nature Inspired Computing*, Advances in Intelligent Systems and Computing 652, https://doi.org/10.1007/978-981-10-6747-1_19

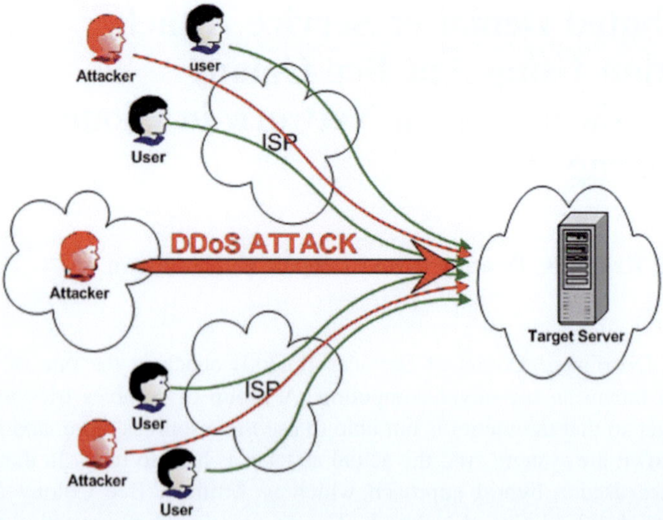

Fig. 1 Distributed Denial of Services Attack

The cloud architecture contains IaaS, PaaS and SaaS where I stand for infrastructure, P stand for platforms and S stand for software [3]. The basic need of the cloud computing is the connection of the Internet [4]. It is used to make dynamic clone of the virtual machines which are performed quickly in the cloud platform. For example; it creates the clone of gigabyte-level server within few seconds [3].

Despite from there all advantages, it also has security concerns in cloud computing [3]. One of the security issues is DDoS attack. DoS (Denial of Services) attack is the old version of DDoS. There are two types of Web attack which halt the server. They are DoS and DDoS. The DDoS attack makes the resources unavailable so that no legitimate user can use it. The DDoS attack prevents the working of the server, and also, it operates by the remote location so that no one can detect the attacker. Many zombies attack a target server and makes server unavailable for legitimate user. The zombies transfer the floods of traffic packets to the target server and make it shutdown [5] (Fig. 1).

DDoS attacks are performed in two levels, basically. The first level applies to make the system not usable. It forces the server to go to halt state so that the legitimate users are not able to use the resources from the server. It is done by making the legitimate users system in compromised systems [6]. A malicious programme is installed in the system of legitimate user, and this makes users system compromised. This compromised system is known as "zombies". The second level is applied in hiding the actual identity of the main attacker and gives instruction to the zombies to attack the victim [6].

1.1 Artificial Neural Network (ANN)

Machine learning (ML) is the type of the data mining technique [7]. The machine learning technique is basically used to find the data with relationships, and then, it analyses the process for extraction. The ML technique is categorized into 3 parts, i.e. SL, RL and UL. The SL (supervised learning) is a learning technique which is learned with the guidance. In other words, any supervisor helps in learning process. The UL (unsupervised learning) is a learning technique which is performed without any guidance. In other words, there is no help provided in the learning process [8].

The Artificial Neural Network is the type of ML technique. The ANN is based on the biological neural networks. The ANN is able to learn and understand data same as human beings. It is capable to learn things by itself [9]. ANN is made up of multiple neurons, and the neurons are connected with each other by using links. The ANN has an aim to find the useful outputs from the inputs. The output is produced with the help of weights. The weights are entered in the links [10].

ANN is made up of three layers, i.e. input, hidden and output layer. The hidden layer can be a single or multiple layers. The output of the input layer becomes the input of the hidden layer. And the output of the hidden layer becomes the input of the output layer. That is the input data is given to input layer, then it transfers to the hidden layer and finally it is received by the output layer and from the output layer we get the output data [11].

1.2 Artificial Bee Colony (ABC)

In ABC, there are three types of bees in colony. First the employed bees, it is related to the particular type of food source. The second is onlooker bees, they are seeing the activity of employed bees. Third and last is scout bees, there work is to find the new food source for the colony. There is another word for onlookers and employed bees which are unemployed bees. The scout bees identify the initial position of the food source in the environment. The onlooker and employed bees exploit the nectar of the initial food source. And this changes the food source into the exhausted food source. After that, the bees have to find a new food source. So the employed bee is changed into scout bee which has the exhausted food source. Then, this changed scout bee goes to find a new food source.

The position and the nectar amount of the food source, maximum loops, the size of population, number of variables and limit value are an important parameter. It shows the answer of optimized trouble or problem and fitness level of the associated solution. The no. of the solutions (food source) is always same as the no. of the onlookers or employed bees in the colony. The one employed bee is able to relate with one food source [12].

In ABC algorithm, the transferred scout bee is not able to find any solution which is not able to explore more from the limit that is the number of loops which is predefined. The food source is declared as abandoned [13].

The steps of the artificial bee colony are given below:

1. Initialize the quantity of the solution x_{ij} which is determined using the following formula

$$x_i^j = x_{\min}^j + \text{rand}(0,1)\left(x_{\max}^j - x_{\min}^j\right) \tag{1}$$

where x_i^j is number of the possible position of food source and $i = \{1, 2, \ldots, \text{PC}/2\}$ and $j = \{1, 2, \ldots, V\}$. V represents number of variable and PC represents the population of the colony.

2. The employed bee searches for the new solution v_{ij} around x_{ij}. v_{ij} is calculated by using the following equation

$$v_{ij} = x_{ij} + \varphi_{ij}(x_{ij} - x_{kj}) \tag{2}$$

where φ_{ij} represents random number which is between [−1, 1] and $k = \{1, 2, \ldots, \text{PC}\}$.

3. The greedy policy is used to choose the improved food source between x_{ij} and v_{ij}.
4. Calculate the fitness value by using the following equation

$$\text{FIT}_i = \begin{cases} \frac{f_i}{1+f_i} & 0 \le f_i \\ 1 + |f_i| & 0 > f_i \end{cases} \tag{3}$$

where f_i represents the value of the predefined objective function of position of the food source.

The probability is calculated on the basis of the fitness value as shown in the below equation

$$\text{Prob}_i = \frac{\text{FIT}_i}{\sum_{n=1}^{\text{PC}} \text{FIT}_i} \tag{4}$$

5. A new position of the food source v_i is produced on the basis Prob_i.
6. According to the greedy criterion, a new position of the food source is selected between x_{ij} and v_{ij} by the onlooker bees.
7. If there is an abandoned food source x_i, it is replaced by the new food source by using equation one.
8. Choose the best position of the food source and continue until the number of the cycle is equal to maximum number of cycle which is denoted as MCN.

1.3 Abbreviations

DDoS: Distributed Denial of Services, ANN: Artificial Neural Network, BP: Back Propagation, DoS: Denial of Services, ML: Machine Learning, ABC: Artificial Bee Colony.

2 Literature Review

In 2015, Mahmod S. Mahmod, Zakaria A. Hamed Alnaish and Ismail Ahmed A. Alhadi have proposed intrusion detection system. In this paper, an efficient network-based IDS is proposed. It combines the ABC algorithm and neural network. The neural network is trained by using MLP. The ABC is used for optimizing the leakage in the weights and bias. The MLP neural network is used to detect the attack and non-attack traffic packets. The MLP is designed on the basis of the features in dataset. The dataset used in implementation of this algorithm is NSL-KDD 99. The final result of this experiment gives high accuracy in detection of attack. The proposed method has exact detected data about 87.5% and low error percentage, i.e. 0.124% [13].

In 2014, Quan Qian, Jing Cai and Rui Zhang have proposed an intrusion detection system. In proposed method, the system is used to defence the malicious activity in the network, both internal and external. And to reduce the falling of the neural network into a local optimum, it uses neural network. The slow convergence speed of the neural network algorithm can be solved. In this paper, the optimization of the neural network is done by using Artificial Bee Colony algorithm. They also use ABC algorithm for the optimization of thresholds and weights of Back Propagation Neural Network. The feature of mapping is increase in the BP (Back Propagation) neural network. It also creates the faster convergence, and capability of the BP neural network is strong learning. It can be also used to obtain the optimal solution for unidentified data sets by using BP neural network. Therefore, the intrusion detection using the neural network is a very efficient way [9].

In 2014, Mehdi Barati, Ramlan Mahmod, Azizol Abdullah, Norwati Mustapha and Nur Izura Udzir have proposed a method for the detection of Distributed denial of services. It uses a hybrid method by combining genetic algorithm and neural network. The genetic algorithm is applied for choosing of the features, and the neural network is used for the detection of the attack. The most efficient feature is selected by using the GA based on the wrapping method. The ANN training is done by using multilayer perceptron which provides an effective way of learning. In this method, there is an improvement in the detection of the attack. It increases the accuracy of the system, and the false alarm rate is low [14].

In 2014, N.Ch.S.N. Iyengar, Arindam Banerjee and Gopinath Ganapathy proposed a defence mechanism. This defence mechanism is used for the detection of DDoS attack in cloud computing. The defence mechanism uses fuzzy logic to detect the attack. This defence mechanism is made by the set of predefined rules. The set contains the rules which help to detect the malicious packets in the network. And this paper also contains the DDoS attack types and defences which are present to protect the details about them. The fuzzy logic is trained, and then the rules are defined. They have some dataset which is having normal and abnormal traffic pattern. On the basis of that they define the rules in the fuzzy logic defence mechanism [15].

In 2014, Seemab Latif and Javed Ashraf proposed a system which is used to detect the intrusion and DDoS attack. They show the machine learning techniques which are used for detection in software-defined network. In this paper, the various machine learning technique advantages and disadvantages are shown [16].

In 2014, Dr. S. Malliga and R. Aishwarya proposed an intrusion detection system which is used for the detection of DDoS attack. It is the defence mechanism for DDoS attack in cloud computing. It prevents the DDoS attack which is occurred by the attack the TCP by using SYN cookies. In this proposed method, the security is divided into two layers. The rules are defined to find whether the legitimate clients are requesting for connection or not. The first layer is made up of these rules. It also has the filtering mechanism. Then the sequence of the SYN packet is encrypted. Only the legitimate user can decrypt this packet. This is the steps performed in second layer. It also uses message authentication code (MAC) to give the packets. In this way, the user is authenticated [4].

In 2013, Ali Sharifi Boroujerdi and Saeed Ayat proposed a detection system. This system is used to detect the DDoS attack in the network. It uses the adaptive neuro-fuzzy classifier for the detection of DDoS attack. It also uses Marliboost which is an effective boosting technique. The proposed method increases the accuracy and reduces the false positive alarm. The experiment is done by using NSL-KDD dataset. By comparing with the other technique of machine learning used for the detection, the accuracy of detection is 96% in proposed method [17].

3 Proposed Method

In the proposed method, the hybrid approach is used. In this, Artificial Bee Colony algorithm and Artificial Neural Network are combined together to increase the accuracy in detection of DDoS attacks [18–23]. It is also used to increase convergence speed. It also includes the step of feature selection by using ABC algorithm. The selected feature is taken as an input of the ANN. The Artificial Bee Colony is used to select the weights and thresholds which are best for training of ANN. The ABC selects the best weights and thresholds to find the solution.

Artificial Bee Colony algorithm is a type of evolutionary algorithms. These algorithms are based on the biological evolution. The ABC algorithm mixes easily with other algorithms or different technologies because it is flexible. The ABC algorithm is capable to find the solution faster for the optimized problem [5].

In the proposed method, firstly ABC algorithm is performed. First initialize the parameters of the ABC and then find the nectar amount and choose the best food source on the basis of requirement. The output of the ABC algorithm is the initial weights and thresholds of the BP-ANN, here BP is Back Propagation.

The Back Propagation Artificial Neural Network (BP-ANN) is used for training for the detection of the DDoS attack. The Back Propagation network consists of three layers which are input, hidden and the output. The input is fed into the input layer. Many inputs can be fed into the layer at a time. These layers are joined with each other using links. The links contain weights. The hidden layer is hidden, and it takes the output of the input layer as input. And the output of the hidden layer is the input of the output layer. And the final output comes from the output layer.

The BP-ANN also has an additional step that when the final output is obtained it checks the error in the output, and if there is no error then this is taken as the final output otherwise adjust the weights and thresholds and again repeats all the steps. And this step is used to find the desired output.

The BP-ANN takes the optimized solution of ABC as an input. In other words, the output of the ABC becomes the input of the BP-ANN. The BP-ANN starts training of the neural network. After that, it checks whether it contains error or not if it contains the error, the weights and the thresholds are adjusted, and it repeats all the process again otherwise it becomes the final output. This is performed again and again until the final output is produced. And the neural network completes its training on the basis of it. In this way, the final output is produced (Fig. 2).

The proposed method algorithm is shown below:

1. Initialize the population of the food source and set the other parameter for ABC algorithm.
2. Initialize the thresholds and weights for the links of the BP-ANN.
3. Calculate the mean square error which represents fitness function. And it is calculated by using the following equation

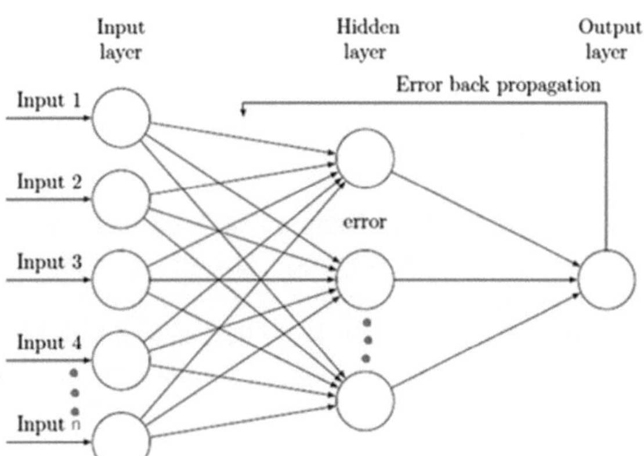

Fig. 2 Back propagation neural network architecture

$$\text{mse} = \frac{1}{2}\sum_{i=1}^{n} (t_i - o_i)^2, \tag{5}$$

where n indicates the total number of input instances. o_i represents the output which is expected of the ith value and t_i represents the output we get for the ith value. o_i

4. And then optimized the weights and thresholds for the BP-ANN.
5. Repeat step 3 and 4 until the maximum number of iteration is reached.
6. From the final output of the ABC algorithm, choose the best weights and a threshold whose mean square error is minimum.
7. Train the BP-ANN with the weights and thresholds.
8. Check the accuracy by finding the error which is calculated by the below equation

$$E^k = \sum_{k=1}^{n} (D_k - Y_k)^2, \tag{6}$$

where Y_k is the output which we get from the output layer. And k represents number of nodes which is used for output. D_k represents the expected output from the k node.

9. If the accuracy is not acceptable then adjust weights and thresholds by using the below equation

$$\Delta W_{ij} = \partial(D_k - Y_k)Y_k(1 - Y_k)Y_i \tag{7}$$

$$\Delta\theta_k = \partial(D_k - Y_k)Y_k(1 - Y_k). \tag{8}$$

In this way, we adjust weights between the hidden and output and then between the input and hidden layer.
Where ∂ represents the constant of proportionality between interval [0,1].

10. Repeat steps 7 to 9 until the accuracy is reached (Fig. 3).

4 Results

The expected results of this method are increasing the efficiency in detection of DDoS attack. In this approach, the speed of the detection can also increase and accuracy rate can also be high. It can produce low error rates. This approach can be able to reduce the occurrence of false alarm. It can improve the rate of detection of DDoS attack. It can have low computational complexity.

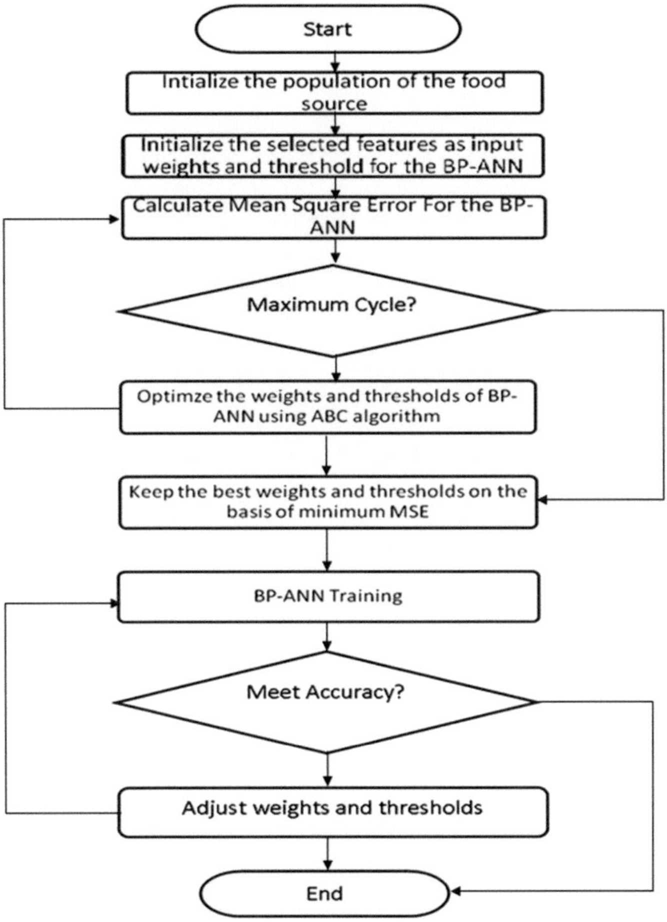

Fig. 3 Flow chart of the proposed model (ABC and BP-ANN)

Feature selection can increase the accuracy and speed up the process of detection. The Artificial Neural Networks are a significant technique to detect new attacks. Detection of DDoS attacks using proposed algorithm can take less time as compared to other approaches. Security loopholes can be reduced in cloud domain using this approach. A standard model representation would allow all the data that is to be mapped in an effective and easiest way. Once detection is successful, prevention method for the same domain can be applied.

5 Conclusion

The proposed method is a hybrid technique in which it uses the Artificial Bee Colony and Artificial Neural Network. The Artificial Bee Colony is the optimization technique which is used to find the optimized solution of the problem, and the Artificial Neural Network is trained in the proposed method with the Back Propagation technique. In this way, the algorithm is proposed in this paper to detect the DDoS attack.

The feature selection step can increase more speed and accuracy. The expected result of proposed method is to increase the efficiency and speed of the detection of the DDoS attack. It can also be used to increase the accuracy rate. The proposed hybrid technique can produce low false alarm rate. This approach can be able to increase the accuracy and reduce the error rates.

6 Future Enhancement

The future enhancement of this proposed method is the implementation of the algorithm, and it checks the accuracy and efficiency. It can also be implemented to detect more attacks like other malicious activity in the cloud computing.

References

1. Shikha, K.M., Sharma, R.: A review on DDoS attack and its detection and defence method. Int. J. Sci. Technol. Manag. (IJSTM), Landran, Punjab (2015)
2. Yu, S.: Distributed denial of services attack and defense. Springer (2014)
3. Vidya, V.: A review of DDoS attack in cloud computing. IOSR J. Comput. Eng. (IOSR-JCE) **16**(5), 32–35 (2014)
4. Aishwarya, R., Malliga, S.: Intrusion detection system-an efficient way to thwart against Dos/DDos attack in the cloud environment. In: IEEE International Conference on Recent Trends in Information Technology (2014)
5. Sahu, S.S., Pandey, M.: Distributed denial of service attacks: a review. Int. J. Mod. Educ. Comput. Sci. 65–71 (2014)
6. Mittal, A., Shrivastava, A.K., Manoria, M.: A review of DDOS attack and its countermeasures in TCP based networks. Int. J. Comput. Sci. Eng. Surv. (IJCSES) **2**(4) (2011)
7. Subaira, A.S., Anitha, P.: A survey: network intrusion detection system based on data mining techniques. Int. J. Comput. Sci. Mob. Comput. **2**(10), 145–153 (2013)
8. Kale, M., Choudhari, D.M.: DDOS attack detection based on an ensemble of neural classifier. IJCSNS Int. J. Comput. Sci. Netw. Secur. **14**(7) (2014)
9. Qian, Q., Cai, J., Zhang, R.: Intrusion detection based on neural networks and artificial bee. In: IEEE ICIS, Taiyun, China (2014)
10. Jaggi, R., Sangade, J.: Detecting and classifying attacks using artificial neural network. Int. J. Recent Innov. Trends Comput. Commun. **2**(5), 1136–1142 (2014)
11. Qiu, C., Shan, J.: Research on intrusion detection algorithm based on BP neural network. Int. J. Secur. Appl. **9**(4), 247–258 (2015)

12. Karaboga, D., Gorkemli, B., Ozturk, C., Karaboga, N.: A comprehensive survey: artificial bee colony (ABC) algorithm and applications. Springer (2014)
13. Mahmod, S.M., Alnaish, Z.A.H., Al-Hadi, I.A.A.: Hybrid intrusion detection system using artificial bee colony algorithm and multi-layer perceptron. Int. J. Comput. Sci. Inf. Secur (IJCSIS) **13**(2) (2015)
14. Abdullah, A., Barati, M., Mahmod, R., Udzir, N.I., Mustapha, N.: Distributed denial of services detection using hybrid machine learning technique. In: IEEE International Symposium on Biometrics and Security Technologies (ISBAST) (2014)
15. Iyengar, N.Ch.S.N., Banerjee, A., Ganapathy, G.: A fuzzy logic based defense mechanism against distributed denial of service attack in cloud computing environment. Int. J. Commun. Netw. Inf. Secur. (IJCNIS), **6**(3) (2014)
16. Latif, S., Ashraf, J.: Handling intrusion and DDoS attacks in software defined networks using machine learning techniques. In: IEEE National Software Engineering Conference (2014)
17. Boroujerdi, A.S., Ayat, S.: A robust ensemble of neuro-fuzzy classifiers for DDoS attack detection. In: IEEE International Conference on Computer Science and Network Technology (2013)
18. Kshirsagar, V.K., Tidke, S.M., Vishnu, S.: Intrusion detection system using genetic algorithm and data mining: an overview. Int. J. Comput. Sci. Inform. **1**(4) (2012)
19. Odac: A dynamic analog concurrently-processing adaptive chip, http://www.odec.ca/projects/2006/stag6m2/background.html
20. TEX: Drawing Back Propagation Neural Network, http://tex.stackexchange.com/questions/162326/drawing-back-propagation-neural-network
21. Itadvicex: Hacker attacks DDOS (distributed denial of service), http://itadvicex.com/hacker-attacks-ddos-distributed-denial-of-service
22. O'Connor, E., Smeaton, A.F., O'Connor, N.E., Regan, F.: A neural network approach to smarter sensor networks for water quality monitoring. Sensors **12**(4), 4605–4632 (2012)
23. Alfantookh, A.A.: DoS attacks intelligent detection using neural networks. J. King Saud Univ. Comput. Inf. Sci. **18**, 27–45 (2006)

Performance Evaluation of Neural Network Training Algorithms in Redirection Spam Detection

Kanchan Hans, Laxmi Ahuja and S.K. Muttoo

Abstract Redirection spam is a technique whereby a genuine search user is forced to pass through a series of redirections and finally land on a compromised Web site that may present an unwanted content or download malware on his machine. Such malicious redirections are a threat to Web security and must be detected. In this paper, we explore the Artificial Neural Network algorithms for modeling redirection spam detection by conducting the performance evaluation of the three most used training algorithms, namely scaled conjugate gradient (trainscg), Bayesian regularization (trainbr), and Levenberg–Marquardt (trainlm). Our results indicate that the network trained using Bayesian regularization outperformed the other two algorithms. To establish the success of our results, we have used two datasets comprising of 2200 URLs and 2000 URLs, respectively.

Keywords Redirection spam · Spam detection · Malicious redirection · Neural network · Information retrieval · Web security

1 Introduction

Redirection spam is a technique whereby a genuine search user is forced to pass through a series of redirections and finally land on a compromised Web site that may present an unwanted content or download malware on his machine. According to Benczur et al. [1], redirections are generally presented as a doorway page to the user, which on clicking triggers the redirection attack. Detecting such malicious

K. Hans (✉) · L. Ahuja
Amity Institute of Information Technology, Amity University, Noida, India
e-mail: khans@amity.edu

L. Ahuja
e-mail: lahuja@amity.edu

S.K. Muttoo
Department of Computer Science, University of Delhi, New Delhi, India
e-mail: skmuttoo@cs.du.ac.in

B.K. Panigrahi et al. (eds.), *Nature Inspired Computing*, Advances in Intelligent Systems and Computing 652, https://doi.org/10.1007/978-981-10-6747-1_20

redirections is important for the entire Web community. But, it is very difficult to detect malicious redirections because redirections are also made intentionally for benign purposes like load balancing. In this paper, we conduct the performance evaluation of various neural network training algorithms in modeling the redirection spam detection. We have used three most popular training algorithms and compared their results.

The paper is organized as follows: Sect. 2 discusses the research background and Sect. 3 outlines the algorithms considered for performance evaluation. Section 4 explains the experimental design. Section 5 demonstrates the experimental results. Section 6 presents the discussion on observations. Section 7 presents the conclusion.

2 Research Background

Spam is a big challenge for search engines [2], and its detection has been an area of research for both industry and academia. Many approaches have been used to detect malicious redirections. But still spammers continue to develop new techniques to induce spam onto Web. Spammers craft the redirection code and very intelligently hide it into scripts [3], taking benefit of the fact that search engines are not capable to detect code embedded into scripts [4].

Wu and Davison [5] conducted a preliminary study on Web redirections. Chellapilla and Maykov [6] gave a detailed taxonomy of JavaScript redirections and stated that JavaScript consists of some code obfuscation abilities which make the redirection detection a very difficult task. Bhargrava et al. [7] observed that redirections are being used in both spam as well as legitimate URLs which make spam detection a difficult task. It was observed in an experimental study [8] that more than 40% redirections were landing on adware pages. Leontiadis et al. [9] detected redirections in pharmacy by checking the referrer and tracking back to identify intermediaries. Zarras et al. [10] constructed the user activity tree and recorded the network traffic while traversing through the tree. This traffic information was used to detect redirections. Takata [11] used sequence of packets for referrer look up and conducted a host test for detecting redirections. In another work [12], authors used a C4.5 classifier to classify the recorded network traffic information in each browsing session to detect cases of search poisoning.

Kurt et al. [13] used a binary classifier to detect malicious URLs that lead to spam. Artificial Neural Network is considered as a very efficient technique for pattern classification [14]. Silva et al. [15] applied various models of Artificial Neural Networks in spam classification and showed that neural networks were able to perform better than decision trees and state vector machine (SVM). Silva et al. [16] used different neural-based algorithms in detecting spam content on Web.

3 Artificial Neural Networks

Artificial Neural Network is analogous to biological nervous system of human brain. The system acquires knowledge by the process called training or learning which depends on strength of connections between neurons called weights [17]. Every ANN model is characterized by its learning function, number of hidden layers, and the number of neurons in each layer. The algorithms of ANN used in our work are described as follows:

- **Levenberg–Marquardt (trainlm)**: This algorithm uses Levenberg–Marquardt method of optimization for updating the weights and bias. It is considered as a very fast algorithm, but its memory requirement is more as compared to other algorithms.
- **Bayesian regularization (trainbr)**: This method uses Bayesian regularization which is known to minimize the combination of squared errors and weights. It helps in generalizing the network and minimizing the chances of overfitting.
- **Scaled conjugate gradient (trainscg)**: This method is also the choice of many researchers because it requires no line search which is generally time taking and a complex procedure [18].

4 Experimental Design

We used a feed forward multilayer perceptron network [18] architecture representing six input features, a single hidden layer having 20 neurons and an output layer representing two classes, namely redirection spam URLs and legitimate URLs. We have applied three most popular algorithms, namely scaled conjugate gradient (trainscg), Bayesian regularization (trainbr), and Levenberg–Marquardt (trainlm) for performance evaluation in redirection spam detection. We employed Matlab neural network toolbox [19, 20] for conducting the experiments.

4.1 Features

We identified the six most relevant features that help in detection of malicious redirections and extracted them using our feature extraction program developed in Java. The features used in our experiment are number of different domains, http status code, number of suspicious functions in JavaScript, path length, use of meta refresh tag, and use of iframe tag for redirection.

Table 1 Details of datasets

Description	Dataset 1	Dataset 2
Total URLs	2200	2000
Redirection spam URLs	1037	872
Legitimate URLs	1163	1128
Number of training samples	1540	1400
Number of testing samples	330	300
Number of validation samples	330	300

4.2 Dataset Used

To evaluate the performance of different algorithms, we used two datasets of URLs collected from PhishTank [21]. A total of 2200 URLs were downloaded on June 3, 2015, for Dataset 1 and another 2000 URLs for the Dataset 2 were downloaded on August 1, 2015. The details of the datasets obtained are in Table 1.

We extracted the identified features using our feature extraction program developed in Java. We performed the semi-manual labeling of these datasets. We divided the dataset into training, testing, and validation data in the ratio 3:1:1.

5 Experimental Results of Different Algorithms

We conducted the experiment on two datasets, the results of which are demonstrated as follows. Tables 2 and 3 show the values of various performance parameters like root mean square error (RMSE), recall, precision, accuracy, and performance error obtained on applying the algorithms on Dataset 1 and Dataset 2, respectively.

Table 2 Results with Dataset 1

Algorithm	RMSE	Recall (%)	Precision (%)	Accuracy (%)	Performance error
Trainscg	0.0530	99.24	98.70	99.50	0.000756
Trainbr	**0.0522**	**99.57**	**99.91**	**99.70**	**0.000567**
Trainlm	0.0548	99.10	99.20	99.30	0.000880

Table 3 Results with Dataset 2

Algorithm	RMSE	Recall (%)	Precision (%)	Accuracy (%)	Performance error
Trainscg	0.0753	99.80	97.75	99.2	0.004638
Trainbr	**0.0736**	**99.91**	**98.75**	**99.3**	**0.004512**
Trainlm	0.1279	99.55	97.65	99.1	0.014663

Figures 1 and 2 show the confusion matrix obtained by applying the trainbr algorithm on Dataset 1 and Dataset 2, respectively. We derived the confusion matrix for all three algorithms in similar manner.

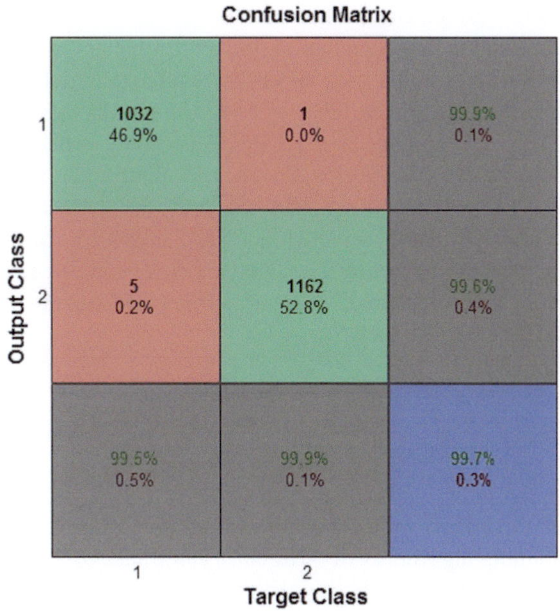

Fig. 1 Confusion matrix (Dataset 1)

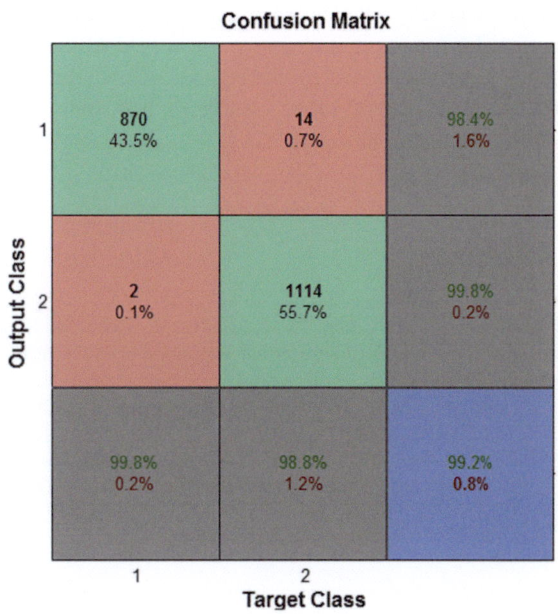

Fig. 2 Confusion matrix (Dataset 2)

6 Observations

On experimentation, it is observed that the best results are achieved when the data is trained with Bayesian regularization algorithm (trainbr). The algorithm trainbr gives the root mean square error (RMSE) value as 0.0522 for Dataset 1 and RMSE value as 0.0736 for Dataset 2, which is minimum when compared to RMSE of other two algorithms. On comparing the performance error, we observed that again the algorithm trained with Bayesian regularization showed the least error value when compared with the other two algorithms, though the difference is very small. In Dataset 1, trainbr achieved 99.7% accuracy, whereas trainscg achieved 99.5% and trainlm achieved 99.3% accuracy. Similarly, the results of trainbr outperformed in case of recall and precision for both the datasets under consideration. From the confusion matrix depicted in Figs. 1 and 2 for the trainbr algorithm, we observed that the number of misclassified cases is very less. However, trainbr algorithm takes long execution time, whereas trainscg and trainlm are relatively faster algorithms with good accuracy.

7 Conclusion and Future Work

In this paper, we have conducted the performance evaluation of three most popular training algorithms of Artificial Neural Networks in detection of redirection spam on Web. Our results showed that if execution time is not a constraint, then a neural network trained with the Bayesian regularization method produces the best result among the three algorithms under consideration. Our work also proved that neural network is very efficient in modeling the redirection spam detection and classification. In our future endeavors, we would explore the use of neural network with fuzzy logic so as to obtain the benefits of both the approaches. We may also explore the performance of other classifiers like state vector machine in modeling of redirection spam detection.

References

1. Benczur, A.A., Csalogany, K., Sarlos, T., Uher, M.: SpamRank–fully automatic link spam detection. In: First International Workshop on Adversarial Information Retrieval on the Web, pp. 25–38. Chiba, Japan (2006)
2. Henzinger, M.R., Motwani, R., Silverstein, C.: Challenges in web search engines. In: ACM SIGIR Forum, vol. 36, no. 2 (2003)
3. Zhou, J., Ding, Y.: An analysis of URLs generated from javascript code. In: 11th International Conference on Computer and Information Science (ICIS), Shanghai, China, pp. 688–693. IEEE/ACIS (2012)

4. Prieto, V.M., Alvarez, M., López-García, R., Cacheda, F.: Analysing the effectiveness of crawlers on the client-side hidden web. In: Trends in Practical Applications of Agents and Multiagent Systems, pp. 141–148. Springer, Berlin (2006)
5. Wu, B., Davison, B.D.: Cloaking and redirection: a preliminary study. In: First International Workshop on Adversarial Information Retrieval on the Web, pp. 7–16. Japan (2005)
6. Chellapilla, K., Maykov, A.: A taxonomy of JavaScript redirection spam. In: 3rd International Workshop on Adversarial Information Retrieval on the Web, ACM, Canada (2007)
7. Bhargrava, K., Brewer, D., Li, K.: A study of URL redirection indicating spam. In: Sixth Conference on Email and Anti-Spam, California (2009)
8. Hans, K., Ahuja, L., Muttoo, S.K.: Characterization and detection of redirection spam. In: International Conference on Computer and Communications, pp 325–331. Elsevier, India (2013)
9. Leontiadis, N., Moore, T., Christin, N.: Measuring and analyzing search-redirection attacks in the illicit online prescription drug trade. In: 20th USENIX Conference on Security, San Francisco, CA (2011)
10. Zarras, A., Kapravelos, A., Stringhini, G., Holz, T., Kruegel, C., Vigna, G.: The dark alleys of Madison avenue: understanding malicious advertisements. In Conference on Internet Measurement Conference, pp. 373–380. ACM (2014)
11. Takata, Y., Goto, S., Mori, T.: Analysis of redirection caused by web-based Malware. Asia-Pacific Adv. Netw. **32**(1), 53–62 (2011)
12. Lu, L., Perdisci, R., Lee, W.: SURF: detecting and measuring search poisoning. In: 18th Conference on Computer and Communications Security, pp. 467–476. ACM (2006)
13. Thomas, K., Grier, C., Ma, J., Paxson, V., Song, D.: Design and evaluation of a real-time URL spam filtering service. In: Symposium on Security and Privacy. IEEE (2011)
14. Haykin, S.: Neural Networks. A Comprehensive Foundation. Prentice Hall, India (2003)
15. Silva, R.M., Almeida, T.A., Yamakami, A.: Artificial neural networks for content-based web spam detection. In: 14th International Conference on Artificial Intelligence, pp. 1–7 (2012)
16. Silva, R.M., Almeida, T.A., Yamakami, A.: Towards web spam filtering with neural-based approaches. In: Advances in Artificial Intelligence–IBERAMIA, pp. 199–209. Springer, Berlin (2012)
17. Bishop, C.M.: Neural Networks for Pattern Recognition, 1st edn. Oxford Press, Oxford (1995)
18. Johansson, E.M., Dowla, F.U., Goodman, D.M.: Backpropagation learning for multilayer feed-forward neural networks using the conjugate gradient method. Int. J. Neural Syst. **2**, 291–301 (1991)
19. Demuth, H., Beale M.: Neural Network Toolbox for Use with MATLAB (1993)
20. Neural Network Toolbox—MATLAB—MathWorks. www.mathworks.com/producs/neural-network/
21. Open DNS. PhishTank. http://www.phishtank.com/developer_info.php

Novel Method for Predicting Academic Performance of Students by Using Modified Particle Swarm Optimization (PSO)

Satyajee Srivastava

Abstract There are numerous methods for extracting useful information from data. This paper describes a method for predicting performance of students. This method modifies the basic particle swarm optimization (PSO) algorithm using a set of rules. An attribute is selected from a set of performance attributes of the students. This attribute is used to frame rules. These rules determine the value of a modifying factor. This factor changes the mathematical expression of the function used in PSO for finding the solution. These rules are based on number of students in a particular shift. Other attributes are assigned different indexes. These indexes indicate number of students deviating from average value. The modified PSO algorithm takes the values of these indexes as inputs and generates a solution set which minimizes the values of indexes. A comparison of the solution set given by modified PSO and the solution set with unmodified PSO is presented. A brief outline of the modified PSO is given. The selection of the modifying factor and design of rules is described. These rules are based on the number of students in a particular shift. The different possible classes for the shift attribute are given. Thus, a decision strategy for predicting performance is described.

Keywords Modified PSO · Performance attributes · Rules, knowledge discovery, data mining

1 Introduction

Predicting the performance of the students involves analysis of various attributes. These attributes constitute a problem space. Predicting the performance based on these attributes requires an analysis of this space. Numerous techniques can be used to provide an insight into problem space. This paper used a modified PSO algorithm to devise a way for predicting performance. The performance of the students is moni-

S. Srivastava (✉)
School of Computer Science & Engineering, Galgotias University, Greater Noida, India
e-mail: drsatyajee@gmail.com

B.K. Panigrahi et al. (eds.), *Nature Inspired Computing*, Advances in Intelligent Systems and Computing 652, https://doi.org/10.1007/978-981-10-6747-1_21

tored using a set of attributes. The attributes used for the purpose in this paper are shift, subject, teacher, and class. The shift can be morning or evening shift. The shift attribute is chosen for devising a scheme and generating a modifying factor. This modifying factor changes the mathematical expression of the function that is being used in the modified PSO to find a solution for each of the attribute, an index is calculated. This index represents number of students who are below the average value of an attribute. The indexes used for the subject attribute represent number of students who are below the average score in that particular subject. Thus, this method has three indexes for subject, teacher, and class attribute. The modified PSO takes these three indexes as input and generates a solution where the equation representing a cost associated with each index has a minimum value. The shift attribute is used to find a modifying factor. This factor changes value of the function being used by modified PSO for finding the minimum value. A comparison of the solution of modified PSO and unmodified PSO is done. This can give essential information required for predicting performance. Whether the shift contribute to a change in performance or not? Which of the other attributes from subject, teacher, and class change significantly with a change in value of the index of shift attribute? These issues are analyzed in this paper. The prediction of performances as well as other parameter related to underperformance is described in [1]. The usage of various classifications technique is presented in [2]. The performance of the students can be improved using data mining techniques. A description of this technique is given in [3]. Various heuristic techniques can be employed in classification of data. Outline of this optimization technique is given in [4]. Predicting the performance of the students with the application of various techniques is discussed in [5]. This paper has a description of classification and clustering techniques. The importance of PSO for applications related to mining of data is given in [6]. The prediction of performance and behavior of the students are presented in [7]. Using different scenarios of the network for social usage has been illustrated in [8].

2 Description of Rules Used in Modified PSO

The various parameters are used for predicting the performance. These are given below:

A subject attribute indicates the particular subject. A teacher attribute indicates that particular faculty conducting the subject. A class attribute indicates the particular class to which a student belongs. Three other performance indices are used for indicating number of student who is below average score.

Performance index 1 indicates the number of students who are below average for subject attribute.
Performance index 2 indicates the number of students who are below average for class attribute.
Performance index 3 indicates the number of students who are below average for faculty attribute.

The shift attribute is being used for representing the number of students who are below average for attendance attribute. Three classes are used for representing these numbers of students that are below average value in a shift.

$Class_1$: This quantifier is used to depict the number of students who are below average for attendance attribute, and this quantifier will be applicable if 70% or more students in a shift of 100 students are below average.
$Class_2$: This quantifier will be used if less than 70% and greater than 60% students in a shift of 100 students are below average for attendance attribute.
$Class_3$: This quantifier will be used if less than 60% and greater than 40% students in a shift of 100 students are below average for attendance attribute.

3 Modified PSO Algorithm Based on Rules

Step1 Declare the parameters used in the algorithm number of data points, total index value, coefficient ad_i, bd_i, cd_i, timax, and timin values.

Step2 Define the following classes I. $Class_1$

II. $Class_2$
III. $Class_3$

Step3 Input the number of students who are below average in attendance attribute.

Step4 Input the values of the following parameters used for framing rules:
M_1 = Number of students who are below average in attendance and are in $Class_1$.
M_2 = Number of students who are below average in attendance and are in $Class_2$.
M_3 = Number of students who are below average in attendance and are in $Class_3$.

Step5 Input the total number of students (T_1) who are below average in attendance.
The following rules are devised:
Rule1: If ($T_1 >= M_1$), then calculate value of the modifying factor from $Class_1$.
Rule2: If ($T_1 < M_1$) and ($T_1 >= M_2$), then calculate value of the modifying factor from $Class_2$.
Rule3: If ($T_1 < M_2$) and ($T_1 >= M_3$), then calculate the value of modifying factor from $Class_3$.

Step6 Convert coefficients ad_i, bd_i, and cd_i from vector into matrix form.

Step7 Initialize vector from values of the parameters. N = number of students

Initial value of factor = 100
Q_1, Q_2, w_{max}, w_{min}
It_{max} = maximum number of iteration

Step8 Initialize parameters:

$\text{Vector}_{1\max}$ = matrix using $\text{ti}_{\max}$ $\text{Vector}_{1\min}$ = matrix using $\text{ti}_{\min}$ $\text{Vector}_{2\max} = 0.5 \times \text{Vector}_{1\max}$ $\text{Vector}_{2\min} = -\text{Vector}_{2\max}$

Step9 It = 1 to It_max

Weight_function = Weight_max − (Weight_max − Weight_min) × It / It_max

Step10 Calculate initial position of agents

$\text{Vector}_1 = \text{Vector}_{1\min} + (\text{Vector}_{1\max} - \text{Vector}_{1\min}) \times Y$. Y = random number;

Step11 Calculate initial velocity of agents $\text{Vector}_1 = \text{Vector}_{2\min} + (\text{Vector}_{2\max} - \text{Vector}_{2\min}) \times Y$.

Step12 Specify the function to be minimized main function = $\text{Term}_1 + \text{Term}_2$

$\text{Term}_1 = \sum (a_i + b_i \times \text{Vector1} + c_i \times \text{Vector1}^2)$ $\text{Term}_2 = \text{Factor}_1 \times (T_1 - \sum \text{Vector1})^2$ Factor1 = Initial value × Modified factor

Step13 Find the initial best value for position. P_1 is found from Vector1

Find Fpbest from main function Fgbest = minimum of fpbest Index = index of minimum value $P_2 = P_1$ (index)

Step14 Store the historic value of the best position: Gbest = gbest, Fgbest = fgbest

Step15 Initialize parameter for iteration

Error_max
Max_error
Iteration = 1

Step16 $\text{Vector}_2 = \text{Term}_3 + \text{Term}_4 + \text{Term}_5$

Term_3= Weight_function × $(N - 1) \times \text{Vector}_2$ $\text{Term}_4 = Q_1 \times$ random number $\times (P_1 - \text{Vector}_1)$ $\text{Term}_5 = Q_2 \times$ random number $\times P_2 - \text{Vector}_1$

Step17 Find global best position of all the agent Fgbest_1 = fgbest

Fgbest = min of fpbest
Index = index of this min value $P_2 = P_1$ (index)

Step18 Calculate max error

Maxerr = max (absolute value (ti − $\sum$ gbest) absolute value (fgbest − fgbest − 1))
Gbest = gbest Fgbest(k) = fgbest

}
End of while statements

Step19 Display the result value of k, max err, P_2

In this paper, the following parameters have been taken.
T = Total number of student in a class

$$\text{Index}_i = aN_i^2 + bN_i + C_i$$

AAV grade indicates above average score in an attribute, and BAV grade indicates below average score.

N_1 indicates number of students having BAV grade in the subject attribute.
N_2 indicates the number students having BAV grade in the teacher attribute.
N_3 indicates the number of students having BAV grade in the class attribute.

$$\text{Index}_1 = a_1N_1^2 + b1N_1 + c_1$$
$$\text{Index}_2 = a_2N_2^2 + b1N_2 + c_2$$
$$\text{Index}_3 = a_3N_3^2 + b3N_3 + c_3$$

$$\text{Total index cost} = \text{Index}_1 + \text{Index}_2 + \text{Index}_3$$

4 Result

The proposed method is being used for a data set of 48 students is given in [9]. From the data set of 48 students, two grades are assigned to each attribute—AAV grade indicates above average score in an attribute, and BAV grade indicates below average score.

Number of students having BAV grade in attendance = 12

$$N_1 = 20, \qquad N_2 = 15 + 22 + 10 = 47, \qquad N_3 = 17$$

AAV represents above average status of the student. BAV represents below average status of the student.

In the Table 1 given above, the attribute attendance has AAV grade if in the data set [9] attendance is good or average. The attribute attendance has BAV grade if attendance is poor.

The attribute subject has AAV grade if end semester marks in data set [9] have first or second class. The attribute subject has BAV grade if end semester marks are third or fail.

The attribute class has AAV grade if in the data set [9] class test grade is good or average. The attribute class has BAV grade if class test grade is poor.

For assigning grade to teacher attribute, the following colons from data set [9] are used:

Table 1 Input data for predicting (till 48 as table) performance of the students

Input data	Grade for an attribute			
S. No.	Subject	Attendance	Teacher	Class
1	AAV	AAV	AAV	AAV
2	AAV	AAV	AAV	AAV
3	AAV	AAV	BAV	AAV
4	AAV	AAV	AAV	AAV
5	AAV	AAV	AAV	AAV
6	AAV	AAV	AAV	BAV
7	AAV	BAV	AAV	BAV
8	AAV	AAV	BAV	AAV
9	BAV	BAV	BAV	BAV
10	AAV	AAV	AAV	AAV

Assignment, seminar, and laboratory work. If any two of these colons have poor and no grade, then teacher attribute is assigned BAV. Otherwise, the teacher attribute is assigned AAV grade

5 Illustration and Discussion

The propose method is being used for a data set of 48 students [9]. The data showing grades of 48 students which are given in Table 1. The value of various parameter used in the modified PSO is given below.

Total index = 84			
Value of a_i coefficients	$a_1 = 60$	$a_2 = 31$	$a_3 = 40$
Value of b_i coefficients	$b_1 = 06$	$b_2 = 08$	$b_3 = 08$
Value of c_i coefficients	$c_1 = 01$	$c_2 = 02$	$c_3 = 01$

For selecting the maximum value of parameter N_1, N_2, and N_3, the data for 48 students is being used and the values used are given below.

$$N_1\text{max} = 20, \qquad N_2\text{max} = 47, \qquad N_3\text{max} = 17$$

The minimum value for N_1, N_2, and N_3 is selected which is less than N_1 max.

The total index cost for the modified PSO algorithm is 5391.821. In the modified PSO algorithm, the attendance attribute is used. The solution generated by modified PSO is given below (Table 2).

The solution generated by unmodified PSO is given below (Table 3).

Table 2 Output of modified PSO

Modified PSO	Index and output				
S. No.	Number of students having BAV grade in attendance	N_1	N_2	N_3	Total index cost
1	12	20	44.49	17	5391.821
2	13	20	45.30	17	5542.955
3	15	20	45.96	17	5669.641
4	17	20	45.96	17	5669.641
5	20	20	45.96	17	5669.641

Table 3 Output of unmodified PSO

Unmodified PSO	Index and output			
S. No.	N_1	N_2	N_3	Total index cost
1	20	46.03	17	5683.532

6 Conclusion

These results indicate that controlling the attendance attribute has profound impact on the performance of the students. The total index cost is reduced if less number of students is having BAV grade in attendance. Also, the value of N_2 is less than the value obtained by unmodified PSO. Thus, the proposed algorithm can effectively use for predicting the performance of the students.

References

1. Pandey, U.K., Pal, S.: Data mining: a prediction of performer or underperformer using classification. Int. J. Comput. Sci. Inform. Technol. **2**(2), 686–690 (2011)
2. Ahmed, A.B.E.D., Elaraby, I.S., Data mining: a prediction for student's performance using classification method. World J. Comput. Appl. Technol. **2**(2), 43–47 (2014)
3. Tair, M.M.A., El-Halees, A.M.: Mining educational data to improve student's performance: a case study. Int. J Inform. Commun. Technol. Res. **2**(2) (2012)
4. Lee, K.Y., El-Sharkawi, M.A.: Modern Heuristic Optimization Technique, Theory and Application to Power System. IEEE press, Willey-Interscience publication. (4), pp. 71–86
5. Sembiring, S., Zarlis, M., Hartama, D., Ramliana, S., Wani, E.: Prediction of students academic performance by an application of data mining technique. In: International Conference on management and artificial intelligence, IPDER, vol. 6, IACSIT Press, Bali, Indonesia (2011)
6. Sousa, T., Nevas, A., Silva, A., Swarm optimisation as a new Tool for data Mining. In: Proceeding of the International Parallel and Distributed Processing Symposium (IPDPS03). IEEE Computer Society
7. Ali, M.M.: Role of Data Mining in Education Sector. Int. J. Comput. Sci. Mob. Comput. IJCSMC **2**(4), 374–383 (2013) (ISSN 2320-088X)

8. Oskouei, R.J.: Analysing Different Aspect of Social Network Usage on Students Behaviors and Academic Performance, IEEE (2010)
9. Yadav, S.K., Bhardwaj, B., Pal, S.: Data mining applications: a comparative study for predicting student's performance. Int. J. Innov. Technol. Creative Eng. **1**(12) (2012) (ISSN: 2045-711)

Medical Diagnosing of Canine Diseases Using Genetic Programming and Neural Networks

Cosmena Mahapatra

Abstract Neural networks and genetic programming have long since helped humans in diagnoses and treatment of human diseases. However, not much has been done for man's best friend—the canine's. This paper thus aims to explore and find the possibility of building software which is based on the use of neural network and Cartesian genetic programming to diagnose the various diseases of canine population. During the study, its outcomes were also compared and contrasted with the results of a neural network combined with simple genetic programming-based system, the results of which confirmed the high success rate of neural network training when it is modified with Cartesian genetic programming for the use of diagnosis of various categories of canine diseases.

Keywords Neural networks · Genetic programming · MLP · Trainbr · CGP · ANN · Perceptron · MATLAB · Software · GA · MLPGA

1 Introduction to Neural Networks

Neural networks is a field of computer science that has from time to time helped humans in many fields such as network security, gaming, banking, stock marketing. It when clubbed with genetic programming has given an edge to the computing world which no other technique has ever done; it has helped the systems to become more human.

Neural networks also known as artificial neural networks were first conceptualized by McCulloch, a neuroscientist Walter Pitts, a mathematician in 1943. They introduced to the world a concept of a single-cell neuron which could take input and provide output. Further research pushed this concept single-layered perception whose success ultimately led to the concept of multilayered perception (MLP) which is a feed-forward neural network that maps the set of inputs onto an

C. Mahapatra (✉)
MCA Department, VSIT, VIPS, Pitampura, New Delhi, India
e-mail: cosmenamahapatra1@gmail.com

B.K. Panigrahi et al. (eds.), *Nature Inspired Computing*, Advances in Intelligent Systems and Computing 652, https://doi.org/10.1007/978-981-10-6747-1_22

Fig. 1 Multilayered perceptron structure

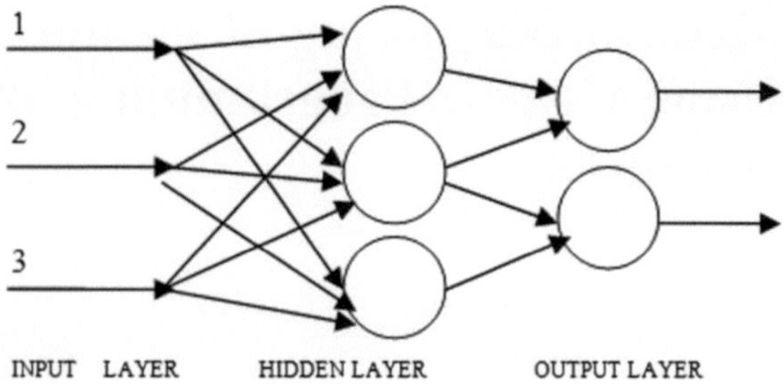

appropriate set of data outputs decided through learning. A feed-forward neural network is a network of neurons connected together as a directed graph such as Fig. 1 [1].

MLP has a three-layered structure. First layer comprises of the input layer, which is responsible for feeding the input into the perceptron, second layer is the hidden layer which is responsible for implementing machine learning, and third layer is the output layer which gives the desired result. Machine learning is implemented in the third layer, by first training the machine, by feeding it dataset consisting of inputs and their expected outputs. For the same, many training algorithms have been devised such as trainlm, trainbr, or traincfg [2] and once the training gets completed successfully, the resulting MLP network is put into learning by using learning algorithms such as learngdm, etc., which then gives the desired output when fed a correct set of inputs.

2 Genetic Algorithm

2.1 Introduction to Genetic Programming

Genetic algorithm or GA where introduced as part of neural network studies in 1960 generally compliments the success of MLP network. This method works by solving the constrained and unconstrained optimization problems of natural selection. At each step, GA selects individual data values from current population to generate children values. Thus over successive populations, we are able to get optimized results. The GA uses three categories of rules for optimized results [3]; these are the following:

1. Selection Rule: Select the parent values that will generate the future children.
2. Crossover Rule: This combines two parent values to generate children for next generation.
3. Mutation Rule: This GA applies random changes to current parent values to generate optimized children values.

2.2 The Algorithm

A. Initialize randomly population (k)
B. Measure the robustness of the population (k)
C. Repeat

    i. Parents are selected from population (k)
    ii. Carry out crossover on K parent population thus creating population ($k + 1$)
    iii. Complete mutation of population ($k + 1$)
    iv. Measure fitness of population ($k + 1$)

D. until the best individual is found

Though the GA has been used and verified to generate optimized solution by them, this study involves the GA to finalize and give an optimized result from the output of MLP network.

2.3 GA-MLP Algorithm

```
% STEP 1: INITIALIZE THE NEURAL NETWORK PROBLEM %
% STEP 2: Read inputs for the neural net
% STEP 3: Identify the targets for the neural net
% STEP 4: Fix the number of neurons in hidden layer
% STEP 5: create a neural network feedforward network
% STEP 6: Configure & create function to the MSE_TEST for
calculating MSE.
% STEP 7: Fix the setting of the Genetic Algorithms tolerance
to minimum for change in fitness function before termination
to 1e-8.
% STEP 8: Running the genetic algorithm with desired options
for optimized results.
```

The above genetic algorithm will take input as the weights and basis of hidden layer of MLP feed-forward networks and thus give optimized result.

2.4 Cartesian Genetic Programming Technique

Cartesian genetic programming is a modified genetic programming technique invented by Julian Miller in the year 1999. The technique uses graph structure for representation of a computer program. In this graph, “Genes” (integer values) are used to determine the functions in the graph, their internal connections to nodes and inputs and location of all outputs [4]. In CGP, a Cartesian program is given by CP which is a set of {T, m_i, m_o, m_n, Fn, m_f, m_r, m_c, l}, where T is genotype, m_i represents a set of program inputs, m_n represents node input and functions, m_o represents program output conditions, m_f is function of the nodes and belongs to set Fn, the total number of nodes in a given column or row is given by m_r, m_c, and lastly "l" is responsible for deciding the number of cells that may connect their outputs to current columns. The algorithm for CGP may be summarized as [5]:

a. Subject to constraints, generate initial population.
b. Fitness of genotype of population must be evaluated.
c. New population is to be formed by promoting the fittest genotype.
d. Mutated version of the fittest now must be used to fill the renaming places in the population.
e. Repeat step b–d till abort condition reached, i.e., optimum solution reached.

In the above algorithm, constraints are the conditions that only those nodes which are in separate columns may be allowed to connect with each other.

3 Literature Review

Madhuna R., Shilpa Mehta, "Hybridization of Neural Network Using Genetic Algorithm for Heart Disease Detection," IJAIEM, Vol. 3, January 2014, ISSN: 2319–4847.

This paper uses genetic programming with neural networks to validate hybrid learning for prediction of heart diseases. The research successfully implemented simple learning pattern with neural networks and genetic programming.

Maryam Mahsal Khan a, Arbab Masood Ahmad etl, "Fast Learning Neural Networks using Cartesian genetic programming," Elsevier, Neurocomputing (2013), pp. 274–289.

In this paper, a revolutionary neural network-based language is proposed in which the authors make use of feed-forward networks with recurrent networks. This method was originally inspired by Cartesian genetic programming technique. The said algorithm was successfully tested on the bench work (pole balancing) for diagnosis of breast cancer in women.

Arpit Bhardwaj, Aruna Tiwari, "Performance Improvement in Genetic Programming using Modified Crossover and Node Mutation," GECCO' 13, ACM DL, pp. 1721–1722, ISBN: 978-1-4503-1964-5.

This paper proposes a modified plus point mutation crossover in GP so that it reduces the problem faced by many GA learning systems, wherein the performance of the system falls even though the tree size of the best solution increases substantially. The research gave excellent results.

David J. Montana, Lawrence Davis Davis, "Training Feedforward Neural Networks Using Genetic Algorithms," ACM DL, IJCAI'89, pp. 762–767.

This study was one of the earliest researches done on training of a feed-forward network using genetic programming. It introduced the idea of joining these two very powerful techniques to find the values which are very closer to global optimum solution. The experiment successfully illustrated the improvement that GA gave on feed-forward network, and furthermore it helped the GA to evolve ever more.

4 Data Files Used

The input data of this study has been finalized after deep study of dog's diseases. The data comprises of disease, and symptoms. A snapshot of the disease database is shown in Fig. 2.

The training database has been formed by referring to veterinary books [6] and is composed of 11 columns in which columns 1–2 are for disease name and category to which it belongs such as skin problem, immune disease, etc [7–13]. Columns 3–9 are used for listing out the various symptoms of the canine disease. Columns 10–11 are used for storing possible treatment and reasons behind the disease.

Disease	Category	Symptom 1	Symptom 2	Symptom 3	Symptom 4
Lyme	Parasetic	Leg Lamness	Kidney Failure	Vomiting	Diarrhea
Demodectic	Skin	Skin lesions	genetic disorders	Hairloss	redness of skin
Urolithiasis	Urology	blood in urine	incontinance	reduced appetite	lack of energy
Depression	pychatric	Not eating	hiding	sleeping	Sadness
Canine distemper	viral	eye discharge	nose discharge	high fever	lethargy
gingivitis	Dental	Bleeding Gums	Plaque	bad breath	sore mouth
Degenerative Myelopathy	immune disease	weak hind legs	paralysis	damaged toe nails in hind legs	hip displasia
Pseudorabies	Viral	seizures	intense itching	jaw paralysis	pharyngeal paralysis
Rabies	Viral	Aggression	hypensenstive	paralysis at neck and jaw	foaming at mouth

Fig. 2 Snapshot of database used for training

5 Result of the Study

The CGP algorithm was successfully used in training the neural network for a sample data size of 120 inputs in MATLAB software. Additionally, algorithm generated an optimized result by minimizing the mean squared error (MSE). The results of the study were compared with the outputs generated when the neural network was combined with simple GA, and it was found that ANN with CGP gave faster and more accurate results as compared to ANN with GA (Table 1).

The outputs of the study are in Fig. 3, and the result of the MLP network can further be verified by generating R value which is in Fig. 4.

Furthermore in Fig. 4, "R" refers to regression value of the MLP network. If $R = 1$, the regression of the MLP network is said to be 100%, i.e., the network is able to generate 100% true result as per the training data provided during training resulting in successful learning. The above was only possible due to the boost provided by CGP in giving optimized results.

Table 1 Results of simulation run in MATLAB for MLP with CGP and GA respectively

Algorithm used with MLP	Elapsed time (s)	Best validation performance	Training stopped at Epoch (Max = 500)	Regression All (R = ?)
CGP	219.13	7.3489 at 500 Epochs	500	1
GA	176.37	0.016465 at 131 Epoch	146	0.90

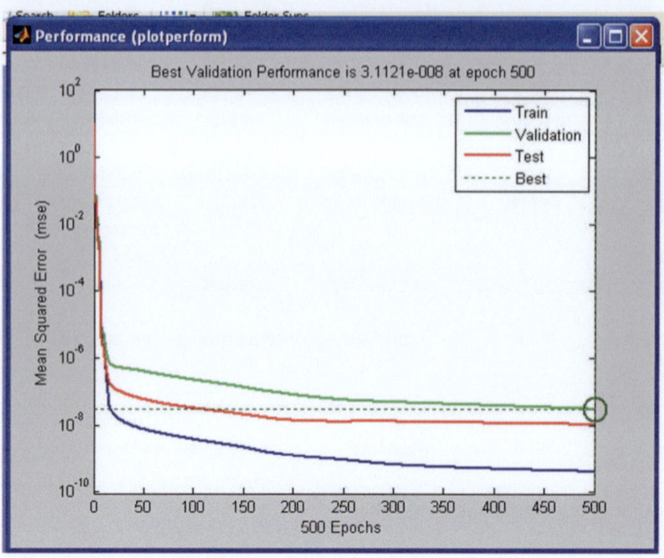

Fig. 3 Snapshot of optimized MSE with CGP

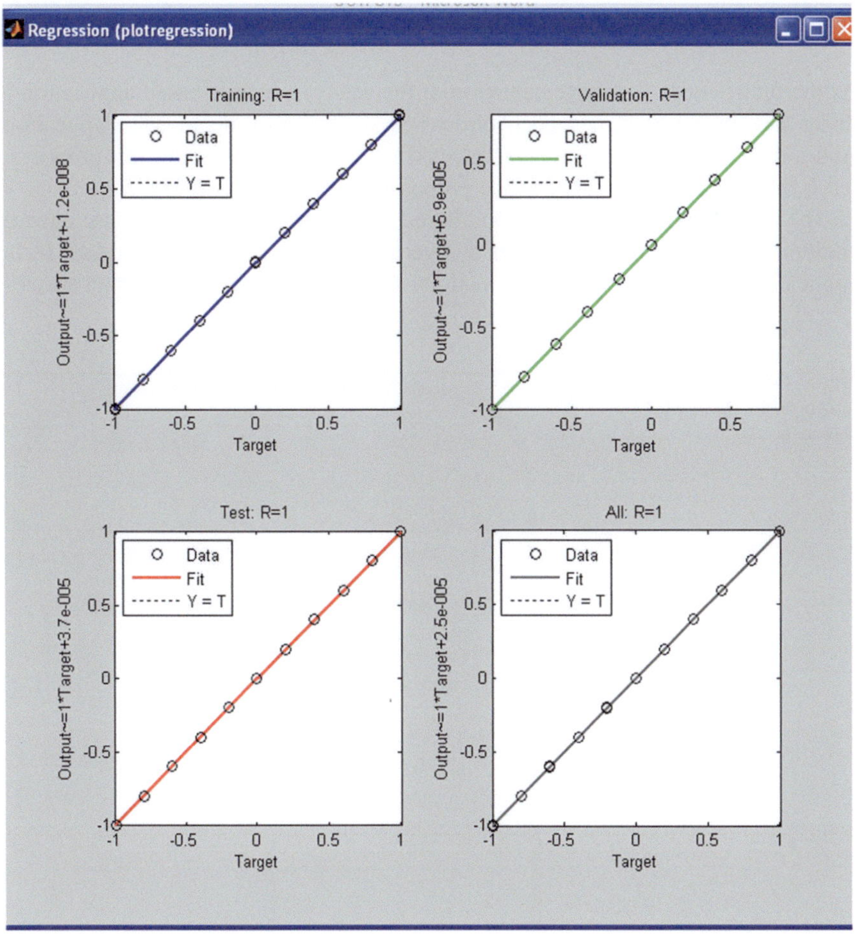

Fig. 4 Snapshot of *R* optimized

6 Conclusion

The result of the study confirmed that global optimum results were possible for medical diagnosing of canine diseases using CGP or Cartesian genetic programming. It also proved that faster results are generated when the neural network is implemented with Cartesian genetic programming rather than simple genetic algorithm.

7 Future Scope

As the future scope for implementation of this study, a mobile-based application is under development. It has been christened as MLPGA diagnostic application. Android operating system has been selected as the platform to enable this product to reach the masses. A snapshot of the proposed App is shown in Fig. 5.

The application shall have a cloud-based architecture with the database open to addition of diseases by public after due verification by the same at our end. If the application is found to be popular, modules may be added for other animal species.

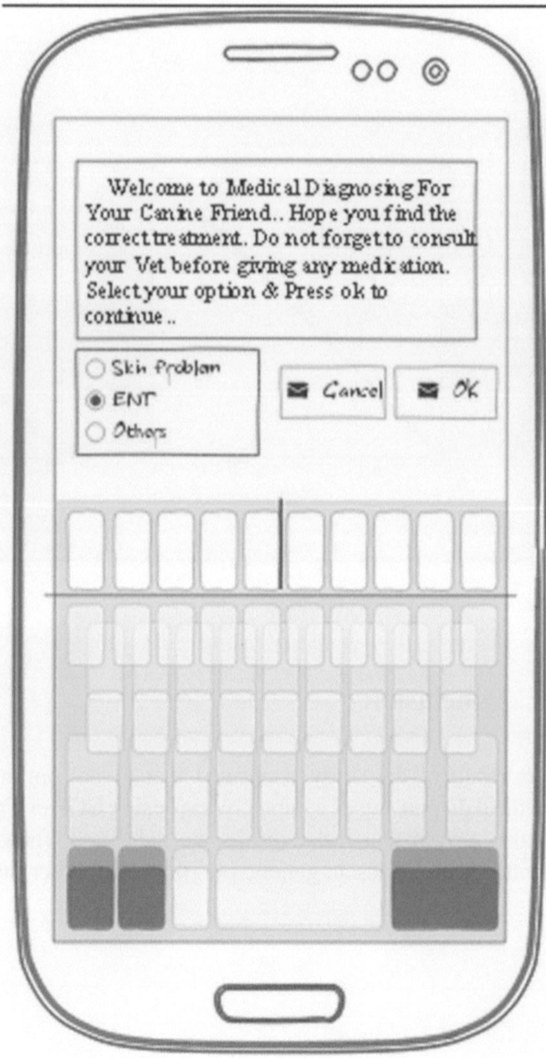

Fig. 5 Snapshot of front screen of proposed MLPGA diagnostic App

References

1. Yadav, N., et al.: An Introduction to Neural Network Methods for Differential Equations. Springer Briefs in Computational Intelligence. doi:10.1007/978-94-017-9816-7_2
2. Yao, X.: Evolving artificial neural networks. In: Proceedings of IEEE, vol. 87, no. 9, pp. 1423–1447 (1999)
3. Mitchell, M.: An introduction to genetic algorithm. In: A Bradford Book. The MIT Press, London, Fifth Printing (1999)
4. Miller, J.F. (ed.): Cartesian Genetic Programming, Natural Computing Series. doi:10.1007/978-3-642-17310-3 2, © Springer, Berlin (2011)
5. Kincaid, C.W.: Numerical Analysis Mathematics of Scientific Computing, 3rd edn. American Mathematical Society, Providence (2010)
6. Tilley, L.P., Smith, F.W.K. Jr.: Blackwell's Five-Minute Veterinary Consult: Canine and Feline, Hardcover, 28 Oct 2011
7. Tsoulos, I.G., Gavrilis, D., Glavas, E.: Solving differential equations with constructed neural networks. Neurocomputing **72**, 2385–2391 (2009)
8. Kaushik, D., Singh, U., Singhal, P., Singh, V.: Medical image segmentation using genetic algorithm. Int. J. Comput. Appl. **81**(18), 10–15 (2013)
9. Masmoudi, N.K., Rekik, C., Djemel, M., Derbel, N.: Two coupled neural network based solution of the Hamilton-Jacobi-Bellman equation. Appl. Soft Comput. **11**, 2946–2963 (2011)
10. Kumar, M., Yadav, N.: Multilayer perceptrons and radial basis function neural network methods for the solution of differential equations: a survey. Comput. Math. Appl. **62**, 3796–3811 (2011)
11. Kumar, M., Yadav, N.: Buckling analysis of a beam column using multilayer perceptron neural network technique. J. Franklin Inst. **350**(10), 3188–3204 (2013)
12. Dukkipati, R.V.: Applied Numerical Methods Using MATLAB. New Age International Publisher, New Delhi (2011)
13. Kumar, M., Yadav, N., Deep, K.: Artificial neural network technique for solution of nonlinear elliptic boundary value problems. In: Proceedings of Fourth International Conference on Soft Computing for Problem Solving, Advances in Intelligent Systems and Computing, vol. 335, pp. 113–121 (2015)

A Comparative Study on Decision-Making Capability Between Human and Artificial Intelligence

Soham Banerjee, Pradeep Kumar Singh and Jaya Bajpai

Abstract The power of reasoning and the ability to make better decisions has been the best gift God has bestowed upon mankind. When we developed artificial intelligence (AI) systems with the goal to think and act rationally, the focus has always been as to how the AI system can replicate the natural decision-making process as compared to humans. However, in adverse situations, the efficiency of making a decision is affected by many factors such as emotional impact which do not affect an AI system. In this paper, we will identify and draw out the factors that affect human decision making and investigate the same on an AI chatbot. Later, a comparative analysis is done to draw out where AI or the human mind excels with those factors.

Keywords Decision making · Chatbot · Reasoning · Artificial intelligence · Emotional impact

1 Introduction

Emotions behave like a cover for the human nature. We generally express our decisions of everyday life based on emotions and consequences of certain actions [1]. Our decisions might result in adapting in a new environment or perform some task. Machines on the other hand analyze a set of rules to draw a particular conclusion. These rules can be programmed, and using a procedural approach we can develop small programs that might reflect a machine, intelligent [2]. But then, there

S. Banerjee (✉) · P.K. Singh · J. Bajpai
Department of Computer Science & Engineering, Amity School of Engineering & Technology, Amity University Uttar Pradesh, Noida, India
e-mail: official.soham@gmail.com

P.K. Singh
e-mail: pksingh16@amity.edu

J. Bajpai
e-mail: er.jayabajpai@gmail.com

B.K. Panigrahi et al. (eds.), *Nature Inspired Computing*, Advances in Intelligent Systems and Computing 652, https://doi.org/10.1007/978-981-10-6747-1_23

are moments when we humans cannot make decisions properly while experiencing negative emotions or when the capacity to analyze facts and reason diminishes due to unforeseen events like an accident or when stress succumbs us. It has been identified that an AI system has the most important role of assisting its human counterpart to tackle the situation. The question arises whether at some point the AI system can think just like a normal human being under similar conditions.

2 Background Study

In order to do the background study, we have followed the work done by Singh et al. [3]. It is important to know how the human mind works whenever we experience some reaction from our environment. The human brain is a complex structure which stimulates various signals that help us to make decisions. Human mind captures data from natural sensors like eyes, ears, skin, smell. This data is a pattern which is compiled and is properly evaluated by individual processing units known as neurons. These neurons based on the sensor data generate some output in the form a stimulating signal which if surpasses the minimum critical threshold of compiled data generates a decision [4]. But every decision is based on how and in which region the brain is processing the data. For example, some scientists have concluded that decision which relies on visual information is processed in the parietal lobe. Therefore, decision somewhat originates based on a rapid complex probability-based calculation by neurons [5].

In the case of machines, decision making depends on classifying data using various classifiers in the case of statistical supervised learning. In the scenario where no data is available, the machine uses unsupervised learning techniques to gain knowledge. The most important factor to realize over here is that during the learning process, a machine can never imitate the thinking process of a human being. Hence, different soft computing or traditional hard computing approaches are there to help the machines make decisions.

Consider a simple scenario where two players are playing a game of chess. One of the participants is a human being, while the other one is an AI agent. The question arises as to how the two players play the game. It is critical to understand that both the participants are aware of the rules of the game. So how will the artificial agent play? Based on a set of rules, it will generate a state due to which it will move a piece of the chessboard. Hence, the agent can generate multiple states for the same move and such a collection of states forms a state space. The fundamental approach for an agent is determining the optimal move using local or guided search algorithms.

This procedure is somewhat analogous to how a human mind will work. Generally, we have better cognitive skills [1] than machines due to which our intelligence insight is stronger than machines. The human participant will also generate a state space but with a probability that the state space generated by a human mind might be of better quality as compared to an agent. However, a point will arise where the agent will perform better due to iterative learning of the human participant's move.

2.1 *Experience*

In this section, we will try to understand how experience plays an important role in the decision-making process. The important question is as to how an experience can affect a decision.

Experience is a paramount parameter of importance. It forms the backbone of learning and is responsible for determining the correctness of any decisions. Imagine the case of a newborn child. Initially, it responds to its own environment using hand actions and observes the actions of its parents and mimics it. As the child grows, social and perceived experience helps in the adaption of new skills (supervised or unsupervised learning) based on experience. For example, the child learns to babble and later improve it to speaking its mother tongue.

In the case of a machine, artificial consciousness adopts machine learning techniques to learn objects of the real world [6]. In case of supervised learning, a prior data set is provided based on which the machine is made to learn the ability to classify and learn objects (gain experience). In case of unsupervised learning where no prior information is available, the machine may learn by committing errors (adaptive experience) [7]. Neuroscience has decrypted the mysteries as to how the learning process helps to develop experience.

2.2 *Learning*

In this section, we will uncover the various types of learning and try to understand the impact of learning in decision-making process.

Learning has many standard definitions based on different domains. Some say learning is a natural process to comprehend objects, while some may coin it as a technique to identify and understand and gain experience from something new. Perhaps the simplest definition that can be derived is that learning is the process of identifying, remembering, and comprehending anything. Nature has put forward countless examples of how learning is intangible. From animals to human beings, everyone learns to adapt and exist in the environment. For example, a newborn child learns to speak, crawl, and then walk. Learning is never rapid, and it is the experience that forms the knowledge that we store in our brains. Learning often takes place in stages rather than being continuous.

In the case of machines, learning can be implemented by presenting data to the system and train it just like a child. Machines can gain experience by the help of programs that accumulate data and generate patterns. Whenever new data is presented, and then based on the generated patterns, it either classifies the data or creates a new pattern to remember. This is somewhat analogous to how the neurons store information inside our brain [5]. Different kinds of learning are adopted by reasoning systems based on the kind of working environment they operate in. Also, it is important to understand that we human often deal with complex problems that combine subproblems from two or more different domains.

We come across three types of learning which can be adopted by any system. The first type is known as supervised learning where a program is provided with training data that helps it to generate and learn patterns. Whenever such systems are introduced with new data, it will either classify the data according to one of the memorized patterns or generate a new class for the new data. Typically, the training data serves the role of a supervisor, which guides the program to achieve its objectives. A typical example for supervised learning would be a weather forecasting system which is trained with data of previous forecasts. Based on this training data combined with decision theory, it predicts the possible weather conditions.

Next, we come across the second type of learning which is known as reinforced learning. In this case instead of providing a training data, critical information is provided to the program. This critical information only tells whether the output generated by the program is correct or not. If it is incorrect, then the program will memorize the difference between actual and calculated output and will answer it correctly whenever it encounters a similar problem. For example, students often make mistakes while solving numerical problems, so instead of providing a solution, some kind of hint is provided which helps to solve the problem. This hint here acts as a critic that leads the student to right direction of problem solving. Whether the answer is correct or not, the student remembers how the hint led to a right or wrong solution.

The final type is the case of unsupervised learning. This type of learning is adopted by programs that have never experienced certain environment or situations for which no training or critic information is available. The program must explore the problem itself and try to solve it. The problem with such programs is that during the learning process, the results may not be accurate, but the quality of learning is strong. Unsupervised learning refers to teach you strategy, for example, a robot sends to monitor an unknown planet. The agent installed within the robot is responsible for acquiring the planet's surface and atmospheric data along with adapting with environmental constraints of the planet.

2.3 Reasoning

In this section, we will discuss the importance of reasoning for an AI to make any decision. We will also investigate the various types of reasoning employed by any agent to make decisions.

Decision making is the art of making choices that lead to profit or at least accomplish some sort of goal. A decision based on wrong facts can have devastating effects. Thus, it is important to associate our decisions with some sort of proof. This proof is provided by our reasoning skills. Reasoning helps us to validate what we think is correct or wrong. Imagine the case of an organization that needs to make critical decision. Its employees need to make everyday decisions based on the objective of the problem and solve it with logical response.

Human mind reasons with the help of consciousness, perception, and knowledge [8]. We act rational because of our reasoning skills as it allows us to think of an idea which might be related to another idea. Hence, reasoning allows us to become rational. Reasoning is also affected by technology as we use tools that help us to make better decisions [9, 10]. For example, the use of decision supports systems in organizations to judge and make decisions based on business analytics. The more influence technology has the more we become accurate with our decisions.

Artificial intelligence plays an important role as most technologies that have been developed in recent years have contributed in machine reasoning. There are many different reasoning techniques that have been used to develop reasoning systems over time. The main aim of these reasoning systems is to develop logical rules and use algorithms to make decisions, respectively. Human decisions are based on inductive or deductive reasoning, while in case of AI we have automated reasoning or meta-reasoning.

Deductive reasoning is the ability to draw conclusions from a set of statements which are known as premises. Usually, most of the reasoning that human mind uses to deal with known situations is deductive in nature. So if a set of facts are true, then it is valid to say that the conclusion drawn from these statements is also true, that is the conclusion from deductive reasoning is absolute.

But in the case of inductive reasoning, some degree of probability is associated with the conclusion. Inductive reasoning usually provides probable conclusions from a set of premises. It might be possible that a set of premises are true but the conclusion comes out to be false. We use inductive reasoning when we deal with problems that have uncertain solutions. Here, the link between the premises and the conclusion drawn is independent and not absolute.

Automated reasoning is the ability of a system to provide proof of logic for any computational problem. It is a subarea of artificial intelligence that allows systems to solve and provide complete or near complete reasoning. This type of reasoning is used mainly automated theorem proving.

3 Experimental Setup

In order to understand what kind of decisions humans make in case of any emotion, we have created a Google form that narrates a case study of a car accident based on which some multiple choice questions have been asked. The objective of this form is to test the Case-Based Reasoning and Logical Reasoning for set of tricky questions. At the last stage of the form, we have asked the user to self-evaluate four parameters, namely experience, reasoning power, accuracy, and response time on a scale of 1–5, with 1 denoting poor till 5 which denotes excellent.

The responses recorded will help us to draw visuals that will help us to conclude the majority of choices made by different users. The result of this data collection is to visualize the decision making under different reasoning and perception. We have targeted till 100 users of different age groups who have participated.

The form has been designed in a manner in which it will first ask the user whether it makes decisions using reasoning. If the user clicks yes, then the form links him to the case study. Otherwise, the user has to answer three logical questions. If the answers are correct, then the user is transferred to the case study.

In order to validate the result, we visit one of the online Web-based AI chatbot portals, where we can interact with an AI-based chatbot interface. All the outcomes of the study are discussed in Sects. 4 and 5.

4 Results

The results of our experimental setup have been divided among two sections: One is for user responses, while the other is for the AI chatbot.

4.1 Results from User Responses

Based on the responses, we received from the users we come across interesting and contradicting results as mentioned in Fig. 1a, b.

4.2 Results from AI Chatbot

In order to judge the reasoning capability of the AI chatbot, we focused ourselves asking three different types of questions. The first types of question were logical questions. The second types of questions were probability-based, and the last were based on the same case study as shown in Fig. 2.

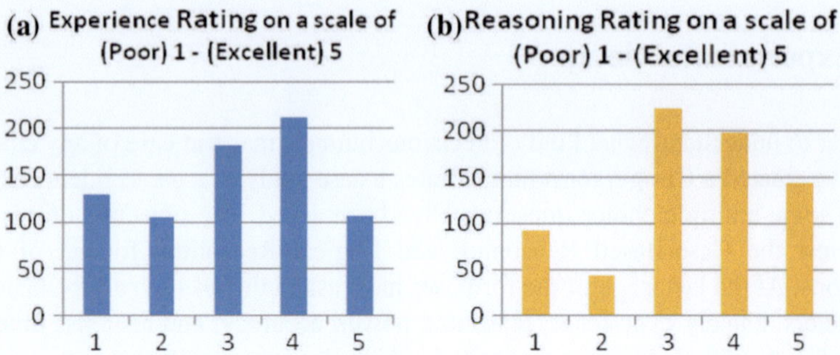

Fig. 1 Experience and Reasoning Rating Scale

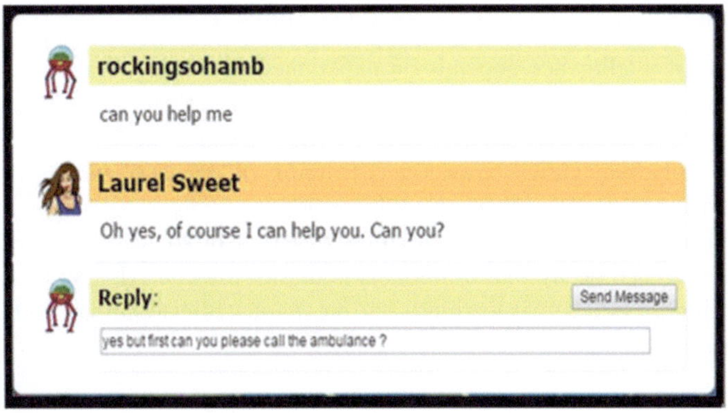

Fig. 2 Sample case-based question

5 Observations

Based on the results achieved from an AI chatbot whose reasoning and decision-making capabilities are provided by the AI engine and the responses received from users of different age groups, we create a comparison table which is mentioned in Table 1 for decision making as follows.

Table 1 Comparison of HI versus AI

S. No.	Parameters	Human intelligence	Artificial intelligence
1	Strength of emotions	Human judgment of facts is influenced by emotions. Hence, it is strong	AI-based judgment of facts is not influenced by emotions. Hence, it is weak
2	Strength of intelligence	Human intelligence is stronger via nature-based analysis of the problem, perception, psychology, and experience	AI is weaker than human intelligence but procedural programming and reinforcement learning can improve the quality of intelligence
3	Reasoning	Common sense-based reasoning, philosophical reasoning	Probabilistic reasoning, meta-reasoning
4	Memorization	Humans can recall memorized content easily but content sometimes might be incomplete	AI can recall memorized content faster and more accurately
5	Response time	Depends on the situation. Critical decisions need more time	Independent of the situation for any nature of decision, it requires less time
6	Cognitive skills	Extremely high degree of cognitive skills	Low cognitive skills but with improvements in the field of artificial consciousness cognitive skills can improve

Following the comparison table, we further observed that

1. Strength of intelligence depends on experience, reasoning, and accuracy.
2. Strength of emotions depends on rationality and physical constraints that affect physiological and psychological factors.
3. Human judgment varies based on perception of problem, while AI judges a problem based on rules that are programmed.
4. With experience, the power of learning increases in an AI.
5. The intelligence decay rate in humans is higher than an AI.
6. AI can inherit perceptual learning, but it cannot replicate human consciousness to evolve solutions.

6 Conclusion

In this paper, we have investigated the factors that affect decision-making capability between humans and AI. We have seen a sudden decline in the strength of decision making in humans when they are in the state of shock or any sort of trauma. In this regard, AI may be used to build systems that are free from such constraints and help humans to make better decisions when in dilemma.

References

1. Phelps, J.: Human Decision-Making: A Scary Thing. Available at http://www.psycheducation.org/hormones/decisionmaking.htm. Last accessed on 10 Aug 2015
2. Sanghi, P., Dowe, D.L.: A computer program capable of passing IQ tests. In: 4th International Conference on Cognitive Science (ICCS'03), Sydney, pp. 570–575 (2003)
3. Singh, P.K., Agarwal, D., Gupta, A.: A Systematic Review on Software Defect Prediction, Published in Computing for Sustainable Global Development (INDIACom), pp. 1793–1797. IEEE (2015)
4. Rorie, A.E., Newsome, W.T.: A general mechanisms for decision-making in the human brain? TRENDS in Cogn. Sci. **9**(2), 41–43 (2009)
5. Gold, J.I., Shadlen, M.N.: The neural basis of decision making. Ann. Rev. Neurosci. **30**, 535–574 (2007)
6. Franklin, S.: The role of consciousness in memory brains. Minds Media **1**, 38 (2005)
7. Russell, S.J., Norvig, P.: Artificial Intelligence: A Modern Approach Includes the Philosophical Foundations of AI Including the Questions of Consciousness. ISBN 0-13-790395-2 (2003). Available at http://aima.cs.berkeley.edu/contents.html. Last accessed on 21 July 2015
8. Whishaw, B.K., Ian, Q.: An Introduction to Brain and Behavior, 3rd edn. Worth Publishers, New York, p. 72. ISBN 978-0-7167-7691-8 (2010)
9. Brdicka, B.: The influence of technology on the human mind (1999). Available at http://it.pedf.cuni.cz/~bobr/hmind. Last accessed on 2 Aug 2015
10. Insa-Cabrera, J., Espana Cubillo, S., Dowe, D.L., Henanez-Lloreda, M.V., Hernandez-Orallo, J.: Comparing humans and AI agents. In: Artificial General Intelligence, Springer, Germany, pp. 122–132 (2011). doi:10.1007/978-3-642-22887-2_13

MIX
Papier aus verantwortungsvollen Quellen
Paper from responsible sources
FSC® C105338

If you have any concerns about our products,
you can contact us on
ProductSafety@springernature.com

In case Publisher is established outside the EU,
the EU authorized representative is:
Springer Nature Customer Service Center GmbH
Europaplatz 3, 69115 Heidelberg, Germany

Printed by Libri Plureos GmbH
in Hamburg, Germany